Denny Howard has dedicated his career t[...] [...] to being fully credentialed, he has a heart for tho[...] a people-helper, this is a must-read. Denny [...] ce and gives suggestions for overcoming th[...] [...].

— [...]LC

After thirty years of domestic and international leadership experience in both non- and for-profit sectors, I can say with great confidence that no one is better suited or equipped to have written this book. Denny's lifelong commitment to those who serve—and his unparalleled insights into the challenges, struggles, and battles they face—make every page of this book worth reading and digesting. He has rescued me from leadership heartaches more times than I can count, and has given me, my wife, and our family wise direction and hope on many occasions.

—Kelly Byrd, executive leadership development at Sweetwater Sound

As an elite mountain climber, Denny Howard has literally been to the mountaintop. But more importantly, as an elite counselor, he has spent decades learning the art of guiding weary ministers safely back to base camp. That's good news for anyone who has dared to risk the heights of vocational ministry and inevitably found themselves on a ledge physically, emotionally, or spiritually. With this book, Denny combines groundbreaking research, wisdom from soul-care literature, and a lifetime of field experience to provide a manual for surviving and thriving in vocational ministry. Peaks and valleys will come for us all; I am grateful for this reliable guidebook.

—Del Fehsenfeld, LMFT, senior editor of *Revive*, pastoral services director at Life Action Ministries

Weekly, I hear from pastors, missionaries, ministry spouses, and their children seeking guidance in navigating potential landmines and scars from the front lines of ministry. As I come alongside these servants and their families, I am so grateful for Denny Howard's experience, research, discernment, and practical tools to help in recognizing pitfalls and bolstering resiliency—so instead of becoming collateral damage, they remain healthy and vital. What a strategic and valuable work!

—Linda Kline, director of Psalm One Ministries

If you are exploring this book, then we share a similar interest of care for those who serve in ministry. Drawing from many years of counseling with over 6,000 ministry leaders, Denny offers exceptional insights and unique perspectives from his vast pool of experience. His meaningful perceptions enable us to grasp these life-giving concepts and become better equipped to stay near full strength while navigating the many relational, spiritual, moral, emotional, and directional challenges of ministry.

—Rod Kraybill, PCC leadership coach, training and leadership development coordinator at AIM International

Methods are many and principles are few; methods always change but principles never do! Thanks, Denny, for a book focused on principles—principles that will help those who serve others stay in the game for the long haul. If you are new to ministry or involved in any people-serving vocation, you need this book. If you are on the final turn of your career, you need this book. Why? Because the ideas, suggestions, recommendations, and directives are all true! Denny's writings speak truth gained from a lifetime of service to others. Let's stay in the game.

—Larry Lance, CEO of Youth for Christ of Northern Indiana

Insightful, practical, researched, and helpful; biblically solid and immediately applicable to a leader's life. Denny Howard is a long-time expert in the field of caring for Christian leaders and it shows in his work. Packed with wisdom, insight, and real-life applications that work, this book could be a difference-maker in the lives of many Christian leaders.

—Michael MacKenzie, clinical director of Marble Retreat

The wave of burnout, depression, and attrition among ministry leaders and caregivers is alarming. Denny and Hugh hit the nail on the head with *At Full Strength*. Both the preventive and prescriptive tools offered will help any leader or caregiver extend their leadership shelf-life, while enjoying their journey more!

—John Opalewski, owner of Converge Coaching

As a pastor personally impacted by Denny and his work, I believe in the message of this book. Ministry is a marathon, not a sprint. Anyone wanting to run for the long haul should devour this game-changing resource immediately.

—Kevin Rivers, lead pastor of Blackhawk Ministries

There is an epidemic today among church leaders who struggle, burn out, and ultimately drop out of ministry. *At Full Strength* provides hope for turning this tide. From a wealth of practical experience and a heart for those leaders, Denny Howard has given us a gift that identifies the warning signs and offers safeguards to proactively navigate the pitfalls unique to those in people-helping vocations. This book brings hope that will positively change the course of individual leaders and entire organizations.

—Rocky Rocholl, president of The Fellowship of Evangelical Churches

— At —
Full
Strength

NAVIGATING THE RISKS
ALL PASTORS FACE

....

The Complete Survival Guide for Those Who
Serve in Ministry and Other Caregiving Vocations

....

Denny Howard, LMHC, LMFT,
Licensed Clinical Counselor

with Hugh White, MDiv

Copyright © 2018 by Education and Clergy Development, The Wesleyan Church
Published by Education and Clergy Development, Thrive Financial Initiative, Full
Strength Network, and Wesleyan Publishing House
Indianapolis, Indiana 46250
Printed in the United States of America
Writers: Denny Howard with Hugh White
ISBN: 978-1-63257-322-3
ISBN (e-book): 978-1-63257-323-0

Library of Congress Cataloging-in-Publication Data

Names: Howard, Denny, 1955- author.
Title: At full strength : navigating the risks all pastors face : the
   complete survival guide for those who serve in ministry and other
   caregiving vocations / Denny Howard, LMHC, LMFT, Licensed Clinical
   Counselor, with Hugh White, MDiv.
Description: Indianapolis : Wesleyan Publishing House, 2019. | Includes
   bibliographical references. |
Identifiers: LCCN 2018049605 (print) | LCCN 2018050413 (ebook) | ISBN
   9781632573230 | ISBN 9781632573223
Subjects: LCSH: Pastoral theology.
Classification: LCC BV4011.3 (ebook) | LCC BV4011.3 .H69 2019 (print) | DDC
   253/.2--dc23
LC record available at https://lccn.loc.gov/2018049605

Contents

Part 3: Navigating Spiritual and Moral Challenges

Part 4: Navigating Emotional and Directional Challenges

Part 5: Navigating toward Gaining and Maintaining Vitality

Introduction

Let us not become weary in doing good, for at the proper time we will reap a harvest if we do not give up.
—GALATIANS 6:9

For over three decades, I've been involved in a counseling and coaching ministry for nonprofit leaders as well as those serving in people-helping vocations. Over the years, I have formed some deeply held convictions around what it takes for them to sustain their vitality for a lifetime of caring service to others. Captured in this book are many of my insights on the risks and perils of ministry that must be understood and managed for these good people to thrive and flourish.

Youthful enthusiasm alone—that thrill commonly experienced when they first begin a career of vocational service—will not sustain a lifetime of ministry. I've heard the same story countless times of leaders who have announced their resignations simply because they had burned out. There was no moral failure, no major crisis event, no major family or health issues—they were just worn out. They reached a point in their sacred vocation where ministry became either a mundane drudgery or they were so overwhelmed, they couldn't cope with another day, week, or month of ministry leadership.

These fine people remind me of dedicated soldiers who stay engaged in the battle under all kinds of adverse circumstances. The scars from wounds suffered, combined with a relentless fatigue, have exacted an insidious toll over time. These good soldiers continued to advance the cause faithfully, eventually *bleeding out* from a thousand little paper cuts. They perished from a condition that could have been easily treated.

In my younger years, running marathons and mountain climbing were personal passions; I had an innate drive to reach the summits and cross the finish lines. For me, there was no thrill greater than being on a mountain wall looking down through my climbing boots at giant pine trees that looked like stalks of grass.

While on a major mountain ascent in Switzerland, an unexpected electric storm engulfed various climbing teams ascending the mountain; all were impacted by lightning strikes. Several members of one team were removed from the mountain in body bags. Several climbers plummeted thousands of feet to their death in the valley below. My own body trembled uncontrollably as our team worked to place climbing hardware into cracks in the wall, to secure our positions, and rest until our nerves calmed enough to continue our ascent. We continued climbing after this harrowing experience, but never without having a secure escape route in mind, should something unexpected occur again.

There are several climbing proverbs or aphorisms that can apply to all those who serve in people-helping professions, including ministry work.

Reaching the summit is optional. Getting down is mandatory.[1]

There are old climbers and bold climbers, but no old and bold climbers.[2]

Youthful enthusiasm and lofty intentions are a great way to start an endeavor, but alone are insufficient to help you reach the summit or cross the finish line of a successful ministry career in fulfillment of God's calling on your life. In ministry, unexpected storms will occur. You will be tested to the limit of your endurance. You will encounter obstacles that seem impossible to overcome. Every vocation has terms to describe these career-threatening moments. Here are some examples:

- Marathon runners *hit the wall.*
- Aspiring writers experience *writer's block.*
- Mountain climbers encounter *false summits.*
- Students taking exams *choke* and perform poorly.
- Aspiring professionals encounter *glass ceilings.*
- Deep-sea divers *hit rock bottom.*
- Psychologists' patients have *brain freeze*, making clarity of thought impossible.
- The psalmist discussed *the valley of the shadow of death.*
- St. John of the Cross called it *the dark night of the soul.*
- Kierkegaard wrote about *fear and trembling* and *sickness unto death.*

All these expressions describe that dangerous place where motivation to continue completely *disappears into thin air.*

Scripture is filled with examples of leaders who encountered blocked goals leading to discouragement and despair:

- Abraham waited twenty-five years for a promised son to be born.
- Moses wandered forty years in the wilderness and only viewed the promised land from afar.
- Job lost all his ten children, his health, and his possessions in a single week.
- David fled from jealous Saul for over twelve years.
- Isaiah was undone.
- Elijah wanted to die.
- The apostle Paul reported, "There was no rest for us. We faced conflict from every direction, with battles on the outside and fear on the inside" (2 Cor. 7:5 NLT).

In the "Faith Hall of Fame" chapter in Hebrews 11, we read:

Some were jeered at, and their backs were cut open with whips. Others were chained in prisons. Some died by stoning, some were sawed in half, and others were killed with the sword. Some went about wearing skins of sheep and goats, destitute and oppressed and mistreated. They were too good for this world, wandering over deserts and mountains, hiding in caves and holes in the ground. All these people earned a good reputation because of their faith, yet none of them received all that God had promised. For God had something better in mind for us, so that they would not reach perfection without us. Therefore, since we are surrounded by such a huge crowd of witnesses to the life of faith, let us strip off every weight that slows us down, especially the sin that so easily trips us up. And let us run with endurance the race God has set before us. We do this keeping our eyes on Jesus, the champion who initiates and perfects our faith. (Heb. 11:36—12:2 NLT)

The heroes described in Scripture are all characterized by a *hope* that empowered them to endure and persevere in their calling. Not all reached the summit or crossed the finish line, but all maintained that unquenchable spark of hope that kept them moving forward, knowing that God lovingly awaited them on the other side.

The desires (or gods) of this world are exposed and summarized by the apostle John in his first epistle:

For the world offers only a craving for physical pleasure, a craving for everything we see, and pride in our achievements and possessions. These are not from the Father, but are from this world. (1 John 2:16 NLT)

These desires or worldly cravings may promise fulfillment, but they never deliver on what they promise. They do not fulfill; they only enslave. What our Father in heaven offers *does* fulfill. He asks us to fulfill our stewardship. In so doing, we will experience life and vitality when our human spirits grow weary in the journey.

Viktor Frankl, an Austrian neurologist and psychiatrist, and his wife, Tilly, were detained in Nazi concentration camps. Frankl worked as a slave laborer in the Dachau camp. Tilly perished in the Bergen-Belsen concentration camp. Frankl's mother, Elsa, was executed at Auschwitz. His brother died as a slave in the mining operations at Auschwitz. In his book, *Man's Search for Meaning*, Dr. Frankl penned these words:

We who lived in concentration camps can remember the men who walked through the huts comforting others, giving away their last piece of bread. They may have been few in number, but they offer sufficient proof that everything can be taken from a man but one thing: the last of the human freedoms—to choose one's attitude in any given set of circumstances, to choose one's own way.[3]

Jesus talked about the kind of life that he desired for his followers, including those he called to shepherd or lead others: "The thief's purpose is to steal and kill and destroy. My purpose is to give them a rich and satisfying life" (John 10:10 NLT).

The apostle Paul, when mentoring his young protégé on how to instruct people to use their wealth properly for kingdom purposes, gave Timothy the explanation or rationale with these words: ". . . so that they may take hold of the life that is truly life" (1 Tim. 6:19).

What did Jesus mean when he said, "I have come that they may have life, and have it to the full" (John 10:10)?

What was the apostle Paul referring to when he said to Timothy: ". . . epi lambanomai tes ontos zoes," which is translated *"to grasp hold of the life that is truly living"*?[4]

How does this apply to those who are called to serve God and others in ministry or other caregiving vocations? Are we living the life that we call others to live?

Statistics on clergy burnout as well as the fallout from other caregiving vocations is alarmingly high. Of those men and women who go to seminary (postgraduate, two to three years beyond college), only one out of six are still in ministry at retirement age. Hardly a week goes by that I don't hear another story of a burnout victim in ministry. Why? What is unique to ministry-related vocations that have such a dramatic dropout rate?

This book is based on the findings of a twelve-year longitudinal study called the Crosshairs Research Project, which began in 2001 to discover why people drop out of the ministry profession and vocations related to caregiving. The outcome of the research project was startling, yet amazingly simple. This book is about the findings and seeks to answer the question: What does one do to curb the fallout?

Consider those people who serve in ministry and people-helping vocations as marathon runners. The distribution curve indicates that more marathoners drop out of the race between miles eighteen and twenty-one than during the other twenty-two miles. Knowing the statistics can help prepare runners for what they'll face during those critical four miles. Similarly, knowing the indicators of trouble in ministerial and other people-helping vocations can help individuals take preemptive action.

This book is for those of you who . . .

- Choose a life of serving others.
- Live a life marked by the ministry of interruptions and inconvenience.
- Realize that the true paycheck of life this side of heaven does not reach a bank account.
- Recognize that life is full of opportunities to make an incorruptible eternal investment.
- Want to reach their full strength in every area of life.

Why was this book written? God wants his children to experience a sustaining, abundant life *now*, on this part of our journey, not only later when we transition to the next life. Ministry leaders and caregivers, if they are to effectively lead and disciple others, must come to understand and experience what God desires for them . . . now!

In the chapters that deal with navigating specific risks of ministry, very few of the ideas, concepts, and strategies originate with me. They represent wisdom and insight I have gleaned from countless authors and other sources, and of course from my experience with thousands of clients across my career.

The topics are included here because they were found to be helpful in counseling and coaching leaders and vocational caregivers. I have learned to see life through the eyes of my clients. I have vicariously experienced their stumbles and failures. I have felt the agony and pain when leaders have chosen not to trust or believe God about the path to abundant life, thinking one of the world's systems more beneficial and rewarding than God's ways.

If you are a pastor, church staff, nonprofit ministry leader, involved in a people-helping profession, or a professional counselor or coach, then it is my prayer that the content of this book will be helpful to you.

This book is dedicated to God's servants who desire to be proactive in maintaining their health and wellbeing throughout their lifetime of service to others.

This book is for those who want to better understand, predict, and prepare to navigate through the low times in life without being derailed or taken off purpose with God's calling on their life.

This book is also dedicated to those who desire helpful strategies that lead to the resiliency, sustainability, and vitality that are essential for lifelong service to others in a way that honors God.

Acknowledgments

Writing this book was clearly not an individual effort. It involved influencers who have spoken into my life over a lifetime. Without them, there would be no book to write. My gratitude goes out to those friends who have spoken into my life over many breakfasts for more than thirty years—Bob, Tug, and Tom. I deeply appreciate Hugh, a gifted word-smith, who did a rewrite of my draft that read more like a dissertation to publish in a psychological journal. Many thanks go to Susan and her editorial team at Wesleyan Publishing House who only increased my appreciation of publishing. I am deeply grateful to my parents, Bob and Jan, who were living examples of love and service over my lifetime. To my love, Debbie, you have gracefully engraved so many good things on my heart with an inner beauty and gentle and quiet spirit. To my favorite vocational people helpers, sons and daughters—Josh, Becca, and Tim (wife, Kelsey)—you inspire me with your lives of love for God and service to others.

—Denny Howard

PART 1

The Crosshairs Research Project

Warning: Danger Ahead!

Peril is unavoidable in life. Wherever you live, conditions may arise that create natural peril with the potential to produce catastrophic life-changing impact, disrupting or destroying the normal routine of life. In coastal regions, it may be the risk of a tsunami, hurricane, or storm surge. Inland it could be a tornado, earthquake, blizzard, or wildfire. Others face lightning, sinkholes, mudslides, disease—the list could go on.

Fortunately, early warning systems now give people time to prepare for or evade most potentially catastrophic events. This has not always been the case. As recent as the early twentieth century, many of these life-threatening natural phenomena would arrive with little warning. For example, the hurricane of 1900 made landfall on September 8 in the United States (US) city of Galveston, Texas. Its estimated winds of 145 miles per hour made it a Category 4 storm. It was the deadliest hurricane in the history of US and the second costliest. The hurricane caused the deaths of an estimated 6,000 to 12,000 people, mostly due to either a lack of warning or a foolish disregard for warnings.

Similarly, history is replete with accounts of ministry leaders whose lives, reputations, and families were devastated or destroyed when they fell victim to the catastrophic spiritual, emotional, or relational dangers related to their professions. Just like unexpected natural perils, *inner perils* can manifest themselves when least expected, catching these leaders unprepared and leaving them desperately scrambling to survive in the wake of a disastrous event.

Based on research, we now know that there are predictable dangers and low times, once hidden, for those who serve in ministry and other people-helping vocations. With a new understanding, we can be pre-emptive in navigating these times.

The Challenge Question

Most people who are constantly exposed to the threat of a natural peril take precautionary measures and make advance preparations to weather the storm. In many cases, preparation involves leaving the threat zone entirely, following evaluation routes established to bring people out of harm's way.

The challenge question is this: As one who serves in a ministry or another people-helping vocation:

- If you could anticipate the hidden dangers and low periods of life, would you heed the warning?
- Would you prepare for the impending dangers and low times? Or would you, like some facing hurricanes, tornadoes, blizzards, and earthquakes, ignore the warnings?

Hopefully, your answer is emphatic: *Yes, I would heed and prepare.* When we possess a deeper understanding and anticipate the challenges before us, we can be better prepared to deal with those challenges. Being prepared is your best defense and offense in meeting those challenges you will inevitability face in a vocation of caring for others.

A Common Malady

The greater share of my life's work has involved counseling and coaching those who serve in people-helping vocations. Who are *people helpers*? They include ministry leaders, clergy, humanitarian workers, nonprofit workers, missionaries, healthcare workers, and others in similar career fields. These people have spent a great deal of time, financial resources, and energy to gain education and credentials in their respective fields.

In the last two decades, I have conducted face-to-face counseling and coaching appointments with more than 6,000 ministry leaders both inside and outside the US. What I have discovered is that many of them are afflicted with a common malady. Countless times I've heard words similar to the following phrases spoken by ministry leaders and other people-helping professionals:

- "I don't know what is wrong with me. I can't seem to get back in the game."
- "I'm just not with it! It's like my rhythm is off or something."
- "I don't want to do this anymore, but what else can I do?"
- "I'm successful, but it isn't satisfying anymore."
- "I'm bored! I want to do something different."

What they didn't realize was that they were caught in the crosshairs.

The Crosshairs

A distinct and predictable low period in life, often without a known cause, is a crosshair. These low times are marked by a lack of resiliency, satisfaction, vitality, and vision.

During a crosshair period, a particular circumstance can cause the vocational people helper to be in a state of extreme spiritual, emotional, or relational vulnerability. A crosshair can diminish sound judgment, impair decision making, or compromise one's self-control. All the while, the person caught in a crosshair may not be able to get his or her heart and mind around the *why* of their low period. There is just a sense of not being "with it."

In this chapter, you will gain an overview of the Crosshairs Research Study. This information is intended to increase your awareness and help you prepare for the crosshair moments unique to those who serve in caregiving and ministry professions.

I have a deep-felt gratitude for the leaders and vocational people helpers for the mutual wisdom acquired as they invited me into their private worlds in order to help them navigate the challenges before them. This long and winding journey with others has taken me, in a sense, through a thousand depressions, betrayals, infidelities, moral failures, disillusionments, and fears.

Some of these good people in different parts of the world have experienced being jailed, persecuted, and tortured for their faith—fingers chopped off one at a time, slowly burned in the hot sun while chained to a stake, or even burned with a hot iron. Others have had knuckles broken or flesh pulled from their bodies with pliers. Yet it was not these severe adversities that caused so many of them to abandon the mission. In fact, those who have been through such adversities seem to be endowed with a grace that fuels a remarkable resiliency. Though many suffer from post-traumatic stress disorder, they possess an inner reserve that drives them back to the front lines of the fray.

Instead, it was the subtle, hidden dangers—the unexpected snipers and landmines of ministry or serving in people-helping vocations—that prevented them from meeting the long-term challenges of serving others for a lifetime.

The Study

There seems to be a predictable pattern of low times among those who serve in vocations such as the pastorate, nonprofit work, missions, education, and other helping professions. The Crosshairs Research Study includes the gathering of data from more than 663 participants in counseling and coaching who have exited their vocations during these predictable low periods.

In the remainder of this chapter, you'll find an overview of the Crosshairs Research, including its hypothesis and findings. This may help you begin to understand the low and challenging seasons in your life that did not seem to make sense to you at the time. The rest of the book, then, attempts to answer the questions: *So what? What can I do about the crosshairs?*

As you read, keep in mind that two significant mistakes can be made in regards to research projects and their outcomes. The first is to ignore the results and not take them seriously. The second is to take them too seriously, as if they were gospel truth. Both extremes are potentially harmful.

The invitation and challenge to you as the reader is to first understand the Crosshairs Research outcomes and then consider the ramifications in your own life. In the same way that people prepare for natural disasters like tornadoes, hurricanes, and tsunamis—these research findings can help you be proactive and preemptive in preparing for times when you may be vulnerable, thereby minimizing their potential damaging impact.

The Hypothesis

There are distinct periods of low times for those who serve in ministry and other people-helping vocations throughout their career. It is possible to establish a way to predict these distinct low periods. If these seasons of low vitality are predictable and can be anticipated, then it may be within the realm of possibilities to discover ways to navigate these challenging seasons more effectively.[1]

The Findings

Over a twelve-year period of tracking 663 ministry and nonprofit workers, 83 percent of those who sought counseling did so in one of five distinct periods of service in their career field. The Crosshairs Research relied on surveys, inventories, and case studies for the data collection.

The counseling and coaching pointed to troubling dynamics that seemed to fall somewhere in a cycle of six to seven years of serving. In other words, years six through seven, thirteen through fourteen, twenty-one through twenty-two, twenty-eight through twenty-nine, and thirty-six through thirty-seven were when people seemed to struggle the most. The issues they experienced could be professional or personal in nature, and seemed to apply in relationship to a current assignment as well as to the overall years of service.

- The first crosshair pertained to the total number of years in the vocation.
- The second crosshair pertained to the total number of years in the current assignment.
- The third crosshair pertained to the total number of years of marriage.[2]

For example, Angela has been in ministry for fourteen years total at two churches. She served in youth ministry for six years at her first church assignment and then served in women's ministry for eight years at her second assignment. The first assignment just ran its course, and she was done with youth ministry. After all, Angela's training and dream was to lead a women's ministry. But after eight years in women's ministry, she found herself thinking, "I'm tired of this. It seems like the same old thing over and over. I think it's time to move on."

Angela was caught in the crosshairs.

When presenting the research data to vocational people helpers, frequently someone will say, "Oh, the seven-year itch!" However, this seven-year itch is just a reference to a movie from long ago and has no bearing on the Crosshairs Research. Other individuals responded by making reference to the Bible on the significance of the number seven or the Year of Jubilee. However, the only preconceived notion that called for the research project was the repeated and cyclic patterns of when counseling or coaching were sought by clients who served in people-helping vocations. The data was collected inductively. The counselor who worked with vocational people helpers seemed to experience a "here we go again" dynamic, which begged to question as to whether it was just coincidence or an actual pattern.

The study revealed that these low periods emerged in patterns that could be anticipated and therefore predictable. If these low periods could be clearly established and anticipated, then it might be possible to be better prepared in advance.

Marks of Being Caught in the Crosshairs

Crosshairs moments—those predictable and identifiable low periods when most exits from ministry and nonprofit leadership occur—involve the low times, the valley experiences, or what we refer to as *bad days*. As the research was compiled involving hundreds of case files, the following patterns began to emerge that seemed to predict when these vulnerable low times would surface in the life of the vocational people helper.

These low times were characterized by the following indicators:

- **Lack of personal resiliency** characterized by difficulty in "bouncing back" from the rigors and blows of everyday ministry life.
- **Lack of personal satisfaction** characterized by depleted enjoyment in working with and serving people's spiritual needs through love.

- ◉ **Lack of overall vitality** characterized by low or no energy to embrace the day with enthusiasm and joy in fulfilling the call to shepherd others in their walks with God.
- ◉ **A clouded vision of the future** characterized by uncertainty about how to lead one's congregation into the future.[3]

From this research, we believe that such low times are predictable enough to issue warnings, just like we would if catastrophic damage was likely if storm preparations were not made. If these patterns can be identified and anticipated, then preparation can be made in advance to weather the storm, do cleanup work, and resume life as normal.

A Crosshairs Time Continuum

A word picture may be helpful to understand the crosshairs dynamic as it applies to your life. White-water rafting and kayaking can be a very rewarding adventure. There is nothing like the adrenaline rush when going down the small waterfalls and crashing through the wild rapids. However, at times, the adrenaline rush turns into fear and one wonders if the chosen route was a mistake. Some people consider the rush in the stomach an exhilarating feeling. Others call it "the butterflies" while others consider it sheer panic.

By examining the Crosshairs Research findings on a time continuum, you can see the predictable low times much like a river rafting map can indicate the dangerous areas while rafting or kayaking. Having a guide anticipate the difficult rapids, allows a person to navigate the challenges more effectively. The rapids make life interesting. However, the rapids can also take a life.

Let's take a look at the time-continuum map of the predictable low times and danger points as we navigate the rapids of ministry and other people-helping vocations. Eighty-three percent of vocational people helpers who sought ongoing counseling or coaching did so within a six-month range of these five distinct periods. We will examine those periods up close later.

Full Years of Service

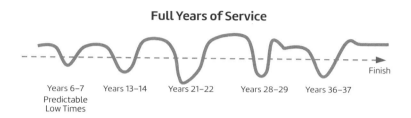

Years 6–7   Years 13–14   Years 21–22   Years 28–29   Years 36–37
Predictable
Low Times

A Word of Encouragement

We encourage you to do your own crosshairs analysis. If you take nothing else from this research, please never lose sight of the low-time indicators. Proactive and preemptive action can save your ministry and your marriage as you respond with rest, restoration, and renewal activities.

You may not be in a crosshair at the current season of life. However, just in the same way we can prepare for a hurricane or tornado, we can be prepared for the crosshairs. In this next chapter, we will take a closer look at the indicators of being caught in the crosshairs. The remainder of the book will help you answer these questions:

- So why should this be important to me?
- What can I do to more effectively navigate the crosshairs?
- How can I help a friend or colleague grow through a crosshairs experience?

Before moving on, see the "Personal Insight Exercise" in chapter 1 of the At Full Strength Workbook. *The workbook also includes an expanded version of the research statistics presented in this chapter.* At Full Strength Workbook *is available for free download at:* FullStrength.org/ AtFullStrength.

Additional Stats and Insights from Our Research

- Eighty-three percent of the ministry leader participants who sought formalized counseling or coaching met the criteria of being in one or more crosshairs when they sought assistance. It may indicate that professional people helpers (ministers in particular), seek help only when they are in a very complicated situation. There were some indications that personal pride and image management may have deterred some from seeking preemptive help.
- Over 65 percent of the moral failures, forced terminations, and distressed resignations involved a crosshairs moment.
- Surprisingly to the people helpers, the moral failures, forced terminations, and distressed resignations were not the problem, but rather, symptoms of a deeply hidden issue. For example, a ministry leader who had an affair may assume that when the marriage was back on track that the problem was solved. However, the adultery needed to be treated as the symptom of a deeper problem. The relationship to the true problem is similar to a headache when one actually has a brain tumor.

- The participants who had served in ministry and other types of people helping indicated that long term, everyone will eventually experience at least one or more crosshairs experience.
- The crosshairs experiences were not necessarily accompanied or triggered by any particular precipitating situations. For example, a ministry or nonprofit leader (outside the crosshairs experience) could be going through terrible circumstances, but still maintain resilience and satisfaction in the overall mission, vitality, and clear vision. Paradoxically, a person could have a thriving ministry and be in a crosshairs experience.[4]

Early Warning Signs: Difficult Challenges Ahead!

In my early adulthood, I spent more than 200 days backpacking and climbing in the wilderness. My first real job was with a high-adventure wilderness program called Project Impact. By the age of twenty-six, more than five months of my life had been spent in the wilderness backcountry, with nearly half of that time trudging through snow and setting camp in freezing temperatures. Imagine trying to tie your boots with mittens!

ROUGH ROAD

The Project Impact team worked with serious juvenile offenders placed in our program in lieu of incarceration. It was like a military boot camp. It was interesting how these hard, intimidating, delinquent youth became quite docile after several days out in the wilderness surrounded by unfamiliar terrain.

The youth often took our map and compass for granted, but the staff knew to guard them like gold. Without map and compass in a frozen wilderness, an expedition group is very likely to become stranded. Over the years, we had encountered whiteouts where snow and fog limited visibility to almost nothing. Trails were blanketed by snow, completely hidden. Extreme cold was a constant adversary.

We also experienced deceptively beautiful days when a weather front formed around the mountain peaks, changing the conditions from fair to severe. Temperatures could plunge forty to fifty degrees and the rain would turn to ice, making a retreat to safety nearly impossible.

Such circumstances were precarious, but the youth in our program would have otherwise been behind bars in an even more volatile and threatening environment. Safety was our highest priority in this high-adventure program. But how could safety be guaranteed with so much at risk? The answer is *preparation*.

Mountaineering and climbing became a passion for me outside of work, where I could pursue more significant adventures that required even greater preparation. Having the right equipment, including adequate hiking boots, gloves, coats, and rain gear for extreme weather was of utmost importance. We would check our climbing ropes inch by inch before an ascent up the mountain. We double-checked our carabineers, seat harnesses, ice crampons, and other hardware for defects. Each participant was trained in rock-climbing techniques, glacier ice-climbing safety, and the administration of wilderness first aid.

In mountaineering, safety is always the highest goal. Calculated risk is the name of the game. However, even with the best efforts, adversity eventually finds everyone. We would prepare for every possibility, but still occasionally find ourselves in awkward predicaments. Sometimes they were due to elements outside our control or influence. Other times they were caused by a foolish judgment on the part of a climbing team member—high-altitude climbing in bitter cold has a way of impairing one's judgment.

Our team has been hit by lightning. We have carried hikers out of the wilderness with the flesh surrounding their joints torn wide open. Others were evacuated with significant high-altitude illnesses and giardia from bad water. Personally, I have experienced a fall of about thirty feet while climbing, followed by a trip to the emergency room.

Some would ask, "Why do you do it?" The reasons are similar to why many people pursue ministry and other people-helping vocations: *the power of the call and the mission.* These vocations are high stress, high demand, and lower compensation than most other professional careers. But those who have experienced the call, truly understand making sacrifices on behalf of others.

However, we who answer a *dangerous call* must be proactive about preparing for the challenges that we will inevitably face.

Be Proactive

Benjamin Franklin is attributed with saying, "An ounce of prevention is worth a pound of cure!"

Some people seem to have the attitude, "We will deal with it as we go!" or "Let's just wing it!" But that's a rather careless approach to facing circumstances that can be anticipated. Imagine applying this philosophy in some very common scenarios:

- The best time to buy a snow shovel or snow blower is in the middle of a blizzard.
- Let's just wait and see how bad the hurricane gets before we board up our windows.
- Oh, the dashboard oil light just came on. We can probably make it another hundred miles.
- I've had this large painful lump in my neck for about a month now. If it isn't better by spring, I might set an appointment with my doctor.
- When she starts talking about divorce, that's when I'll know it's time to get counseling.

Let's revisit the challenge question that was stated earlier concerning the crosshairs: If you could anticipate the hidden dangers and low times as one who serves in a vocation of ministry or other people-helping vocations, would you heed the warning?

The Crosshairs Research findings can serve as a predictor, both alerting and allowing you to prepare for challenging low times ahead. By being proactive and preemptive, we can navigate the challenges more effectively and maintain both personal and professional vitality.

In addition to the cycles mentioned earlier, these crosshairs, or low times, have other indicators as well. First, we'll provide an overview of these characteristics and then later define them with each crosshair. After that, we will identify how we can be more proactive and preemptive in navigating the crosshairs in our life of service.

Know the Signs

The defining indicators and symptoms of the crosshairs can serve as your *early warning signs* (EWS) of the coming crosshairs ahead. Data for the EWS was gathered as a part of the Crosshairs Research Project. Based on the data collected from 663 participants, the objective was to identify the most common characteristics of the low cycles we refer to as the crosshairs. These indicators and symptoms are not in any way a comprehensive list. They are some of the most common complaints from a wide range of vocational people helpers and ministry workers.

If you know the signs, you can take the appropriate action that will allow the highest level of vitality through these challenging low cycles. Effective navigation of each crosshair is, in part, dependent upon each person recognizing the impending dangers. Being proactive and prepared can minimize the potentially damaging impact of these seasons of low vitality in ministry and other people-helping vocations.

When a person was experiencing one or more of the crosshairs, several indicators and symptoms were present. The number and intensity of the indicators varied with the number of overlapping crosshairs.

The indicators and symptoms of being caught in the crosshairs were divided into these domains:

- Relational domain
- Spiritual and moral domains

- ⦿ Emotional and physical domains
- ⦿ Mental focus and life direction domains[1]

Do a Self-Check

Checklist Exercise: On the following page is an inventory checklist of the crosshairs indicators and symptoms frequently reported by those who participated in the Crosshairs Research Study. We encourage you to take inventory to monitor your own wellbeing. Take a few minutes to reflect on each one and ask yourself whether it is descriptive of your situation over the last thirty days or more.

An expanded version of the research outcomes and statistics can be found in the free online At Full Strength Workbook, *chapter 2 appendix. You can find the research by going to:* FullStrength.org/AtFullStrength.

The Indicators and Symptom Checklist of Being in the Crosshairs

Potential EWS in the Relationship Domain
- ☐ Lack of marital vitality
- ☐ An increase in the frequency or intensity of relational distress
- ☐ A tendency to become easily disappointed by others
- ☐ A decrease in the ability to recover from relational challenges and disappointments
- ☐ At least one bothersome relationship that is considered toxic and energy draining[2]

Potential EWS in the Spiritual/Moral Domain

☐ A return to former bad habits or getting involved in a single activity to excess

☐ An increase in the level of temptation experienced

☐ A diminished accountability marked by *hiddenness* and often for no particular reason

☐ Increased susceptibility toward *counterfeits* (something other than what God intended) for relief or a sense of satisfaction

☐ Investing emotional energy in self-justifying rather than healthy self-evaluating[3]

Potential EWS in the Mental Focus/Life Direction Domain

☐ Extended times of low mood, depression, and/or a diminished level of emotional and/or physical vitality

☐ Frequent somatic (physical health) complaints that might be chronic in nature

☐ Significant episodes of self-doubt or an elevated sense of self-importance

☐ Frequent episodes of concern or anxiety over one's future direction that keeps you awake during the night

☐ Experiences of extremes as evidenced by feelings of boredom or making risky choices

☐ Easily disappointed or discouraged

☐ Struggling with being self-absorbed or self-focused[4]

Potential EWS in the Emotional/Physical

☐ A predominant lack of clarity in one's direction or life plan

☐ A strong yearning for something new or different

☐ Disillusionment or disappointment with the outcome of life and/or career

☐ Priorities become fragmented
☐ A loss of mental focus or hyper focus in one area of life to the neglect of others[5]

Analyze the Results

◉ **If you marked one to four signs,** consider what kind of strengthening resources might help you gain and maintain your vitality. Pay attention and explore strategies and strengthening resources in the remainder of this book.

◉ **If you marked five to eight signs,** you are struggling and may be in a crosshair. Consider who you can talk to, such as a trusted advisor, coach, or counselor. Consider the strengthening resources available to you.

◉ **If you marked nine or more,** take decisive and intentional action to invest in your wellbeing.

Understand Each Crosshair: An Overview

Let's dig deeper into the concerns, conditions, self-talk, and underlying themes that surround each crosshair experience.

The First Crosshair (Years 6–7)

By the time most people enter into years six and seven of an endeavor, the enthusiasm and good intentions that served as a source of energy in the early years often become depleted. Lofty expectations have been dashed against the rocks of disappointment. It is like the marathon runner who hits the wall.

The emotional energy and focus has turned to realistic questions about the balancing of marriage, children, bills, and the mortgage: "Can I afford to take care of a family on this salary?" Small irritations and hurts related to balancing life may become magnified in the marriage.

Earlier ventures and activities that were once highly rewarding, have become dull and commonplace. Much of the work feels like "Here we go again!" The discontent, if not dealt with constructively, can give way to unhealthy practices and bad habits. Individuals experience a yearning for something new or different—a new challenge, a new role. Based on the Crosshairs Research, this period is when most of the participants changed job descriptions or exited the field all together.

The overall theme in the first crosshair based on the research was: *Can I really afford to keep doing this? Why am I discontent with a good job?*

The Second Crosshair (Years 13–14)

In years thirteen and fourteen, many participants indicated that their careers had become dull and uninteresting, but they didn't know what else they could do. It felt like they were on a treadmill, doing the same types of activities endlessly. Work seemed to be the same old thing over and over.

Many began to feel like an old soldier bearing the scars of multiple battles with difficult people in their work world. Some were starting to bleed out emotionally, spiritually, and relationally. Relational disappointments were becoming more of a burden and beginning to wear on them, like a faucet dripping water on a stone and slowly wearing a hole through it.

Their minds were filled with thoughts like, *If only I could do something different! But who would want to hire me in another field? I would have to start over financially.* Many felt trapped in their career field due to their financial needs. Even though the salary was not significant in relation to their peers' salaries, it was enough to keep them in their field of work.

The overall theme in the second crosshair based on the research was: *I feel stuck. There has got to be something else for me. Is there something else I could (should) be doing?*

The Third Crosshair (Years 21–22)

By years twenty-one and twenty-two, boredom has become a frequent visitor and never far away. A lack of creative energy and emotional stamina—and even the onset of depression—may settle around them like a cloud that stays for days or weeks. Self-doubt includes thoughts like, *Why am I not doing as well as I had hoped?* or *I'm successful, but so what?*

This season is when many tend to move into a midlife evaluation. Along with disillusionment or disappointment in their work situation, a good number of participants indicated an increasing difficulty in discerning what their priority should be, because they felt pulled in many directions. Many participants definitely wanted to do something new and different but felt trapped. They had thoughts like, *Who is going to hire me after twenty-plus years in this vocation? It is too late to change!* However, many indicated that during this season of life, they had a strong desire to add to or take from the recipe of their work context. Attitudes about work may be characterized by extremes. On one end of the continuum, individuals might have a strong drive to prove themselves with an obsession over work. At the other extreme, they might abdicate responsibility and seek out avenues to just be free of the pressure.

Like weary soldiers, they find themselves groping for some source of sustenance. The persistent and accumulative impact of the wounds, disappointments, and betrayals have taken its toll on the most faithful soldiers who have persevered through the years.

The overall theme in the third crosshair based on the research was: *I am not sure if life is turning out as I had hoped. I need to evaluate! I wonder what is missing.*

The Fourth Crosshair (Years 28–29)

In years twenty-eight and twenty-nine, the most noticeable change is that a person's body doesn't seem to do what it used to. Energy becomes a valued commodity. The persistent, continual stress of serving over many years is beginning to show up in the physical body. In many cases, they perceive that younger, more gifted people are rising up everywhere, willing to work for a much lower salary. They become concerned that their wisdom will be traded in for youthful energy and enthusiasm. By this time, however, the participants know that they are likely to finish in the current career regardless of any desire to change. Still, they may feel a need to add something to or take something out of their work experience.

Self-doubt or concerns take on the form of questions like:

- Why don't I seem to have the time to do all that I hope to accomplish?
- Why is my body so unreliable?
- How do I adjust to the changes in my marriage and family?
- Am I on track financially to retire?
- What does God have for me in the future?

The overall theme in the fourth crosshair based on the research was: *How do I keep up when I feel so tired? Will this tiredness ever go away?*

The Fifth Crosshair (Years 36–37)

The fifth crosshair, occurring in years thirty-six and thirty-seven, looks a lot like the third crosshair but with much less energy. There is often a tension between wanting to accomplish more and just coasting to the finish line. A person's overall energy—physically, mentally, and emotionally—may be short in supply. Some experience an unexplained weariness that is sometimes referred to as being "soul weary." In some instances, it may have a biological basis. In any case, the person experiences a lasting sense of tiredness, and wonders whether it will ever go away. This soul weariness will be addressed in later chapters.

During this time, there may be extended times of low mood or even depression. Physical complaints become more frequent, likely due to the onset of potential health issues. A once-strong leader may drift into an acquiescence posture with a diminished ability to make clear decisions and take the appropriate actions. Decisions over the future may keep the person awake at night. Self-doubt may take on the form of questions such as:

- How can I slow down my pace and still feel significant?
- Am I going to be replaced by someone younger with more energy?
- Am I a has-been?
- When do I stop doing all the things that have defined who I am?
- What will be my legacy?
- What is still left for me to accomplish? Will anyone know who I once was?

Many people experience concern about being displaced or replaced. One well-seasoned ministry leader put it this way, "I feel like an old thoroughbred race horse that is being put out to pasture." A significant number of the participants did find themselves pushed out of their positions to make room for younger leadership. Wisdom was indeed being traded for youthful energy and lower costs.

The overall theme in the fifth crosshair based on the research was: *What can I contribute? Why do I feel ignored by the greater majority of the population? Does wisdom count for anything?*

Take Heed of the Crosshairs and the Marriage Relationship

These cycles and crosshairs are observed in marriage as well as work. The crosshairs indicators and symptoms in marriage are not as clearly defined as in the vocational context, but two factors are important to note:

1. If the vocation-based crosshairs (both years in current assignment and total years of service) overlap with the six- to seven-year dynamic in marriage (when marriages typically go through their first real rough patch), the participants indicated higher levels of distress.
2. The vast majority of moral failures, adultery, and divorces come to light during the second crosshair (within twelve months of year thirteen and fourteen) and third crosshair (within twelve months of year twenty-one through twenty-two). A conclusion that can be drawn from this dynamic is that these two crosshairs can contribute significantly to the lack of vitality in a marriage.

The Crosshairs Research outcomes as it pertains to marriage appear similar to the findings of one of the leading marriage researchers, John Gottman, PhD. Gottman has been conducting a longitudinal research project on marriage for forty years at the University of Washington. Professor Gottman and his team at the Gottman Institute have studied thousands of couples' interaction to determine the key predictors of divorce.

These predictors, which Gottman calls "the Four Horsemen of the Apocalypse" are more common place than one would think. They are:

- First phase: Critical (sharing a complaint while putting the blame on one's spouse)
- Second phase: Contempt (negative thoughts about one's spouse coming from a position of superiority)

- Third phase: Defensiveness (self-protecting either by self-victimization or righteous indignation)
- Fourth and final phase: Stonewalling (emotionally withdrawing from one's spouse)[6]

Gottman's research indicates that many couples take about 5.6 years to reach the fourth phase in which the marriage is in trouble. The research also indicates that the average couple waits six years before seeking help for marital problems.[7] This corresponds to the Crosshairs Research that indicates the first low time in the life of a vocational people helper is within twelve months of years six and seven of marriage.

Gottman's research further indicates that a predictor of a later divorce occurs when couples move into emotional withdrawal, the absence of positive affection during conflict. This comes around 16.2 years after the wedding. The Crosshairs Research indicated that the second low time comes within twelve months of years thirteen and fourteen of marriage. It is just a year or so later that Gottman's research indicates a high potential for divorce.[8]

Apply the Findings to Your Life

It is my hope that you will benefit from the Crosshairs Research findings and the remainder of this book that answers the "So what?" question. However, we want to clarify a number of points before moving on to the following chapters that help you navigate the low times you encounter:

- The Crosshairs Research is not suggesting that every person who serves in ministry or another people-helper vocation will experience the predictive low times referred to as the crosshairs. What is important to note is that those who work within ministries and other people-helping vocations tend to have cycles of low periods that are marked by a lack of resiliency, satisfaction, and vitality, and a loss of clear vision. A preemptive recognition of these predictable low times can help prepare a person for these challenging seasons of life.

◎ *All* the participants in the initial ten years of the Crosshairs Research were in counseling or coaching. However, two additional years were focused on presenting the data to groups of ministry workers and vocational people helpers to explore whether they had experienced cyclic low times similar to the crosshairs. It was not known which of the participants, if any, in the final two years of exploration had been in counseling or coaching. However, more than 80 percent responded that they definitively had experienced the crosshairs, thus affirming the outcomes of the research project.

◎ It was anticipated that many who serve in ministry and other people-helper vocations would be skeptical or resistant to the findings. Instead, the response included repeated and strong recommendations to publish the results, along with strategies that would allow for more effective navigation of these predictable low times.

◎ Some may be skeptical that their low cycles do not fit the pattern found in the Crosshairs Research. I suggest creating a timeline, charting out your service history, and identifying the low seasons. You may discover that it is cyclic in nature, because some individuals experience cycles that are closer together or farther apart than the participants in the research. Yet, it remains true that there seems to be predictable cycles. It is as if a person were kayaking down the rapids of a white-water river. Some move faster than others, which results in reaching difficult rapids sooner. Others move more leisurely and their rough spots on the journey are farther apart than the general population.

Given the findings of the research that the crosshairs dynamic is definitively cyclic in nature, it would be beneficial to identify ways to effectively navigate these predictable low times. The remaining chapters chronicle the perspective, strategies, and activities that many have reported as having been truly helpful in navigating the challenges before them though the most difficult seasons.

My goal is that you would find ways of navigating the challenges before you effectively, as you commit to a life of service. May you discover all you need to gain and maintain the vitality essential for lifelong service to others, and in doing so, live a life that truly honors God. I trust that God will impress upon your heart and mind all that you need to know in order for you to "take hold of the life that is truly life" (1 Tim. 6:19).[9]

Before moving on, find the "Personal Insight Exercise" in chapter 2 of the online workbook at FullStrength.org/AtFullStrength.

Navigating Stress:
Sharp Curves Ahead!

The word *stress*, as it relates to the human experience, was coined in 1936 by Hans Seyle, a Hungarian medical doctor and researcher. After attending school at a Benedictine monastery, at age seventeen, Hans entered medical school in Prague, Czech Republic, where he graduated first in his class. Later, he earned a doctorate in organic chemistry.

Dr. Seyle observed that patients suffering from a wide range of diseases often exhibited similar signs and symptoms. He would say that they just "looked sick." He called their disorder General Adaptation Syndrome (GAS), a way the body responds to the demands and challenges placed upon it. These demands induced hormonal autonomic responses that often lead to ulcers, high blood pressure, arthritis, kidney disease, and allergic reactions.[1]

Though Dr. Seyle was familiar with eight languages, he chose the English word *stress* to characterize this recurring response to the challenges and pressures of daily life. Before that, *stress* had been primarily an engineering term that stood for **STR**uctural **E**ngineering **S**ystem **S**olvers. It was used to refer to the load-bearing capacity of a structure such as a bridge or a building. Structural engineers had to understand, for example, the volume of water that could flow beneath a bridge without weakening the structure or the wind speeds the bridge could sustain and still maintain its integrity over time and against the forces of nature.

Using this engineering term as a metaphor, Seyle began to speculate about the load-bearing capacity of a human being. He was curious as to why some of his patients looked sick, but seemed to have no apparent underlying biological basis for their malady. Dr. Seyle began to speculate that psychological forces must be at work with the capacity to produce a disabling impact in the lives of some people, whereas other people experiencing the same life experiences adapted and navigated through those circumstances without apparent harm or a disabling reaction.

Over time, the nontechnical term *burnout* came to represent the phenomenon first recognized by Dr. Seyle. When a person felt overwhelmed by life circumstances, he or she would say, "I feel as if I'm experiencing burnout." In the 1960s in the United States, those involved in the drug culture referred to certain overuse of drug experiences as burnouts. Today, the term is informally used in reference to a person who has reached the point of his or her exhaustion stemming from sustained exposure to stressors.

Awareness: The First Step in Recovery

In order to recover from the disabling effects of stress and burnout, we must first accurately assess the nature and forces that deplete or tear down our ability to navigate through and survive those forces without sustaining a disabling psychological injury. Accurate diagnosis always precedes a clear treatment or recovery plan.

But first, let's take a deeper look at stress and consider the various ways it manifests itself in our lives. It will be helpful to think about the four different types of stress we encounter in everyday life:

1. Potent stress
2. Persistent stress
3. Perceptual stress
4. Pervasive stress

Potent Stress

A serious car accident is a good way to conceptualize this form of stress. It happens abruptly and unexpectedly, often with devastating and life-altering consequences. This type of stress may manifest itself following a serious medical diagnosis, a major financial setback, the unexpected death of a loved one, losing your job, your child being arrested, or upon learning that your spouse has been unfaithful. The list could go on.

The predominant characteristic of potent stress is its sudden and unexpected onset, blasting its way into the routine of your life. It disrupts all your normal routines, and you feel as if life has suddenly spun out of control. This stress experience has the capacity to alter how you view everything in life. The landscape of the future you once imagined for yourself now looks likes the surface of the moon. The life you once felt you owned now seems lost forever.

Even though potent stress can be deeply painful and life changing, it is often the simplest type to navigate for one simple reason: other people in your circle of family and friends tend to recognize and understand what you are going through. We need to process potent stress by communication—literally *talking it out.* The empathy, encouragement, support, and prayers from those in our circle of relationships help us carry and slowly recover from what at the time seems to be an unbearable and nonsurvivable catastrophe.

Persistent Stress

This form of stress differs from potent stress in a major way. It is like a dripping faucet. Over time dripping water has the power to wear a hole through a block of granite. It isn't the force or strength of the water that brings damage, but the persistent, constant dripping. It can slowly wear a hole in your soul.

This type of stress is the most damaging of all the stresses because it's not obvious or alarming. You may tend to think of it only as an annoying distraction. It doesn't register as a real threat because your mind adapts to and ignores or represses its ever-present drip, drip, dripping force. The subtle and often silent force keeps pounding away until real and serious damage occurs. It slowly pierces and drains your resilience reservoir until you crumble and break apart under the relentless pounding.

An unaffordable monthly mortgage debt, a chronic pain, an unpleasant relationship from which you cannot escape, helping your child day by day overcome a learning disability, providing chronic care to a sick or elderly loved one, dealing with a perfectionist who hour by hour points out every mistake and flaw in your behavior—these are examples of persistent stress that sooner or later may break you.

Persistent stress takes a toll on your physical health by weakening the body's immune system. It depletes your brain's pain and anxiety-management systems. It affects the hormones in your body that are responsible to support resilience and mood stability.

Persistent stress is like bleeding to death from a thousand paper cuts.

In any stress-management program designed to prevent burnout, it's critical that we understand the power of this force, identify all its sources, and develop a protection plan that helps us maintain the resilience and vitality that are critical to healthy living.

Perceptual Stress

A third form of stress is *perceptual* stress. This type of stress is activated based on how we have learned to *perceive* things in our external environment. It is the antithesis of optimism and positive imagination; it is negative imagination and a pessimistic orientation where we constantly perceive external factors to be worse than they really are. This form of stress is highly correlated with our larger world and life view.

What you *think* about your life situations can actually be more potent than the actual circumstance you are encountering. Your life script or perceptual filters often determine your level of stress. Situations that some people may experience as stressful, others might label as challenging, interesting, or even stimulating.

Perception stress results from believing that your imagined or factually distorted reality is real, when the actual facts of your reality are much more benign and much less threatening than you believe them to be. Traveling by air is a good example. Most flyers know that flying is one of the safest forms of travel, and they relax from takeoff to landing. A few of the passengers on each flight are anxious and stressed hours before they board, taking hours to decompress from their stress after they land and disembark. The risk factor for both types of flyers is identical; it's the perception of the risk that varies.

The spiritual implications underlying this form of stress are profound. In Hebrews 11:6, we read: "without faith it is impossible to please God." We mature spiritually only as we learn to surrender and trust God to provide for and protect us in every dimension of our lives. One of the most important ways a person grows spiritually is by allowing the Spirit of God to drive the darkness of unbelief (faithlessness) out of every nook and cranny of our hearts. It's by learning to live and walk by faith in a God who has control over every circumstance of our lives that we thrive and flourish.

Perceptual stress is based upon our expectation concerning life as it should be. We expect certain responses from others or anticipate a particular outcome to events. When our life as it should be is dashed against the rocks of life, we experience disappointment or stress.

We often compare our inner-world experience with the image-managed world of others. On a practical level, the comparison is almost always self-defeating. Comparison is crippling in that we generally compare our life circumstances to someone whom we perceive as being better off. But therapists have the advantage of daily reminders that we would not want to trade places with most people who *appear* to be better off.

The famous NCAA basketball coach John Wooden said this about perceptual stress:

The only pressure that amounts to a hill of beans is the pressure you put on yourself. If you're trying to live up to expectations put on you by the media, parents, fans, your employer, or whatever else there may be, it's going to affect you adversely because it brings on worry and anxiety. I think that is the tendency of people who choke under pressure. They're thinking about living up to the expectations of everybody else instead of just doing their job the best they can.[2]

Perceptual stress is definitely manageable when we can identify whether our expectations are both *reasonable* and *realistic*. However, expectations can have roots in our private and subliminal vows that are buried deep beneath our conscious awareness. They can be intertwined with our deepest motives and intent and rooted in our perception of what others perceive about us. In reality, most people are not thinking about us at all. They're much more concerned about their own situations.

The challenge in managing perceptual stress is that the organic human brain does not know the difference between a nonfactual vividly imagined reality and an actual or fact-based reality. Our brain reacts as if both are legitimately real. A good coach or counselor can help a person learn to know the difference and slowly reorient a person to manage his or her reality assessment processes and minimize and manage illegitimate perception reality.

Pervasive Stress

Pervasive stress is a combination of two or even all three stress types working together in your life at the same time. In a perfect storm scenario like this, you will feel so overwhelmed that you'll need to engage others to help you take defensive or protective action to navigate through the tornado, rising floodwaters, and hailstorm all pounding away at you in the same season.

Four Ways Stress Expresses Itself

Stress, when not managed constructively, will usually manifest itself in common, observable patterns. When you observe any of these behaviors reaching a boil point in your own life or the life of others, a stress warning alarm should sound. Take action to help yourself or others find positive and constructive steps to remove yourself from the forces of stress attacking you.

Here are the four common ways that stress seeks to express or manifest itself. Consider these as clues of the destructive force of stress and replace them with healthier and constructive coping strategies. These four common expressions of stress are:

- **Exploding:** Sudden, emotional explosions
- **Somatization:** Manifesting as physical symptoms and health issues
- **Underhanded:** Corrosive, sarcastic, negative thinking and expressions
- **Whipping Post:** Self-criticism and self-punishment

Exploding

Here, stress manifests in outbursts of anger, frustration, hurt, fear, or other strong emotional reactions. The damage to those who serve in vocations of people helping can be permanent.

Vocational people helpers must deal with unrealistic, unreasonable expectations placed upon them by those they serve. This is especially true for those who serve in ministry. They are expected to receive unkind comments from people whose hostility is disguised as concern, without becoming defensive or discouraged. They are expected never to struggle with resentment or envy. They are to be a model spouse and parent. They are expected never to withdraw, disengage, or seek to control situations in a moment of self-preservation. They are expected to enthusiastically execute an unrealistic job description that would be overwhelming to anyone this side of heaven.

Exploding is outward and aggressive. It is likely intimidating to others. Often the frustration may be vented on someone innocent and unsuspecting like a spouse or child.

This manifestation of stress comes in various forms. You may be in a chronic state of frustration and have small explosions several times a week when your expectations are not met. For you, exploding may function like the vents of a volcano that let off pressure to prevent an extremely damaging explosion. You may let the stress build until it explodes like a volcano from the summit—you blow your stack! As a counselor, I have encountered people who were quiet, calm, and easygoing, but who ended up in jail the very first time they exploded outwardly. The pressure built up over the years and the explosion resulted in physical damage, even murder.

Exploding is viewed as unacceptable in most people-helping vocations, especially for ministry professionals. If you find yourself in a state where you fear it could happen to you, get counseling or coaching help now! Don't let the accumulated effects of stress destroy your life's work.

Somatization

The second way that stress seeks its own expression is called *somatization,* which means "to body-ize." In other words, to somaticize is to express psychological conflict through somatic (body) symptoms. People who somaticize often have body aches and pains for which doctors cannot find a clear medical basis. These individuals may be some of the nicest people we will ever encounter, because they almost never show their stress outwardly. Over time, however, they may simply fall apart under the stress.

A somatic expression of stress is inward and passive. It is most damaging to the individual who is experiencing the symptoms. There are a wide range of somatizations such as headaches, back pain, intestinal disturbances, upset stomachs, insomnia, depression, anxiety, frequent crying spells, and the list goes on.

It may be helpful to consider the mind-body connection as it relates to stress. Stress always affects your body, even if somaticizing is not the primary manifestation of your stress. Your body cannot distinguish the difference between external stressors and those that are from within. Your physical body responds to both in the same way. A perceived offensive word from a work associate may evoke the same reaction as experiencing a potential accident in your automobile.

When you encounter a potential threat (real or perceived), your brain sends messages along two separate pathways. The first message goes to the pituitary gland, which releases a substance called *adrenocorticotropic hormone* (ACTH). This hormone stimulates the adrenal glands. The second message is through the brain stem and the spinal cord sending nerve impulses throughout the body. These messages stimulate the two major parts of the adrenal glands, the cortex and the core.

The *cortex* releases various stress hormones; among them are cortisol and cortisone. Under normal conditions, both hormones serve to fight pain and inflammation. But at higher levels sustained over time, it can have potentially disastrous consequences on your health.

The *core* releases adrenaline and noradrenaline into your bloodstream—stimulating the heart, raising your blood pressure, and preparing your body for the fight or flight emergency response.

Understanding the effect of the *fight or flight* response on your health is extremely important. Elevated adrenaline flowing through your bloodstream produces a number of potentially serious consequences. Just of few of these outcomes include the following:

- Increased production of cholesterol
- Decrease in the body's ability to remove unhealthy cholesterol
- Narrowing of the capillaries and blood vessels reducing the supply of blood to the heart muscle
- Increase in the deposits of plaque on the walls of the arteries

In summary, ongoing stress clogs a person's arteries and contributes to other potentially dangerous conditions.

Unfortunately, somatization is frequently an acceptable—and even laudable—expression of stress in many circles of vocational people helpers. It is a sign of being deeply sacrificial on behalf of others. This stress expression may even bring much-needed empathy from others. But this attention is only a secondary gain. Meanwhile, your own body is in the process of slowly imploding. The cost of somatization can be emotionally, relationally, and even financially devastating, as it results in ever-increasing medical bills.

Underhanded

This expression of stress manifests itself through behaviors involving negative attitudes, sarcasm, pessimism, cynical judging and gossiping, skepticism, a bias to mistrust, and bad-mouthing others behind their backs.

In psychological terms, this manifestation presents itself typically as inward and passive-aggressive behavior, although there can be frequent outward and passive-aggressive manifestations. For those in people-helping and ministry professions, this form of behavior is generally deemed vocationally unacceptable, which forces the person to take it underground. In other words, this behavior is often manifested through pretense or mask-wearing, as the person keeps his or her true negative feelings about people and circumstances hidden.

Underhandedness can involve an outward niceness, while inwardly the person is expending a significant amount of emotional energy depreciating the perceived or real enemy. This form of underhandedness is inward and passive-aggressive. It is like drinking poison and expecting the other person to die.

Another form of underhandedness is outward and passive-aggressive. Being on the receiving end of it is like walking through a field of flowers along a babbling brook, birds singing with beautiful mountains as a backdrop, only to have your leg blown off by an unexpected landmine.

Living with this form of incongruence over time robs a person of vitality, and usually has the effect of pushing people away, far enough away that they feel safe and not vulnerable to being influenced or corrupted by the person's pretense and false humility. Under this stress response pattern, a person may not even be aware that people who once were close are now engaging at a much safer distance.

Whipping Post

This expression of stress manifests itself when people take themselves to the woodshed for a self-inflicted whipping when they come to believe that they have failed or haven't measured up in some significant way. A helpful example is an athlete who pushes himself to the point of a debilitating physical injury in practice as a response to a poor performance in competition. This form of stress is inward and aggressive, mostly damaging the individual; seldom is it projected outward against others.

This expression of stress is often related to performance anxiety or expectations where people experience stress because they believe that they are not measuring up. A helpful self-reflection question is to ask yourself, "Would you treat others the way that you are treating yourself?" The answer is most likely an emphatic *no!*

For more information on this form of stress, please see chapter 10.

Regular Stress Inventory

A wise leader will pause on a regular basis to conduct a personal stress audit or inventory. This assessment can be done by thinking through the forms of stress described above and asking yourself whether you can observe symptoms related to the various forms of stress. Ask yourself:

- ◉ Am I suffering from potent stress?
- ◉ Am I suffering from persistent stress?
- ◉ Am I suffering from perceptual stress?
- ◉ Am I suffering from two or more of these stress forces at the same time?

If you know or suspect that stress at work is affecting your behavior or performance, the next step is to identify the unhealthy ways you are expressing stress toward others. Ask yourself:

- ◉ Do I tend to explode and shower hot words down upon others?
- ◉ Do I sense that my physical health is being impacted by stressful forces in my life?
- ◉ Am I frequently negative, critical, sarcastic, or judgmental toward people in my life?
- ◉ Am I anxious when I don't perform at the level I think I should? Do I tend to inflict punishment on myself to relieve my under-performance anxiety?

Once you have a better understanding of the stress forces at work in your life and a sense of the ways in which that stress expresses itself, here are some suggestions on how to deal with potent and perceptual stress. We will deal with persistent stress later in this book, because it is the most complicated form of the three types of stress.

Remembering Not All Stress is Bad!

First, it's important to realize that not all stress is bad. *Eustress* (*eu* in Latin meaning "good") is the type of stress that an athlete might experience when getting psyched up before a big game. Eustress is what a public speaker or musician feels just before going on stage. This form of stress helps put the performer in an optimal state of preparedness. It involves concentration, focusing your strength, flowing your creativity, and staging yourself for maximum productivity. When danger is present, eustress is involved supporting rescue or allowing escape to occur.

Good stress is like the tension in a bowstring. Stressing the bowstring allows the arrow to fly with force to its intended mark. It's the flexing of muscles to make a heavy lift. This form of stress positions you for success, producing desired results or outcomes.

Good stress is a *fruitful friction*. It allows you to produce the results that you are aiming toward. Eustress is typically productive when manifested for short or controlled periods of time. Sustained or persistent stress does not allow for recovery. It's like over-flexing a muscle to the point where tear and debilitating injury occur. Damage only occurs when the brain and the body are not allowed to return to a state of rest and recovery in preparation for the next round of good stress.

Navigating Potent Stress

The best way to deal with potent stress is to *get it out*. Talking with others about your pain, journaling about your pain, or offering prayer to God about your pain helps release the pressure. As mentioned above, the people in your life generally know that you're in the middle of a potent or extreme stress experience. Let these caring people help you, walk with you, cry with you. The sense of not being alone, with others wanting to help shoulder the stress, helps you survive the potent stress experience.

As someone in a vocational people-helping profession, you may excel at helping others but may not know how to receive help as you experience potent or other forms of stress in your own life. Your "help receiver" may be broken or still in the box, unwrapped and not ready for use.

In bed dying from cancer, a very sacrificial and mature child therapist friend shared these words with me in the final week of her life:

Denny, there is a hardness of heart that eludes our awareness. We think of a hard-hearted person as one who is unwilling to give. But there is also a hardness of heart that makes us unwilling to receive. I wish I had discovered earlier in life how to receive from others more graciously. It was in working with children that I discovered how to graciously receive.

Have you learned to be a gracious receiver? Is your receiver broken or still packed away? It requires humility to receive from others when it is your primary job in life to give to others. We actually bless others as we learn to cultivate the capacity to receive graciously. To disallow receiving robs others of the blessing of giving to us, especially during our potent stress experiences in life.

Though it requires discretion, as a stress-management technique, share your concerns and hurts with others who can receive and hold what you share in faithful confidence. As a professional people helper, your work requires you to express supportive care constantly. You must have relationships in your life where you can receive and be strengthened by the care offered by others. Absent such relationships, you may have no protective relationships to help you cope with the stress that enters your life.

In his book *The Four Loves,* C. S. Lewis offers this warning:

To love at all is to be vulnerable. Love anything, and your heart will be wrung and possibly broken. If you want to make sure of keeping it intact, you must give it to no one, not even an animal. Wrap it carefully round with hobbies and little luxuries; avoid all entanglements. Lock it up safe in the casket or coffin of your selfishness. But in that casket—safe, dark, motionless, airless—it will change. It will not be broken; it will become unbreakable, impenetrable and irredeemable.[3]

For those of us in the people-helping professions, we must not let our professions become our coffins. We run the risk of insulating ourselves from real relationships that support our vitality and help us be resilient through the stresses of life and our vocations. One-way exchanges where we only give are not really relationships. To effectively help us cope with stress, we must have real, trustworthy relationships where we receive as well as give. We must have relationships that allow us to remove our masks and be honest, more honest, and then completely honest and transparent. It's only there that we can experience genuine love.

Show me a vocational people helper who has no one with whom to be open and honest, and I will show you an unhealthy individual.

Responding to the Challenges of Perceptual Stress

Keep in mind that perceptual stress is based on your perception of reality, and it may or may not represent the actual (fact-based) reality of the situation generating stress. Your organic brain is not able to distinguish between something vividly imagined and actual facts gathered through your senses. The brain causes the body and emotions to react to stress whether the stress-producing facts are real or only vividly imagined.

It is quite often the case that disappointment and stress are directly related to our expectations of our life situations. We cannot be disappointed without a preconceived expectation of how life should be. We cannot navigate through life without expectations. Those expectations, embedded in the backdrop of reality, can cause significant stress. This leads us to five helpful strategies to manage perceptual stress.

1. Intentionally change your perspective or vantage point.

The first step is to ask and answer two questions: Is my current expectation surrounding the source of my stress situation reasonable? Is my expectation realistic?

For example, if the source of stress is a boss or a spouse, you can ask yourself: Does this person realistically have the capacity to meet my expectation such that my stress would recede or disappear if he or she conformed to my expectation? Is my expectation toward this person reasonable and realistic? If it does not pass the litmus test of both reasonable and realistic, then it is beneficial to consider other options.

Expecting people to behave toward you in a manner of which they are incapable is bound to bind you perpetually in a stress prison that will damage and harm you. So, move to a more realistic and reasonable vantage point regarding your expectations of others. You really have only these options:

- ⦿ **Cling** to your unrealistic and unreasonable expectations and continue to be frustrated, disappointed, and living with chronic stress.
- ⦿ **Clarify** your expectations.
- ⦿ **Modify** your expectations to make them reasonable and realistic.
- ⦿ **Abandon** your expectations altogether by giving them up or giving them over to God.

Being intentional about the option you choose can actually give you freedom from the negative impact of perceptual stress.

2. Consider how a wise person would view your situation.

The second strategy is to think of the wisest person you know and reflect on how he or she might evaluate your current stress-producing situation. How would they manage their emotional state? How would they maintain objectivity? How would they respond differently to achieve balance and perspective?

This type of analysis has the same effect as strategy number one. It helps you change your vantage point, to see things more objectively, and results in having stress dissipated or drained away. A change of attitude or perspective generally produces a change in our feelings—the prerequisite for finding freedom and deliverance from the stress.

3. Get an eye examination.

Think of this strategy like you would going to the optometrist and doing the A/B lens test: "Can you see better with this lens or this one—which is clearer?" Now, in your mind's eye, the question becomes: *Which lens makes this situation look darker*? *Which lens makes this situation look brighter, clearer, and more hopeful*?

People with declining vision, who see only negative circumstances and dire outcomes, view life through dark and cloudy lenses. By helping the mind's eye view the situation through brighter and clearer lenses, overall vision and clarity about life situations improve. The emotional muscles of the mind's eye can relax and enjoy the view.

There is a coaching exercise referred to as the *LENS exercise*. In this exercise, clients try on different lenses, but over their mind's eye. The dark lens looks at a circumstance from the worst possible outcome. The bright lens illuminates the best possible outcome, the opportunity disguised beneath the surface of the issue.

In this exercise, the inverted lens looks at life from the vantage point of another person, possibly the person that is a challenge for us. The fundamental questions that must be answered are:

⊙ How might the other person see these same circumstances differently?

⊙ In what way does the situation make sense from that person's perspective?

Maybe the perspective of the other person does not make sense to you. However, if you cannot come up with an answer that makes sense from the vantage point of the other person, you have not made a genuine attempt to truly understand that person. This inverted lens exercise is an attempt to discover a practical way of seeking first to understand before being understood. Doing so is essential in solving a challenge or disagreement.

4. Choose to change your attitude.

Every pilot knows that your attitude determines your altitude. Attitude represents an aircraft's axes relative to the line of the plane or the plane's horizon. A negative attitude causes the plane to lose altitude and eventually return to earth, either with a planned and controlled landing, or not. A positive attitude causes the plane to climb to higher altitudes eventually reaching a stall point. Every type of aircraft has a safe cruising altitude, where the plane levels off and makes its way safely to the intended destination. Just as a pilot has control over increasing or decreasing attitude, we too have a similar ability.

Negative attitudes affect a person's neurological and chemical biology. Practically speaking, negativity produces a force field around the person that repels other people. Interacting with such people is like wading through a toxic chemical spill.

As a stress-management technique, evaluate the role your attitude plays in directly or indirectly affecting the relational dynamics that creates the stress load you are experiencing. Negativity begets negativity, and your attitude may be part of the problem in the relationship that is troubling you.

Negativity can devolve into self-pity and in turn can lead to depression. Likewise, an unrealistically positive attitude can damage relationships as well, causing people to question your view of reality and thereby your credibility. People tend to avoid people who seem Pollyanna-ish or out of touch with reality. That's why it's important to keep your plane level with the horizon.

A chronic negative attitude will eventually lead to disastrous con-sequences. Physically, a negative attitude alters the production and release of brain hormones essential for good emotional health such as serotonin, dopamine, and others.

Spiritually, the negative person eventually doubts God. To focus mostly on the negative, results in self-pity. In his award-winning book, *How to Win Over Depression*, Dr. Tim LaHaye says, "Nothing produces depression faster or more deeply than self-pity."[4]

The easiest thing to change about a bad situation is your bad attitude. Nothing good can come of a bad attitude. The fundamental way to change your bad attitude is by making the choice to do so. It begins with being intentional.

To help address your own attitudinal struggles, avoid or regulate your relationships with people who are chronically negative. Carefully consider whether you're one of those people who others are avoiding due to your negative attitude. As your attitude improves, people will move into relational proximity where positive and uplifting relationships can develop. Such relationships are therapeutic and healing, relieving hidden or out-in-the-open sources of relational stress. Such relationships also enhance your ability to be resilient and recover quickly from painful bumps and bruises.

I would be remiss if I failed to address the biochemical component of attitude. Like many clinicians, I believe it is difficult, if not impossible, to simply "snap out" of endogenous, biochemically-based depressions. However, changing your attitude by an act of the will is different from changing your emotional state by an act of the will. Quite often, when you change your attitude, the emotions follow in time. If you wait for your feelings to change, you may be waiting for a very long time.

We've often heard that attitude is everything, and it's true. A positive attitude can and will make all the difference in your outlook and how your life unfolds. There are many ways a positive viewpoint can enhance your life. Here are just a few:

- ◉ You will attract people who are more positive into your life, and it will make it easier for those who are entrenched in negativity to distance themselves from you. Overall, a positive attitude results in more emotional, relational, and mental vitality—and maybe even more physical energy and health.
- ◉ You will handle setbacks more effectively. A good attitude increases your capacity to see options. When circumstances do not go according to your expectations, you won't be nearly as devastated because you know that "This too shall pass."
- ◉ Fundamentally, choosing a good attitude is more *fun*. People who struggle with a chronic negative attitude are not fun to be around, and they just don't have fun themselves.

5. Change your behavior.

Some chronic behaviors and actions are the source of stress. Similar to evaluating the role your own attitudes play in your relational stress dramas, you must also evaluate whether you radiate perturbing behaviors that repel people and disrupt your ability to maintain healthy relationships.

If your behavior is off-putting to begin with, trying harder is not always the answer. Sometimes, we can only impact change by *trying differently.* Henry Ford is credited with saying that, "If you always do what you've always done, you'll always get what you've always got." A behavioral change must occur. The title of executive coach Marshall Goldsmith's book says it this way: *What Got You Here Won't Get You There!*[5]

Among the many brilliant quotes by the leadership guru, Peter Drucker, the wisest may be, "We spend a lot of time teaching leaders what to do. We don't spend enough time teaching leaders what to stop. Half the leaders I have met don't need to learn what to do. They need to learn what to stop."[6]

Most people have good intentions but forcing a change of off-putting behavior is tantamount to changing a habit—and we all know how difficult that is. We're quick to judge others by their actions, but we tend to judge ourselves by our good intentions (whether they ever come to fruition or not). In our mind's eye, we give ourselves credit where credit is not due.

Here's a helpful checklist of behaviors that could be undermining your relationships:

- ◉ Refusing to say, "I'm sorry" and asking to be forgiven
- ◉ Insisting on your way at all times
- ◉ Having to win at all times
- ◉ Speaking out of anger
- ◉ Trying to convince others you're more competent and always correct
- ◉ Failing to listen and just waiting a turn to speak
- ◉ Failure to express gratitude or say, "Thanks!"

- Passing the blame
- Refusing to give credit or acknowledge the contribution of others
- Making excuses
- Negativity and sarcasm
- Speaking ill of others when they aren't present
- Incongruence (saying one thing and doing another)
- Failure to keep promises
- Staying stuck in the past, or refusing to let things go (forgive and forget)
- Dismissing or downplaying the feelings of others

Behavioral blind spots have been the undoing of many otherwise talented people. We all have blind spots—we really don't know or even suspect that they exist in our behaviors.

It is possible to take corrective action and change your behaviors and recurring actions. You can start the change process by identifying your off-putting behaviors and the new behaviors you want to display. Scripture admonishes us to put off certain things and, in their place, put on better things. Here are some illustrations, but be sure to make your own list.

Put Off	Put On
• Lack of gratitude	• Learn to say, "Thank you"
• Injurious conduct	• Apologize and ask for forgiveness
• Failing to listen	• Reflect back what you heard before speaking

If you're really serious about making life changes that will improve your relationships and drain unwanted stress from your life, boldly ask your friends and colleagues, "If you could change something about the way I behave to help me be a better person, what would you change?" Then be still and seriously listen to what they have to say. You don't get to control someone else's opinion of you; you can only influence that opinion for better or worse.

Finally, ask yourself these two questions:

- ◉ What is the one thing I can start doing that if I did it faithfully and consistently would make all the difference in my personal or professional life?
- ◉ What is the one thing I can stop doing by intentional, faithful, and consistent effort that would make all the difference in my personal or professional life?

In the following chapters, we will answer the question of "So what? So what about the Crosshairs Research? What about the types of stress? What can be done about these dynamics?"

We will take a closer look at navigating the relational, emotional, and directional challenges of working in vocations of people helping. You will discover how to develop a strategic plan to both gain and maintain vitality throughout a lifetime of serving others.

To complete your Personal Insight Exercise, go to chapter 3 of the online workbook at FullStrength.org/AtFullStrength.

PART 2

Navigating Relational Challenges

Interpersonal Encounters and the Toxic Triangle

The text came from an unrecognizable phone number and displayed these words: *Please tell me that God cares, that He has not abandoned me! I don't know how I'm going to go on with life!*

My immediate concern was for the physical safety of the person, so I prayerfully redialed the phone number not knowing who or what to expect. It was a ministry leader who was in deep despair over being abandoned by a trusted friend. This person was so distraught that he was wrestling with the idea that his life and ministry might not be worth preserving.

As a counselor specializing in working with ministry leaders, I've had the opportunity to work with thousands of faith leaders in all kinds of ministry settings all over the world. Some of the most painful situations for me involve leaders who have been physically tortured for their faith.

Jonathan ministered in an area of the world where Christians were hunted down and tortured. As a young ministry worker, Jonathan had spent several years in prison for his faith. He viewed this experience as part of the price he had to pay to serve Christ in his part of the African continent. Just when he thought things could get no worse, his second detention was brutal beyond imagination.

Jonathan was chained and staked out completely naked in the courtyard of the prison in the hot African sun. It was a torture technique referred to as the "slow burn." In an attempt to extract information, Jonathan lay exposed for days to the scorching sun and dehydrating heat. Every part of his naked body was severely sunburned. On other occasions,

Jonathan had his flesh pulled from his body with pliers to extract information about the house church he served.

When I first met Jonathan, his entire body was covered with scars. During our time of counseling, I asked Jonathan, "Of all the burdens you've had to bear, what was the most difficult?" His answer surprised me. He replied, "The betrayal of a friend." This friend, a former member of the house church, had disclosed the church's location. He left the fellowship of the house church never to return. Though efforts were made by Jonathan to reconnect, the former member declined to do so.

Among all the types of pain we experience as human beings, relationship-based pain is among the most difficult for humans to endure. Rejection, abandonment, and unresolved conflict that separates people have the capacity to generate one of the most unwanted companions on our life journey. Jesus experienced this in his relationship with Judas. King David addressed this type of pain in the following words:

If an enemy were insulting me, I could endure it; if a foe were rising against me, I could hide. But it is you, a man like myself, my companion, my close friend, with whom I once enjoyed sweet fellowship at the house of God, as we walked about among the worshipers. (Ps. 55:12–14)

Nearly every human has been through heart-wrenching experiences of disloyalty, deception, and betrayal at some point. Scripture seems to indicate that Paul's apprentice Timothy experienced pain like this during his leadership at the bustling megachurch in Ephesus. After three years of investing all he had into the lives of believers at Ephesus, Timothy expected the emerging leaders of the church to be loyal and faithful to him and to the Lord they served.

When Emperor Nero began his reign of intense terror against Christian communities in the empire, many Ephesian believers abandoned the church in Ephesus and returned to the pagan temples and emperor worship. Timothy's pain must have been intense. Paul wrote to encourage Timothy instructing him to choose new leaders, build new friendships, and begin his ministry in Ephesus afresh. In his intimate letter to Timothy, Paul outlined the qualities that Timothy should look for in church leaders.

Relational pain at times seems greater in magnitude than any other type of pain. Rejection, abandonment, and unresolved conflict leaves one on a painful journey, often without adequate closure. Only a friend can betray a friend. Only a friend can cause such pain!

This is well captured in the poetic music of Michael Card who writes this concerning the betrayal of Jesus by Judas:

Why did it have to be a friend
Who chose to betray the Lord
Why did he use a kiss to show them
That's not what a kiss is for

Only a friend can betray a friend
A stranger has nothing to gain
And only a friend comes close enough
To ever cause so much pain[1]

The quintessential illustration of abandonment pain was experienced by Jesus, who knowingly endured the cross to accomplish the will of the Father. It was there that he painfully uttered these words, "My God, my God, why have you forsaken me?" (Matt. 27:46).

It seems poignant that this expression of painful abandonment was the last word to be uttered by Jesus as he ended his earthly ministry. A sense of abandonment is the signature pain that characterizes human existence since the fall. As we navigate this fallen world, our lives will be filled with this kind of pain.

Corrie ten Boom, who survived the atrocities of a Nazi concentration camp, is numbered among the most quotable people who possess the license to speak about adversity and despair. In her reflections of the memories during her time in the concentration camp, she wrote:

There is no pit so deep that He is not deeper still.

Hold everything in your hands lightly, otherwise it hurts when God pries your fingers open.

Never be afraid to trust an unknown future to a known God.[2]

So, how do we navigate the challenges of relational pain? We'll address this question in the following sections.

Dealing with Relational Disappointment

At its core, we experience pain when our expectations of others are not met. This is one of the greatest challenges for leaders. People under your influence will often fail to meet your expectations, or you may not meet the expectations of others who placed you in a position of leadership.

How a leader manages the pain and frustration of unmet expectations is one of the key markers of an effective leader. Paul David Tripp, in his book *Dangerous Calling*, aptly captures the dynamics that generate discouragement and disappointment pain in the life of a pastoral leader. In the following passage, Tripp outlines a "cycle of danger" that flows from wrong assumptions and unrealistic expectations. Tripp writes:

In many cases the cycle of isolation and danger begins when the church that calls the pastor makes incorrect and unhelpful assumptions about the person they have called. Sadly, in many cases the person being called has not lived in protective and productive redemptive community for years. Having separated from the nurture of his home church, where his gifts were recognized, he goes off to a place where the faith has been academized and compartmentalized, being taught by professors who do not presume to function as the pastors of their students. . . .

The biggest [expectation] is that many churches simply don't expect their pastor to struggle with sin. . . .

They don't expect him to get discouraged in the middle of the war for the gospel. They don't expect him to be tempted toward bitterness or envy. They expect him to be a model husband and father. They don't expect him to be lazy or to settle for mediocrity. They don't expect that in moments of self-protection he will be tempted to be antisocial and controlling. They expect that he will be able to joyfully carry an unrealistic job description that would overwhelm anyone this side of Jesus's return. They expect that he will be content with significantly less pay than most people with his level of education. They expect that his wife is so fully committed to ministry herself that his coming to the church is actually a two-for-one deal. They don't expect that there will be moments when he is tempted to doubt the goodness of God. They don't expect that in a meeting or in the pulpit, fear of man will keep him from doing or saying the things that God calls him to do and say. They don't expect to hire a flawed man who is still desperately in need of the very grace that he is called to offer and exegete for others.[3]

Expectation dynamics like this are what sets the stage for toxic relationships to develop and metastasize, even when the relationship began with a sense of optimism and good intentions by all parties. Not knowing how to identify and navigate through these situations is the surest way for leadership effectiveness to be damaged or destroyed, along with the relationships themselves. In the next few sections, let's examine some proven strategies you can employ at the first signs of danger.

Exploring the Toxic Triangle

You may not be able to control the forces that set the stage for relationship stress to emerge, but you do have the ability to influence and prevent the relationship from melting down into a toxic soup that affects larger numbers of people.

In any leadership role, especially a ministry role, the leader has to deal with people who are bitter, controlling, and blind to the part they play in triggering a damaging relational meltdown. Ministry leaders don't have the luxury of choosing the people that God calls them to serve and lead. Within the flock, there will be people who are bitter, controlling, and toxic. These people often wear masks and may not be easy to identify, until something happens that pushes them to pull off their masks and begin poisoning the fellowship.

A wise leader must be able to identify people who appear friendly on the surface, but underneath are dealing with issues such that, if their expectations are not met, can cause them to become a destructive force within the fellowship. In most cases, these people carry deep wounds that they don't recognize or understand, let alone know how to heal. In the right set of circumstances, any of us has the potential to be the proximate cause for a relationship to decline and become toxic.

Following are some of the common signs that a relationship has or is becoming toxic. When you see these indicators, take action to stop further meltdown and allow healing to occur:

- You or the group feel exhausted, exasperated, or angry about the behavior of a particular individual during interactions that involve this person.
- You find yourself emotionally agitated from the drama this person creates.
- You find yourself thinking about how to rescue the situation and neutralize the tension this person creates.
- You dread or fear being in the presence of this person.
- You find yourself avoiding or withdrawing from this person.
- You don't like who you become when this person is present.
- You emotionally disengage when this person is present.
- You feel as if the person does not respect relational boundaries.
- You find yourself wanting to take control to prevent feeling controlled by this person.
- You find yourself feeling like you need to "walk on eggshells" around this person.
- You find yourself becoming angry when this person refuses to accept the emerging consensus of the group.

Though we cannot necessarily *control* the toxic situations or people in our lives, we can exert both a significant and positive *influence* over a situation that is becoming toxic.

THE TOXIC TRIANGLE

An exercise I have used since 1996, referred to as the *Toxic Triangle,* has been a helpful tool in managing situations where a toxic person is disrupting or destroying the harmony of an individual or group relationships.[4]

Let's examine each of the three angles of the triangle in turn, because understanding and wisely addressing one or more of these dynamics may help neutralize the toxic damage being created and restore the relational dynamics to a healthier state.

The Judgmental Angle

These individuals, or groups of individuals, are characterized by their judgmental spirits toward situations or toward others. Their underlying belief is this: *If you would be more like me, everything would be better. Just do things my way, and life will be good.* People who behave this way display a condescending and controlling attitude. People who behave this way are trying to ensure that the future will be better based on their past experiences. These people may be fearful of the future, so they want to take charge to control the future where they will feel more secure.

The belief and self-talk of judgmental people sounds like this:

- ◉ If only you were like me, life would be better!
- ◉ I am right, you are wrong.
- ◉ You are an idiot!
- ◉ It's your fault!

The Martyr or Victim Angle

While a subtler expression, people who play the martyr or victim angle can be just as damaging and controlling as those who are judgmental. These people manifest passive-aggressive behavior and manipulate relationships with messages like: *After all I've done for you, this is what I get?* People who play the victim or martyr role are essentially saying that they are not responsible for their situations (someone or something else is responsible), and they must get their way as they're due preferential consideration due to their circumstances.

The belief and self-talk of martyrs or victims sounds like this:

- ◉ After all I've done for you, this is what I get?
- ◉ I do all the work around here, and what thanks do I get?
- ◉ Nobody ever appreciates me for the sacrifices I make!
- ◉ It's just not fair!

The Rescuing or Fixing Angle

Though the intentions may be helpful, people who play the rescuing or fixing angle become insistent on having their way, believing that they possess a superior knowledge or expertise that will save the others from making a bad or even horrible mistake if they take a different path.

The belief and self-talk of fixers or rescuers sounds like this:

- ◉ I have the solution, but you just won't listen!
- ◉ You should be like me, and then your life would be better!
- ◉ Just do it my way, and life will be good!

If you've been involved in helping others who've been caught up in the Bermuda Triangle of toxic relationships, you know the pain that results when these dynamics play out in people's lives. As a leader, it becomes your responsibility to understand these dynamics, know when relationships have entered the triangle, and know what to do to help people break away from these destructive forces and get back on positive-relationship-building ground. An even more important consideration for leaders is to understand whether to express any of these unproductive postures in individual or group relationships.

Consider using the following statements as an indicator of toxicity in others or even yourself.

Toxic Thinking / Toxic Self–Talk

Judgmental: *If only you were like me . . . life would be better!*
I am right . . . you are wrong! (Black & white thinking)
You are an idiot!
It's your fault! (Blaming)
Martyr or Victim: *After all I have done for you . . . this is what I get!*
I do all the work around here and what thanks do I get!
Nobody ever appreciates me for the sacrifices I make!
It's just not fair!
Fixer or Rescuer: *I have the solution, but you just don't listen.*
You should be like me . . . then your life would be better!
Just do it my way and life will be good! (I have the answer)

When most vocational people helpers explore the dynamics of the Toxic Triangle, our thoughts quickly go to hurtful people and painful circumstances we have encountered. However, it is of great importance to consider the situations that cause us to step into the Toxic Triangle ourselves. We all get there at times and it is difficult to discern the exact moment we enter the Toxic Triangle. However, it is easier to stay out of the danger of the Toxic Triangle when we can clearly identify when we are in it.

Time for Self–Evaluation

Pause for a moment and reflect upon your own toxic behaviors or tendencies. Ask yourself these questions:

- Where do I tend to make my entry into the Toxic Triangle?
- When relationships that involve me grow more toxic, what's my move in the triangle—which posture do I assume next?
- When relationships reach a meltdown point, what's my final posture as I watch the relationship start to self-destruct?

As a leader, if you can't be vulnerable and conduct a self-assessment like this, you'll be part of the problem and not part of the solution to Toxic Triangle situations in life.

In any people-helping profession, you'll be invited or lassoed into very toxic situations and relationships. You'll be invited in as a paramedic, a surgeon, a rehab specialist, or in worst-case scenarios, as a funeral home director. In your leadership role, as you become proficient in understanding and helping people manage the Toxic Triangle, you can and should assume the position as fitness coach by training others to understand these toxic dynamics and develop the wisdom and strength to overcome and manage them proactively. Being like a fitness coach should be your ideal role as a leader seeking to create a healthy relationship culture where you serve.

Journeying to Effective Leadership

To lead others in proactively managing their relationships, you must be healthy yourself, fully in control over the Toxic Triangle issues. Your response patterns, whether you realize it or not, have been shaped by your specific nature and nurture history. This history encodes a response script into your life that begins to operate on autopilot mode over time. You've been conditioned to view your life experience through *filters* that can distort your view of reality. Leaders must come to understand and manage these dynamics that have shaped their lives if they are to lead others effectively into happy or wholesome relationships.

Seeking out help from other caregiving professionals who are trained and gifted in helping coach or counsel you into deeper levels of self-awareness is never a sign of weakness. Such assistance can help you rewrite your unhealthy automatic response scripts and remove certain filters that may be distorting and limiting your leadership ability.

Life's disappointments and discouragements are also powerful shaping forces that affect you in profound ways. How you respond to unmet expectations is a critical factor that impacts your leadership effectiveness.

A third area relating to life scripts deals with our self-talk, especially when confronted with challenging Toxic Triangle situations requiring adept leadership skill. If we have an inordinate need to be liked, approved of, and respected, our self-talk around a need like this affects how we behave, relate, and lead. We'll touch on a few of these self-talk patterns below to help illustrate the power of self-talk.

Understanding Your Response Pattern

First, you must acknowledge that your reaction or response to life's challenges is often scripted by numerous dynamics. You benefit when you recognize that we all have reactions that are often linked to pain in our pasts. To deny it is to sell yourself short in dealing with it in the present.

When dealing with relationship challenges where you are drawn into the Toxic Triangle, you must understand how you react when you yourself are in the triangle helping others to break out. This ability requires you to analyze and to understand your own entry point or posture as you enter the triangle. Do you come in as a judge, a martyr, a fixer, or a rescuer? My pattern is to enter the triangle somewhere between fixer and martyr. Even though I'm considered an expert in my field, the minute other people sense that I am trying to "fix" them, they emotionally begin to pull back or away.

As ministry leaders involved in a people-helping profession, one of the privileges of our profession is that we are granted the high honor of being invited into the private world of others. We are called to journey with them as they deal with life's challenges, particularly those involving toxic relationships. As with any of the toxic angles, the minute we try to fix others, we are complicating rather than helping them on their journey toward healing. When we move from trustworthy advisor to judge, fixer, or victim ourselves, we are attempting to control the person we're trying to help.

It is wise to reflect on and take note of where you tend to enter the triangle when you yourself become involved either as participant or advisor in a toxic relationship situation. What is your initial posture when you first enter the triangle?

In situations where the relationship does not begin to improve, as a participant or advisor, you will migrate to a second posture (angle) to see whether another approach can achieve a breakout response. It will be helpful to understand your next posture or angle. Where do you move next?

If I don't achieve success after multiple attempts of fixing, then my pattern is to drift toward becoming a martyr. These words enter my mind: *After all I've done for you (trying to help or fix you), this is what I get?* Pastors witness this victim or martyr posture every time a parishioner exits the church over some toxic wound. Here's the message the pastor hears: *After all we've done for this church, all the giving, all the volunteering, and this is the treatment we get?* Or maybe the exiting parishioner had a fixer angle, and the exit message is: *We tried to tell you this style of worship wouldn't work! Sorry. We're out of here!* The judgment angle sounds like this: *You need to preach the Bible!*

For some people trying to heal a relationship meltdown, they will even migrate to the third angle or posture in trying to achieve a breakout or breakthrough experience. For me, judging is my third perspective when I'm in the triangle. Though I enter this perspective rarely, it comes in the form of a judgmental warning: *This relationship will end if there's no change of heart!* As an experienced counselor, I've come to understand that my ability to perceive and understand another person fully is incomplete, therefore I tend to avoid making judgments believing that I don't have all the facts.

The essential point of this discussion is simply this: You can never truly heal a toxic relationship by employing any of the three angles or perspectives that define the Toxic Triangle, no matter how sincere you may be in your efforts to bring healing. Let's look now at some of the strategies that do work in helping people break out of the Toxic Triangle.

Managing the Toxic Triangle

Let's start with some guiding principles we must remember when dealing with toxic relationships:

- ◉ **Immunity from entering the Toxic Triangle is not possible, even for spiritually mature people and leaders.** Maturity leads to a reduction in frequency, duration, and intensity of triangle experiences, but does not guarantee freedom from involvement.
- ◉ **Self deception, or lack of perfect perception of reality, applies to everyone, to some extent.** (We assume and therefore believe that certain things may be true or false that in fact are not true

or false.) It's only a matter of where and to what degree we are self-deceived. Humility is required to accept this truth.

◉ **Toxic triggers affect each person uniquely.** Awareness of our triggers positions us for a more rapid escape from the triangle. We must learn to acknowledge honestly that we are always self-deceived; it's only a matter of degree and where.

◉ **Pride is the root attitude of all participants trapped in the triangle.** When wisdom moves us from a posture of self-justification to a posture of self-evaluation, then healing and restoration become possible. If you tend to enter the triangle as a judge, reflect on the truth expressed in Proverbs 16:18: "Pride goes before destruction. . . ." Behaving well outwardly does not justify our prideful hearts. Pride manifesting itself in fixing others is shrouded in a cloak. What appears to be genuine concern is actually concealed pride. Pride demands that the sacrificial martyr be reciprocated with admiration or appreciation. Pride displays a judgmental spirit in a cloak of self-appointed discernment.

◉ **False humility and pretending to be genuinely concerned for others fuels toxicity.** You can't fake genuine concern for people. You will only deepen their mistrust of you with you becoming another part of the problem.

◉ **Exiting the Toxic Triangle is a choice.** We also have the spiritual freedom of choosing not to take offense at the foolishness of others. We do not have to let the poor behavior and attitudes of others write the script of who we are going to be regardless of how ugly we are being treated. We ultimately, with God's help, choose who we want to be. "A person's wisdom yields patience; it is to one's glory to overlook an offense" (Prov. 19:11). Our goal ought to be that we come to the place in our lives that nothing offends us because of our high view of God.

◉ **Allowing principles to guide during toxic interventions keeps emotions from slipping into the driver's seat.** The Bible indicates that when we humble ourselves under God's mighty hand, in his time, he will lift us up. Humility is not a character quality. It is not a fruit of the Spirit. Humility is a posture. One can be humble one moment and arrogant the next.

Exiting the Toxic Triangle

As a leader, to get out of or help others get out of the Toxic Triangle, several things are required:

- **Pause and step back from the situation to get a bigger picture view of what's going on.** You must develop the ability to view the relational conflict through correct spiritual and emotional lenses. Assess what's best for the spiritual wellbeing of the parties at conflict, without being sucked into and becoming a participant in the drama. Emotions must never be denied or repressed, but they must be managed. A helpful analogy is to think about emotions going along for a car ride with you. The proper place for emotions is not in the trunk nor in the driver seat, but as a passenger.
- **Be fully aware of your posture tendencies as you enter a Toxic Triangle.** Do you slip into a judge, fixer/rescuer, or martyr/victim role? If your tendency is to judge, your goal is to make the positive choice of offering discerning insights instead. If your tendency is to fix or rescue, your goal is to shepherd or become a trusted advisor. If your tendency is to become a martyr or victim, your goal is to become sacrificial and supporting.
- **Work to discover God's deeper purpose that will result from a restored and managed relationship.** As a discerning, supportive, sacrificial advisor to the process, your goal is to help the parties begin to define and take the steps necessary to reach a point where God's work is being advanced and not stifled and damaging blows

are not being thrown. The goal is to achieve a state of peace. Only the Holy Spirit can move parties in a relationship to love another, but skilled leaders can help people escape the Toxic Triangle and achieve a state of peaceful and mutual coexistence.

◉ **Embrace humility.** Just as John the Baptist shared with his followers, "He must become greater; I must become less" (John 3:30), this insight must become a natural part of the way we help ourselves and others escape the Toxic Triangle. A humble attitude enables you to stay in the helpful role of advisor and caring friend seeking only the good of the parties in toxic conflict. Pride inspires you to fix or rescue someone else who is not really looking to be fixed or rescued, or worse yet, have the other party or parties in the conflict fix or rescue you when you assume the posture of martyr or victim.

God's Intentions for Us

Now let's take a look at what God intended for us as we encounter challenging relationships and situations. Review the chart below and notice the humility choices that lie outside the Toxic Triangle.

Consider: Why are the positive choices of offering discernment, being a trusted advisor or shepherd, and being sacrificial outside the triangle? Outside the triangle, the possibilities are infinite when birthed out of humility. But postures like judging, fixing, and being the martyr cultivate an erosion of options and possibilities of anything

THE TOXIC TRIANGLE

Justice and Discernment

Humility

Judgmental

Pride

Martyr or Victim

Rescuing or Fixing

Sacrificial

Trusted Advisor Shepherd

fruitful. We become cornered by our own prideful and self-preserving heart. Over time, the triangle becomes smaller and smaller, trapping us in a nearly irreconcilable situation.

Our toxic tendencies can often serve as indicators of what God intended for us—to be discerning, a trusted advisor or shepherd, or to be truly sacrificial. For the person who has a tendency to be judgmental, when led by the Spirit you will desire to be *discerning*. A person with a tendency to fix or rescue, when led by the Spirit, will desire to be a *shepherd* or *trusted advisor*. For the person who can easily feel like a martyr or victim—at heart, when led by the Spirit, will truly desire to be *sacrificial*.

The humble response to the adversity is to choose and commit to become and remain a trusted advisor, discerning, and sacrificial. We must be *intentional*. The person with a humble heart invests in others without conditions nor reciprocation. When lost within the Toxic Triangle, consider these principles as you seek to change from a prideful heart to a humble heart:

- ◉ If you are to be a trusted advisor, understand that the other person is free to accept or reject part or all of what you have to bring to the context. Nobody wants to be fixed. The moment another person senses that you are trying to fix them, they will push away.
- ◉ If you are to be discerning, exercise it with kindness. Use the highest and best discretion in what and how you bring to light the valuable information.
- ◉ If you are to be sacrificial, accept the reality that it may not be reciprocated. If you expect something good in return, then it is not really a sacrifice.

You must choose to be a 100-percenter in relationships without expecting reciprocation. The Bible refers to this as *agape love*, or unconditional love. It is deciding ahead of time what kind of person you want to be before God regardless of how others treat you. It is deciding to choose your actions based on principles rather than emotions of the moment.

Being a 100-percenter based on principles and choosing ahead of time what kind of person you want to be before God is easier said than done. However, incremental success is better than grand failure. The Bible does not say we should try to be Christlike. The Bible refers to being a Christian as having entered training in the same way an athlete trains. First Corinthians 9:25 states that "Everyone who competes in the games goes into strict training. They do it to get a crown that will not last, but we do it to get a crown that will last forever."

Dealing with toxic people and relationships requires training and skill development. The apostle Paul admonishes us in this verse to undergo strict training to win an eternal prize. By diligent study and practice, you'll be amazed at how skilled you can become at helping people escape their Toxic Triangles. Effectively serving people in managing their relationships is one of the most productive ministry leadership functions you can perform to help those you shepherd grow and relationally mature.

A humble response of discernment, being a trusted advisor or shepherd, or being sacrificial expands the possibilities of attaining God's highest and best in our relationships and endeavors. Even when the other person is in the Toxic Triangle, the opportunity is at its best when we choose to respond humbly, moving out or remaining outside the Toxic Triangle. When two or more people navigate within the Toxic Triangle, the opportunities for effectiveness, helpful endeavors, and relationships become greatly diminished.

We are not perfect! We will have failed attempts. But we must seek forgiveness and be willing to grant forgiveness. Remember:

◉ There is only one True Judge who is always just! God the Father, Omnipotent.

⦿ There is only one True Shepherd who never bites the sheep! God's Spirit that guides us.

⦿ There is only one True Sacrifice that is altruistic! Jesus and his Sacrifice.

To complete your Personal Insight Exercise, go to chapter 4 of the online workbook at FullStrength.org/AtFullStrength.

Confronting Difficult People

Who in your life do you experience as a challenging person?
What is it about that person that makes it a challenge?

From time to time, we receive requests to consult with churches or other organizations where there is a low level of trust and a high level of relationship stress. Before considering whether our ministry should get involved, we ask a couple questions:

- Is there an individual or group of individuals in the setting that if they were removed, the dynamics of the culture would instantly change for the better?
- Is anyone willing to confront this individual or group?

The answers to these questions quickly reveal the nature of the organizational challenge.

In an organizational context, people often tend to respond to difficult people in one of two ways: Remain silent, or rush to speak into the difficult person's life prematurely, without adequate insight into what's driving the person's disruptive behavior.

Because of the deep passion to impact others in a fruitful way, we can find ourselves moving to one of two extremes. First, because of the tendency to be genuinely helpful to others, the very thought of confronting can seem unpleasant. Therefore, we remain silent when speaking up might have brought about a catalytic and fruitful change.

The other extreme involves an unhealthy and compulsive need to add value to others, so we speak into their lives prematurely. Timing and context can make the difference in the receptivity of a person in need of a midcourse correction. But instead we sometimes speak into the lives of others, running the red light and crashing through the gate of appropriate timing and context.

We all have people in our lives who pose a challenge for us. We often forget, however, that to some, we may be the challenge. For this very reason, we must have humility mixed into the recipe of confrontation if we want the best chance at a fruitful outcome.

The objective of this chapter is to discover several strategies that will equip us to navigate those challenging relationships effectively. Confronting difficult people does not have to be as uncomfortable as we commonly think. When we have been equipped with effective strategies, we can navigate those challenging relationships and achieve more positive outcomes. But before we examine the strategies, it is important to accept some realities of being in community with others.

In the next chapter, you will receive a toolbox full of practical paradigms and strategies for confronting in a way that can bring about the most fruitful outcomes.

Cultivating a Context of Receptivity

Confronting disruptive behavior is essential for organizational growth to occur. We all have blind spots of which we are not aware. We all from time to time *are* the difficult person in the room. We all tend to feel and react defensively when confronted. We all have moments where we speak or behave foolishly. None of us has the ability fully to perceive and know what's going on inside others. Everyone has knowledge, strength, and skills that others don't have.

Gardening is a good metaphor for reflecting on the need for confrontation. In this metaphor, difficult people are represented by the weeds and pests that work to undermine and diminish the harvest potential. A greater harvest will occur when we test the soil, cultivate the ground, start the garden in the right season, plant healthy seeds, water, weed, feed, and protect the growing plants against pests or grazers, and then harvest at the moment of perfect ripeness.

The first priority in nurturing and caring for our organizational garden is to know and identify who needs to be confronted. Who is undermining and damaging the healthy plants in the garden? Making this assessment is often difficult. Dr. Henry Cloud, in his book *Necessary Endings,* outlines a strategy to identify the kinds of people on the team. He places people in one of three categories: wise, foolish, or evil.[1]

Let's add the fourth and important category of *ignorant* to remember this assessment.

The Wise Person

A person walking in wisdom responds favorably when exposed to knowledge and truth. He or she learns, adjusts, and grows in behavior to become continuously more effective and productive. These team members are teachable and are the backbone members of effective organizations. When confronted, the healthy response of a wise person is to *consider* what is being said, rather than immediately *counter* it, blocking out any opportunity to learn and to grow.

Note that being wise is not the same thing as being smart or gifted. People who are wise navigate relationships without causing friction. They build up and nurture others around them through their faithfulness and productivity. Wise people aren't easily distracted and pulled off course as they work to accomplish their positive purposes in any organizational context.

The Ignorant Person

The person walking in ignorance is simply one who does not know any better. He or she does not have adequate information to make the best choices. This word *ignorance* is not intended in any way to be derogatory. It is simply acknowledging that the person is not aware of the facts necessary to make better decisions.

You might even get the false impression that there is an inherent wisdom applicable to every area of life. But, we are all ignorant in certain ways and gifted in others. My gifts are in the area of counseling and coaching. In reality, you would never want me to do your taxes, fix your automobile, or even help you put a new roof on your home. I am ignorant, or at least very limited in my understanding, of these matters.

When valuable truths are brought into the light, we have the responsibility to make a choice. We can choose to walk in wisdom indicated by the willingness to consider and act accordingly, or we can choose to walk in foolishness and deflect the truth that has come into the light.

The Foolish Person

A foolish person is one who is less (or not at all) interested in gaining truth and learning from feedback that comes to them from people in their environment. They justify and rationalize their underperformance by blaming factors outside themselves. These people are ever learning but never able to come to a deeper knowledge of the truth.

It's important to consider that there's a difference between foolishness and being a fool. We all are capable of foolish moments where we say or do unwise things. In contrast, a fool is one who consistently refuses to acknowledge and align with truth when learning opportunities come his way. The individual walking in foolishness will inevitably counter the new information rather than exhibiting a willingness to consider the new insights.

It is not uncommon for fools to:

- Receive feedback defensively and with countering comments
- Consistently blame others for their circumstances
- Minimize the importance of their underperformance: "What's the big deal?"
- Regularly make excuses
- Be incapable of seeing how their behavior negatively affects productivity
- Be unable to see how their behavior negatively affects others
- Change the subject
- Point out the shortcomings of others

If we have integrity, we courageously need to examine *when* and *where* some of these countering postures apply in our own lives.

There is a statement that I frequently enter into my own personal journal as a reminder when dealing with the foolishness of myself or others. I encourage you to consider the same response when encountering foolishness.

....

God has gifted to us a spiritual option to deal with foolishness that we so often fail to exercise. We can choose to exercise our God-given spiritual freedom to not take offense at the foolishness of others. At the same time, we must realize that they have the spiritual freedom to choose foolishness.

—from my journal (Denny Howard),
May 2009

....

The Evil Person

An evil person (or a person who displays consistently evil characteristics) is one who leaves hurt and wounded people in his or her wake. Evil people have no concern for the damage and negative impact their attitudes and actions cause in the organizational environment. They care only about optimizing their own outcomes, not the overall productivity and outcomes of the organization itself. They care about only one thing: serving and fulfilling their own interests and desires.

It's hard for most of us to accept the notion that genuinely evil people are in our midst, especially inside our churches and other ministry groups. But even some ministry leaders are narcissistic and controlling. For example, the role of clergy can bring with it *imputed authority*, in which some men and women believe that since God called them to ministry leadership, he endowed them with wisdom and privilege to do things as they feel led—mistakenly assuming that this leading is coming from God by virtue of his calling. This view of authority allows more control to be taken than the normal *positional authority* allowed leaders in secular organizations.

It is sad to have to report that in my years of counseling thousands of spiritual leaders, numbered among them were clergy who would later spend time in prison as a result of their destructive indiscretions. Jesus warned us in the Gospel of Matthew concerning wolves that come in sheep's clothing. Some intend to deceive. Others are fully sincere, but self-deceived. This warning was not meant to cause us to mistrust people in positions of spiritual leadership. It does encourage us to have discernment. Under normal circumstances, it is fair to assume that ministry workers and other people helpers are harmless servants of God, and therefore fully worthy of our trust.

Acknowledging the Challenges of Confronting

The first and most important factor in confronting difficult people (especially those who are professing Christians) is to realize that confrontation is a spiritual matter. We are dealing with people who are allowing the desires of this world to control their behaviors, and our task is to help coach them into an awareness of this fact and turn them back into a posture of walking in the Spirit and living out of their new natures.

Confronting Foolish People

The writer of Proverbs tells us that "Wounds from a sincere friend are better than many kisses from an enemy" (Prov. 27:6 NLT). Other proverbs suggest that not all people are good candidates for confrontation:

Anyone who rebukes a mocker will get an insult in return. Anyone who corrects the wicked will get hurt. So don't bother correcting mockers; they will only hate you. But correct the wise, and they will love you. Instruct the wise, and they will be even wiser. Teach the righteous, and they will learn even more. (Prov. 9:7–9 NLT)

The way of a fool is right in his own eyes, but a wise man listens to advice. The vexation of a fool is known at once, but the prudent ignores an insult. (Prov. 12:15–16 ESV)

Scripture gives us warrant to forego confronting foolish people. Jesus instructed his disciples, "Do not throw your pearls to pigs. If you do, they may trample them under their feet, and turn and tear you to pieces" (Matt. 7:6).

How might this be said in a contemporary vernacular? *Do not give your best effort or speak your wisdom into a context where you know it will be trampled. Don't waste your breath! Don't spit in the wind! Don't hold your breath!*

The Bible gives clear instructions on how to deal with the person who lives his life walking in foolishness: Do not persist in conversation to persuade him. The foolish person will not *consider*, but rather, will continue to *counter*. To persevere is to become like the foolish person.

So, here's the hard lesson that we need to draw from these and other passages—do not get drawn into debates and discussions with difficult people who are foolish. Such people will not *consider* what you have to say, they will *counter* and ultimately seek ways to damage or hurt you.

We return again to Dr. Cloud's wisdom in *Necessary Endings* for guidance: "The strategy for foolish people is simple: Quit talking about the problem . . . because talking is not helping. . . . Give [establish] limits that stop the collateral damage of their refusal to change."[2] Cloud goes on, "With these kinds of people, the only time they get it is when it begins to cost them."[3]

Each of us must realize that we all *walk in foolishness* at times. Though some people are *fools* in the truest sense of the word, it is helpful to think of foolishness as a *condition* that is within the possibility of being cured. If we are honest with ourselves, we can reflect back on a time that we thought and acted foolishly, while all the time thinking to be wise in our own eyes. It is about that time that we later ask these rhetorical questions: *What on earth was I thinking? What was wrong with me? How could I ever do such a thing?*

Confronting Evil People

When dealing with a person who is bound up in evil behavior, the management strategy is different. Prayer has to be the first priority, and removal from the ability to influence and damage others the second. Pray for God to supernaturally intervene and miraculously transform this individual, but don't be overly optimistic that the person will change.

These types of people are unsafe and always destructive forces inside your organization or fellowship. They must be avoided to ensure your safety. Stay clear of them. If a confrontation is unavoidable, the person must be intentionally, assertively confronted by more than one person.

People exhibiting evil behavior must be isolated from being allowed routinely to hurt other people, because hurt people they will. This separation may necessarily include various forms of legal restraints. Clear boundaries must be established and consistently enforced. They must experience a deeply felt *cost* as a consequence for bad conduct.

Confronting Wise People

Jesus' teaching in Matthew 18 provides the most concise instruction on confrontation. The key truths are found in verses 15–20, but this passage must be considered in the light of the whole chapter. Here's the chapter outline:

- Greatest (Greatness) in the Kingdom (18:1–11)
- Parable of the Lost Sheep (18:12–14)
- Correcting Another Believer (18:15–20)
- Parable of the Unforgiving Debtor (18:21–35)

The three surrounding sections all have something to teach us about how to interpret the following key verses of 15–17.

If another believer sins against you, go privately and point out the offense. If the other person listens and confesses it, you have won that person back. But if you are unsuccessful, take one or two others with you and go back again, so that everything you say may be confirmed by two or three witnesses. If the person still refuses to listen, take your case to the church. Then if he or she won't accept the church's decision, treat that person as a pagan or a corrupt tax collector. (Matt. 18:15–17 NLT)

The word *sin* generally carries the idea of "missing the mark." In this context, the word likely conveys the idea of another believer offending you in some way that disrupts your ability to relate to the person in a healthy way as a brother or sister in Christ.

Jesus plainly teaches that we are to share our offense only with that person. To do otherwise (complain or gossip about the other person) is a sin in and of itself. In the vast majority of cases, the offender will be grieved that he has caused you this pain and seek immediate forgiveness and reconciliation—which is to be immediately granted.

If reconciliation does not occur, then you must return with one or two observers to document the fact that you are seeking reconciliation and recovery from that which has offended you. If reconciliation still does not occur in the smaller circle involving observers, then the entire body is to be informed—and the group needs to begin to view and relate to the offender not as a fellow Christian, but as someone in need of receiving the transforming power of the gospel, as forgiveness and reconciliation are the hallmark truths of the Christian faith.

This passage is not teaching that we can shun or denounce such people; it's teaching us that we need to view and relate to them as if they are unbelievers in need of trusting Christ as their Savior. They have lost the honor of being considered a member of the family of God, but they should never lose our compassion and desire to lead them into a transforming relationship with Jesus.

See the parable of the unforgiving debtor immediately following verses 15–20. Since God has forgiven so much that it required the substitutionary death of his son, he is angered when a ready spirit of forgiveness and reconciliation does not characterize the life of a professing Christ follower.

There are some key truths we should discern from Jesus' teaching about correcting other believers who offend us:

- Go only to the person who can help you fix the problem and restore broken fellowship. The circle of involvement should remain as small as possible to remedy and restore the damaged relationship. Once fixed, the drama should end and stay there.
- If you fail to handle the offense as Jesus instructs, you unnecessarily set the stage for the offender to experience further isolation and alienation caused by gossip or publicly complaining about the offender. You become part of creating another problem when you do this. You become an offending party.
- When taking observers is necessary, select mature individuals who function as referees and arbiters to help protect an alleged offender from being improperly accused of offensive or harmful conduct. In some instances, as the offended person, you may be in the wrong, and you are the one who must ask forgiveness for bringing a defective allegation and seek reconciliation for improperly accusing another believer.

Knowing When and Where to Confront

Most people have heard the expression, "Timing is everything." When it comes to confronting people, whether they are wise, foolish, ignorant, or evil—timing *is* everything. During my early years of counseling, I learned the hard way that there are right and wrong times to confront behaviors in order to maintain healthy relationships and a healthy culture. In truth, you cannot find an ideal time to give someone bad news. You can however select a wrong time to present bad news.

Confrontation should never occur when emotions are storming, anger is raging, or any of the parties in the conflict are weary and exhausted.

Though not always possible, confrontation ideally takes place on neutral ground where both parties are required to make an investment in meeting in a safe, nonthreatening venue. Neutral ground also has the effect of keeping either party from having negative associations or memories around the experience, such as the pastor's office or the person's home. Being part of a confrontation experience often involves experiencing intense emotions, guilt, and shame with corresponding longer-term memories. In many or most cases, joyful memories should result when reconciliation and restoration occur.

Remembering the End Goal

The offended party must always keep in mind the desired outcome before confronting a fellow believer. Simply stated, the end goal is the full and healthy restoration of relationship and fellowship. Nothing is more important to God than reconciliation and restoration of relationships. It's the story of the Bible.

The offended party must have a clear picture of what restoration looks like before acting. What response are you expecting from the offender? In cases where restitution is sought, if the offended party makes receiving some form of restitution the top priority and does so at the expense of enabling the relationship to be restored, the offended party is playing with the fire of provoking God's anger. This truth is depicted in the parable of the unforgiving debtor that concludes Matthew 18. It's clear that God prefers us to suffer the loss of things and have the relationship restored. Truly forgiving a debt owed by another is a unique way to worship God; it demonstrates the power of his life in yours and is one of the most powerful testimonies you can offer others as long as you don't flaunt your generosity. If you do that, you're simply exchanging one form of repayment for another.

Before confront someone, here are some important questions to ponder:

◉ Can you identify in advance the potential benefits to all who may be involved? If there are no beneficial outcomes for the person being confronted, it is likely to be a difficult and unfruitful interaction.
◉ What is the plan if your confrontation is unfruitful and does not end as expected?
◉ Have you considered varying outcomes that may be acceptable though not ideal?

As a leader, one of your highest duties is to create a culture or community where relational health flourishes, and people who threaten such a healthy culture must be identified and effectively managed God's way. It's our prayer that God will teach and show you how to effectively deal with difficult people. It's one of the most challenging aspects of being a leader.

The Lens Exercise, to which I alluded in chapter 3, can be extremely helpful as it pertains to a difficult or conflicted situation. Again, these tools can help you gain a clearer perspective from different vantage points. So think of a current or past conflicted situation and try on one or more of the six lenses listed below.

6 Lenses to Gain Perspective

The **Dark Lens** helps us see our circumstances from the worst possible scenario.

The **Inverted Lens** allows us to view the same circumstances from the perspective of that other person with whom we are encountering difficulties.

The **Rear-View Lens** allows us to discover how our past may be distorting our perspective.

The **Wide-Angle Lens** helps us see our circumstances based on the perspective of others we deem to be wise.

The **Panorama Lens** helps us see our circumstances from the vantage point of the future.

The **Bright Lens** helps uncover the opportunities that may not be readily apparent to us in the moment.

Choose a challenging situation in your life and try on the different lenses. They will help you gain perspective from different vantage points and open options that may be yet unrealized.

Only the Dark Lens and Bright Lens will be illustrated on the next page. However, you will, like many others, find the remaining four lenses to be very helpful as well. You can find them in the free online workbook in the Personal Insight Exercises for chapter 5 at: FullStrength.org/AtFullStrength.

Dark Lens—Most Negative Outlook

- ◉ Concerning your story, what might be the worst possible scenario?
- ◉ How likely is it that the worst scenario will happen?
- ◉ Could you tolerate it if the worst were to happen?

Bright Lens—The Optimistic Outlook

- ◉ What opportunity may be hidden below the surface or still unrealized in your challenging situation?
- ◉ What might be the benefits of both recognizing and acting on the opportunity?

Based on this chapter, what is one thing that you need to do differently when confronting that can make all the difference in your life situation?

To complete your Personal Insight Exercise, go to chapter 5 of the online workbook at FullStrength.org/AtFullStrength.

Mastering Effective Confrontation Strategies

Effective confrontation and relationship management with difficult people requires more than good intentions. It is imperative to have effective strategies and techniques in your tool box to bring about the most positive outcomes. When leaders confront, extra skill and sensitivity are required because of the power differential.

> **CAUTION**
>
> **SPEED BUMPS AHEAD**

The tools I present here are not intended to be a step-by-step formula. But rather, they are a smorgasbord of paradigms, postures, and strategies that can be helpful in the navigation of challenging relationships.

Let's look at each one of these strategies to address the difficult situations and/or people we encounter that may require confrontation. They are like an assortment of paradigms, postures, and process strategies that have been collected over the years of coaching and counseling high-capacity and brilliant leaders. You may find some of them unpalatable, maybe even controversial. However, if you consider them with your heart and mind open to new possibilities, you may find one or more to be life changing.

You can find additional paradigms, postures, and process strategies of equal importance in the appendices for chapter 6 in the online workbook at: FullStrength.org/AtFullStrength.

The Four Paradigms

Effective treatment of any problem must begin with a clear diagnosis. If you took your automobile to a repair shop because it stalled at traffic lights, you would report the symptoms that would help the auto technicians clearly assess the exact nature of the problem. But imagine that later in the day you go to pick up your automobile, pay the cashier, and drive away just to experience your car stalling again at the first two or three traffic lights. You call back to the repair shop, and they tell you that they rotated the tires, aligned the front end, and changed the oil, but didn't do anything to address the real problem. It might be the last time you use their service.

However, this dynamic happens frequently in the people-helping vocations. Instead of adequately collecting the information necessary to make an accurate diagnosis, assumptions are made concerning the exact nature of the problem. The situation becomes complicated when we confuse our past issues with the current situation. It is easy to fill in the blanks with inadequate information that results in wrong conclusions.

A *paradigm* is a new model, pattern, or example of how to approach our life circumstances. The Four Paradigms can serve as a guide to help you get a clear diagnosis of a difficult situation, confront the issues, and assist in solving the challenges. The Four Paradigms are ways of viewing life that can help you form more accurate conclusions. So let's dig into the paradigms.

Anthropologist Paradigm: Being a Student of Others

This first paradigm, an anthropologist, helps us know how to approach situations that can be awkward or confusing. Because we do counseling or coaching in cross-cultural settings, we must adopt an approach that is suitable in attaining the clearest understanding of another person.

Anthropology is the scientific study of the origin, the behavior, and the physical, social, and cultural development of humans.[1] The anthropologist does this study without passing judgment on the people being studied. The goal is to understand the history and drivers of behavior in the culture being studied.

As an example, let's consider an anthropologist who was a member of the first archeological team uncovering Aztec ruins. The team uncovered evidence that this culture conducted human sacrifices that included innocent children and babies. It would be easy for the anthropologist to conclude that these people were a primitive and unrefined people. As the dig continued, it became more and more evident that these people were actually quite advanced for their time in history. Additional evidence revealed strong family bonds indicating that children were loved and nurtured in the culture, leaving the anthropologist to wonder what caused these people to practice human sacrifice.

As additional evidence surrounding Aztec beliefs emerges, the evidence suggests that the people considered it an honor to be sacrificed to the gods. Their beliefs seemed to suggest that such sacrifices were done for the greater good of the family offering their child to the gods. The anthropologist begins to wonder, "What kind of love and rationale would drive parents to offer their child, especially with the knowledge that the family would suffer deep grief for years to come?"

When we approach challenging or struggling people and situations as an anthropologist by asking investigative questions, without prejudging motives and behaviors, we can uncover a deeper, fuller picture of the life experience of the person. Depending on the nature of the investigative questions asked, we may subconsciously lead the person to share glimpses of themselves that paint a picture of them that we had already formed in our own minds, akin to creating a self-fulfilling prophecy.

Dr. John Gottman, a leading marriage researcher, asserts that the negative energy or damage that arises out of conflict scenarios can be totally averted with two to three well-framed investigative questions, when early intervention occurs. But of great importance to this process is the motive of wanting to understand truly the behavioral drivers by asking objective questions, not those designed to trap the person into giving responses that support a preconceived interpretation of the conflict situation. When truth begins to emerge through honest investigation and understanding, the parties at conflict will soften their defensive postures and begin to feel understood, setting the stage for an improved relationship. To understand and to be understood is the goal of all effective communication and the foundation for healthy relationships.[2]

Enlightenment Paradigm: Bringing to Light Valuable Information

Numerous assessments pertaining to conflict management reveal that over 60 percent of our population tends to be *conflict avoiders*. The Livstyle assessment (Livstyle.com) has indicated consistently over the past decade that 63 percent of the adult population (ages eighteen and over) indicated that avoidance was their primary or secondary way of dealing with conflict. The thought of confronting someone who is offending us is often well developed in our heads, but in reality can manifest in postures of avoidance and being passive-resistive. The word *confrontation* elicits negative feelings. However, if we think of it as *bringing to light valuable information*, a confrontation can become a gift.

For example, one could sincerely say something much like this: "I am not a true friend if I do not bring to light some important information!"

The words have a "work with me" posture. They move an interaction away from a posture of being *against* to a posture that communicates, "We're in this together."

Civility Paradigm: Choosing Regard

We all encounter people who are so difficult it seems impossible to respect them. The Bible commands us to love one another. It is interesting that the Bible does not command or even suggest that we *like* one another. Very few passages even refer to us *respecting* one another.

If you cannot find it within yourself to respect the person who is difficult for you, you have an alternative. This alternative is nearly as effective as respect and does not expend as much emotional, spiritual, and relational energy. When we cannot *respect* a person, we can demonstrate *regard* for that person. Here is the difference:

◉ Respect is earned.
◉ Regard can be a gift.

Why should we demonstrate regard for the value of another person? Because Christ died for even the most difficult individual, we can demonstrate regard for all people. If we devalue them, we are saying to God, "You made a foolish investment!"

In this paradigm, your job is to help the person being conflicted move to a posture of being consistently civil, regarding or loving the other party without allowing him or her to highjack their emotions when together. You are not trying to convince the person you're helping to like or respect the conflict person. You're simply trying to help them be civil toward and love the conflict person, while at the same time creating a force field around the heart where the person you're helping stays in full control of his or her emotions when in the presence of their conflict person.

If Christ died for the conflict person, love requires you to relate to that person with civility and positive regard, even though they possess personality characteristics that you find unpleasant or objectionable. It is no sin to avoid being in the presence of such people when that is possible. When not possible, you must learn to view those people with positive regard and relate to them in a civil manner.

In my counseling career, some of the most difficult interactions I've experienced involve people who have molested children. Part of my counseling involves helping these people prepare a survival plan for likely incarceration. To fulfill my duty, I had to regard such people through the lens of love. I had to help them in a civil manner remembering that Christ died for them as well as for me.

Grace with Truth Paradigm: Idolizing Speaking into Others' Lives

Having to speak into the life of others may be idolatrous. We have all met people who simply must share their opinion in every situation. If we are honest with ourselves, most leaders have been in this dilemma.

Every leader or person in a people-helping role has a fundamental desire to have a positive impact in the lives of those they lead and serve. One of the greatest challenges we face is the desire to speak into the lives of other people. In our true desire to help others, we must avoid developing an unhealthy need or compulsion to add value in each encounter we have with people seeking our help.

Consider the following admonitions from Scripture:

When words are many, transgression is not lacking, but whoever restrains his lips is prudent. (Prov. 10:19 ESV)

Too much talk leads to sin. Be sensible and keep your mouth shut. (Prov. 10:19 NLT)

This paradigm is helpful when dealing with people, even those in leadership or people-helping professions, who just feel compelled to speak their wisdom into your life. These people have an unhealthy or compulsive need or belief that they, from their wisdom reservoir, can add value in every people-helping situation or exchange.

It's natural to want to push back against such people, ignore them, patronize them, pretend to agree with them, or walk away from them. But pursuing one of these options may leave you feeling dishonest and an accomplice to their unhealthy behaviors.

We must pause and avoid leaping to conclusions when we encounter difficult people like this. Their motives may be to control and manipulate others or it could be a sign that the person lacks the skill to express hurt, anxiety, or insecurity in a more positive and constructive way.

Catherine, a nonprofit leader, complained to me during an advice-seeking session that her priest had lied to her when she confronted him on an issue. Catherine went on to offer justification for the rightness of her perspective and for feeling offended by her priest's dishonesty: "How audacious that he would outright lie to me!" She then articulated her plan to "deal with" her priest since he needed to be exposed for his lack of honesty.

Seeking support for her plan, Catherine asked me for my perspective on the situation. I replied that, "Lots of good people lie to you; they are just less obvious about it. So what makes this situation so different that you feel compelled to take action?" My response displeased her greatly and was a moment of reckoning with the truth about her own life and behavior.

Catherine had an unhealthy and compulsive need to speak into the lives of other people. Thinking herself helpful, her behavior forced others to deflect her feedback and helpful insights. Not wanting to hurt her feelings or aggressively confront her offensive behavior, most people avoided confronting Catherine with the truth about herself as an opinionated "truth teller."

As a leader or people helper, you need an effective model to help such people. These people are often good people who care about others. They may be high-capacity people in their knowledge, gifts, and skills. However, these people suffer from an inordinately high opinion of themselves. Combine this with a compulsive need to speak truth into the lives of other people, and you will have a conflict catalyst in your midst.

Here's a response strategy that may be helpful when a truth teller forcefully shares his opinion, expecting compliance with his perspective of truth: "I appreciate you sharing your perspective, and I will weigh it with the information received from others with perspective on this issue." If the truth teller persists, set the boundaries by repeating, "I am certainly going to consider and weigh your perspective with that of others. Again, I am grateful for your willingness to contribute to the discussion." Considering the perspective of others is not agreeing or disagreeing; it's a truthful way to deal with a person who feels that he is genuinely trying to add value or speak into the situation.

Following are some indicators that you may be dealing with a truth teller who has the potential to catalyze conflict or tension in the discussion:

- Though the person may be kind or friendly in sharing, she conveys the message that her perspective is superior to that being offered by others.
- He presents his perspective as if it's the one with the deepest spiritual insight or wisdom.
- She disrupts the discussion by stifling others if they present a different perspective.
- You hear the words, "Yes, but . . ." or "No, that's not right because . . ."
- He always wants the last word.
- You hear language like, "I think there's a better idea."
- You leave the discussion feeling controlled, manipulated, and like your views didn't matter all that much.

At this point, it's good to take a moment and reflect on whether you exhibit any of these characteristics of a truth teller. If you are in a position of authority or leadership, your responsibility is to bring out the best thinking from all the minds involved in the discussion and allow the best ideas to surface, even though such ideas may be different than your thoughts on the topic. You must also manage and neutralize the stifling influence of truth tellers in the room. It's always good to remember and even share the aphorism: *All of us together are smarter than any one of us alone.*

I had one ministry leader who cut short a generous sabbatical to return to the pulpit because he missed the intoxicating high of speaking into the lives of others. For this individual, his self-worth was wrapped up in feeling indispensably valuable as he was instructing others on the path they should walk.

Ask yourself: *Have I learned to speak with both grace and truth?* Truth without grace is cruel. Grace without truth can be misleading. If we cannot speak with both grace and truth, then we may want to consider a prayerful silence until we are able to do so as a leader.

The Four Healthy Leadership Postures

These four postures come from lessons learned over the years of counseling and coaching very gifted leaders and people helpers. They are not firm rules of engagement, but rather suggestions to assist you in dealing with the many conflicted situations you encounter. These postures are helpful tools to have in your toolbox, further equipping you to deal effectively with complicated situations of life.

Be Teachable, Not Just Learn–able

Learn-able is a capacity. Getting straight As in school is an indication of being *learn-able*. But *teachable* is an attitude. Many very brilliant people are actually foolish. Some of the most intelligent and talented people in our

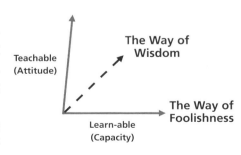

culture can be involved in foolishness. In the same way, you can find simple people who are very teachable and therefore, wise.

Being teachable is the path to wisdom. We must never lose sight of the fact that God wants us to grow in wisdom. Wisdom is the correct application of knowledge with the goal that we exhibit God's love in all our interactions. Loving others means that we relate to them in accord with all the teachings and principles God has shared with us in the Holy Scriptures. Wisdom and the consistent expression of love are deeply connected. The following proverbs illustrate the consequence of foolishness.

The prudent keep their knowledge to themselves, but a fool's heart blurts out folly. (Prov. 12:23)

Fools find no pleasure in understanding but delight in airing their own opinions. (Prov. 18:2)

Do not answer a fool according to his folly, or you yourself will be just like him. (Prov. 26:4)

One of the most profound lessons I've learned in my journey came in a graduate course taught by Dr. V. This beloved professor consistently exemplified an enthusiastic, teachable posture. He truly was a student of life. When he gained a new insight from one of his students, during his class discussion he would turn and say, "I learned this from Mary. Mary, would you share what you taught me with the rest of the class. You will communicate this much better than I would." This posture created such a positive learning atmosphere. Both leaders and students would discover and learn together bringing out the best that each had to offer for the benefit of the rest of the class. Dr. V exhibited a teachable posture worth emulating.

Armed with enough humility, leaders can learn from anyone!

Respectfully Consider, Not Rudely Counter

Have you ever been asked your opinion on a matter only to have the other person abruptly disagree with you? The first thought that flashes through your mind is this, "If you didn't want my opinion, then why did you ask?"

Many leaders are tempted to adopt a posture of quickly countering the opinions of other people when they differ from views held by the leader. For some leaders, they may feel threatened with the belief that "if this idea catches fire, I'll lose control over the organization that I'm leading." In other situations, the leader's arrogance may show through when he simply dismisses a differing opinion as stupid or foolish. Regardless of the motive, a leader who consistently displays a countering demeanor to the views of others is creating an unhealthy team culture. She is squandering the team's greatest resource—the collective wisdom and execution energy of the group.

To become an effective leader, the leader must maintain a posture of respective consideration for every idea and viewpoint offered in a discussion, regardless of how extreme or distracting the viewpoint may seem. Extreme ideas or ideas on the edge of reality are often the very catalysts needed to have a breakthrough moment in understanding.

To respectfully consider the ideas and perspectives of others does not signal or mean that you agree with them, but it does convey the important message that other viewpoints are welcomed, desired, and will not be judged or condemned in front of the group. Adopting a consistent posture of respectful consideration provides these three benefits:

⦿ It affords time for more thoughtful consideration before making a response.

⊙ It restrains you from displaying a negative or judgmental reaction before others.
⊙ It conveys that you value every team member by openly welcoming everyone's ideas.

Here are response suggestions that you can practice, if your normal tendency is to counter, rather than consider viewpoints that differ from yours:

⊙ "Wow! That's an idea I never I would never have considered. Because I respect you like I do, I'd like to take some time to think through your idea before I/we make our decision."
⊙ "What you just said deserves more thought and reflection."
⊙ "I would appreciate some time to think about your perspective. I'll reconnect with you by [date] and share my thoughts after giving your idea respectful consideration."

When we communicate that we consistently value other people, it's very difficult for a person to become or remain offended that their perspective wasn't immediately embraced. Oftentimes, the person may have been "shooting from the hip," and giving more time will allow him to think through and potentially revise his own thoughts about the situation. It also truly gives us more time to consider revising our own perspectives and come to a better solution overall.

Be Propositional, Not Positional

When you become emotionally flooded concerning a situation in your life, it is easy to become *positional* in your emotional posture. You become fixed and inflexible in your stance, unwilling or unable to hear alternative perspectives. It is felt by others as an ultimatum or demand.

A healthy alternative posture is to choose being *propositional*. Here you offer your thoughts as something for consideration or acceptance, which is felt by others more as an appeal to consider.

When anxiety or tension emerges during a discussion, put the issue being discussed in its proper category. Questions like "Will this issue be important a month from now, or a year from now?" are helpful to size up the importance of the issue. To allow emotions to flare over noncritical issues is simply unwise, and something that can easily be managed by the leader.

PastorServe (a clergy coaching ministry) has a helpful exercise that helps establish the importance of an issue and put it in its proper perspective. It is called the Five D exercise.[3] The questions in this tool are:

1. Would we be willing to *die* for this issue?
2. Would we staunchly *defend* this issue, no matter what?
3. Is this an issue that is worthy of serious *debate*?
4. Is this an issue worth our valuable *discussion* time?
5. Should we simply *dismiss* this issue as a distraction?

So when should we be positional? Be positional when the issues are *essential* to God. Here are some simple guidelines to follow:

1. For the essentials in your faith, be willing to *die* and *defend*, maybe *debate*.
2. In the secondary issues, be willing to *discuss*, maybe *debate*.
3. But when the issues are tertiary, be willing to *discuss* and *dismiss*.

Be Discrete: Using the NBA concept

From time to time every leader will encounter messes that will need to be managed and cleaned up for the health of a group of people or organization. A key principle found in Matthew 18 suggests that when controlling damage and restoring a messy situation characterized by sinful or damaging behavior, the circle of involved people should remain as small as needed to resolve the situation.

After car wrecks, people tend to want to slow down, stop, and gawk at the wreck along the roadway. People seem to get some sort of curiosity high by investigating a fresh crash scene. People compromise their attention to driving and intently focus on all the observable details surrounding the crash site—the police lights and sirens, the fire trucks, the ambulances, the damaged vehicles, and injured passengers all become the focus as we pass by a crash scene. It's in our nature to want to understand what just happened and how that will impact the lives of those involved.

While the source of a technique known as NBA is not clear, this mess-management model is a simple and helpful way to remind ourselves how to restore people ensnared in a sin-laden messy situation. While our natural tendency may be to tell everyone what just happened, Scripture advises another model—the NBA model.

Here's a simple outline of the model that serves as a good guide for who to inform or involve in the mess-management process:

1. **Necessary:** Who does necessity indicate be included in the circle of knowledge and involvement in managing the messy situation?
2. **Beneficial:** Will it be beneficial for certain parties to be fully informed of the circumstances surrounding the messy situation?
3. **Appropriate:** How much information about the messy situation is appropriate for various parties to know and understand?

Keeping the Matthew 18 principle in mind, by taking the time to cycle through the NBA analysis, clarity should emerge as to who should be involved and to what extent the details should be shared. This approach reduces the possibility for gawking, gossiping, and judging. It also helps set the stage for recovery and restoration to occur. This approach runs counter to the world's know-all, tell-all, and find-someone-to-blame response to messy situations. It also helps us to reach out for God's highest and best.

The Four Process Strategies

In addition to having the proper paradigms and postures, process strategies will also allow you to navigate those challenging relationships more effectively. These process strategies are timeless, field-tested, and deemed helpful by many of the clients we have had the honor to journey with as they navigated difficult challenges. Though these process strategies are quite simple to understand, they can be difficult to master. However, incremental success is always better than grand failure.

Noting the Importance of Esteeming Others

One important way we can esteem others is to consider such factors as the timing and context in which a confrontation occurs. Before a seed is planted, the gardener must soften and prepare the soil to have any hope that germination, growth, and harvest will occur. To confront someone in the presence of other parties may cause embarrassment and anger in the person being confronted. People will receive unpleasant news about themselves only when and to the extent they feel esteemed and respected by the person bringing confrontation news.

Leadership coach John Maxwell says this about timing and context:

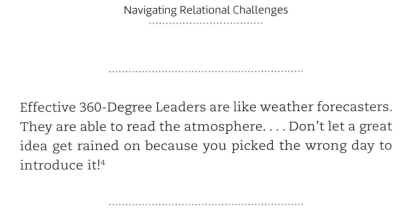

Effective 360-Degree Leaders are like weather forecasters. They are able to read the atmosphere. . . . Don't let a great idea get rained on because you picked the wrong day to introduce it![4]

When confronting, if we are to honor God in the process, our goal is not to diminish the person. It is to address unacceptable behavior that is disruptive to the health of an individual or a group relationship. The tendency of most people when addressing a behavioral issue is to react defensively. For growth and healing to occur, the person must feel and believe that you are confronting them out of love and respect for their health and wellbeing.

Because of our sin nature, we all have a bent toward justice. And justice takes on different shapes. It's that desire to make things right or fair, a need to even the playing field. The negative extremes can include revenge or the desire to punish cloaked in a posture of being one who cares. This underhandedness happens far too often in Christian circles. It is an insidious form of control. With a judgmental mindset, the future can only be a recycled version of the past. Justice in its aberrant form is birthed out of pride, not righteousness.

This need for justice has been evident throughout history. Both Mother Teresa and Adolf Hitler had a justice bent, but the justice for them took on dramatically different forms. Mother Teresa's justice was based in principles greater than herself. Adolf Hitler's aberrant form was based on his own narcissistic needs.

The desire for justice is rooted in a spiritual reality concerning sin. The Bible says, "Without the shedding of blood there is no forgiveness" (Heb. 9:22). Since the beginning of time, there has been war, human sacrifice, animal sacrifice, honor killing, fighting, revenge, and hate—all in the name of attaining some form of justice as an individual or culture defines it. When Jesus took on the sins of man and died on the cross, it was the shedding of his blood that brought justice—the ultimate act of justice. It was also the ultimate act of grace.

We all have justice within us. We want to expose wrong, at least, as we see it. There is a paradox between justice and mercy, truth and grace. When we lack truth, we lack the courage to speak and act with conviction. When we are without grace, we lack the compassion to empathize with the deepest needs and longings of others.[5]

The Gospel of John states that Jesus came "full of grace and truth" (John 1:14). Jesus was not full of grace on some occasions and truth in other circumstances. He was not 50 percent grace and 50 percent truth. Jesus was 100 percent grace and truth. He also esteemed others as indicated by his ultimate sacrifice. From his life, we can glean these principles:

- Truth spoken without grace can be cruel.
- Grace dispensed without truth can be misleading.
- Either truth or grace without demonstrating esteem can be potentially manipulative or controlling.

This concept is evidenced in both the Old and New Testament. For example, Micah 6:8 asserts, "[God] has shown you, O mortal, what is good. And what does the LORD require of you? To act justly and to love mercy and to walk humbly with your God." The correlation here is clear:

- **Act Justly** (Truth-telling)
- **Love Mercy** (Grace-giving)
- **Walk Humbly** with your God (Esteeming others)

We bear testimony of this paradox of grace and truth in the life and death of Jesus. God's justice and truth required a sacrifice to redeem mankind. The price was paid on the cross. It was grace and mercy in Jesus' response to his executioners when he said, "Father, forgive them, for they do not know what they are doing" (Luke 23:34).

It was in his deep pain that Jesus still had the audacity to both esteem and bestow grace upon a nefarious criminal hanging on a cross, "Today you will be with me in paradise" (Luke 23:43). It was his capacity, in excruciating pain, to demonstrate grace and mercy in showing concern for Mary by saying to the disciple John, "Behold, your mother!" (John 19:27 ESV).

Esteeming others as a foundation to healthier relationships is evidenced in the epistles as well. According to Romans 12 and Philippians 2, we are to have regard for others and value them if for no other reason than Christ died for them. We must recognize people's value if we are to walk in obedience.

Confronting others is most likely to produce the best outcomes when the person being confronted experiences being esteemed or valued. Truth is best dispensed when served with grace and truth. If we do not esteem the other person, then we potentially cultivate a context that will not bring about the most fruitful outcome.

Dispensing Information Wisely: The Candor Continuum

One of the most challenging aspects of confrontation is the question of who should know, what they should know, and why they should know it. The question of what or how much should be shared is a very important issue. The Candor Continuum will be helpful for leaders responding to mess ups.

The word *candor* conveys the idea of honesty and forthrightness. However, being candid also allows us to be reserved and discerning about the extent of information that we share. As leaders, we must control any compulsion to tell everyone everything, just because we're "in the know." We may think this impresses people, but without some discretion, we could be harming others or tainting relationships by telling others more that they want or need to know. In many cases, this is a sophisticated form of gossip, rationalized by the musing that not to share every known detail is somehow being deceitful.

Discretion is behaving or speaking in such a way as to avoid causing offense to a weaker believer or sharing information that can be harmfully gossiped by the holder of that information. By not knowing more than they need to know, people cannot purposely or inadvertently share or be harmed by the information.

Discretion is advocated in the wisdom literature and elsewhere in Scripture. Discretion is a God-honoring discipline that is critical to healing messy situations. Always pray and ask God to guide you in how best to apply discretion in every confrontational situation. It involves wisely determining what another person can handle.

For example, it would be very inappropriate to be most honest with a child who has no capacity to process the pain of certain adult realities. True discretion involves practicing NBA. Who needs to know and for what purpose? What is the benefit for others to know? Is it even appropriate for them to know and to what degree?

Consider the options along this continuum:

When I'm presenting on these options in a seminar, some people ask what is meant by the expression *silent lying*. When we become involved in silent lying, it does not suggest that we would speak an outright lie with intent to mislead. However, *silent lying* is the refusal to tell others what they need to know to improve the relationship or situation, when doing so really does matter. It is an acquiescent silence. The impact can be very damaging. It is the strategic approach of the conflict avoider. Some personality types struggle with silent lying because of their aversion to conflict. Some people keep the peace at all cost even at the risk of being unethical.

The line between silent lying and discretion can become blurred. The difference is that discretion is active while silent lying is more of a passive resistance to addressing the truth concerning a person or situation.

Outright deceitfulness is rampant in our culture. Hiddenness and deceit in the form of image management is the adversary's gauntlet on the community of Christ followers. Hiddenness destroys many loyalties and erodes significant relationships. Frankly, it is surprising how commonplace lying has become among clergy and other nonprofit leaders in our culture. Almost weekly we hear the sad story of people who are truly good leaders, but whose credibility and relationships have eroded due to hiddenness and deceit.

Leaders must accept the fact that they will never win the approval or support of all the people when managing messy situations. You will always have resisters, opponents, and saboteurs in the community you are leading. The sooner you accept and acclimate to this reality, the less personal pain you will experience.

Always be consistent or congruent when addressing messy or disruptive behavior, especially when it involves confronting behavior in a highly talented and highly respected member of the team. Even high-capacity and impact members of the team "mess up" from time to time, and it's important that other members of the team not develop the belief that the superstar is exempt from confrontation because of his or her high-impact contribution and capacity. Confronting incongruent behavior is a gift you can share, without exception, with each member of the team.

Exercising the Process of Bracketing

It is difficult to set healthy boundaries with others, when working in ministry and other people-helping vocations. Expectations from others, as well as those expectations we place on ourselves, can be both unreasonable and unrealistic. We are often our own worst enemy as we allow the challenges and problems of the vocation to invade every corner of our thoughts and existence. It can erode our own vitality, which can in turn negatively impact marriage and family. Many couples spend endless hours on the treadmill of processing the burdens of work, caught in a cycle of worry, consuming unending hours of time and depleting their precious vitality.

Bracketing is a strategy to help the individual and couple put some distance between the front stage of the work world and the private backstage of marriage and family. Over many years of counseling and coaching, several couples have told me that the concept of bracketing has been immensely helpful for their marriage and family.

Here is how bracketing works: Whatever the challenge in your work environment, establish a time and place to journal (individually) or discuss (as a couple) the challenge or problem. It is important to process and emotionally discharge complicated and troubling situations that you encounter. The objective in bracketing is that you can be as emotionally upset as necessary, say what needs to be said, and plan what needs to be planned. But when the time is up, and you are not at the designated location, you let it go and involve yourself in the other areas of life such as marriage and family. You give yourself permission to clock out of the work environment.

Think about it! Why would you allow your ministry/work environment to determine how you think and feel in every aspect of your life?

Why would you relinquish your God-given prerogative to decide who you want to be and how you want to live for your enemy to decide? And the entire time you are doing so, your perceived or real enemy isn't even aware you have relinquished this power to him or her. Think it through. You will probably not be working in the same place or position fifteen years from now. But you will hopefully have the same spouse and family.

A second way to bracket your work troubles is through the 20/60/20 principle. This theory is especially helpful for those who struggle with an unhealthy need for approval, respect, or appreciation. The 20/60/20 principle is based on research and works this way: If you are a ministry leader of a church, the top 20 percent of the congregants will be very supportive of what you do and say. They will have a high appreciation for leadership, maybe even if it is unwarranted. Within that top 20 percent according to the research, 6 percent of the congregants will be supportive regardless of how well or poorly the leadership does. For example, a minister could be absolutely foolish and this 6 percent might say, "What a shame. I like my pastor so much. I still believe in him or her!"

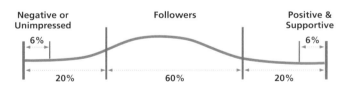

On the other end of the continuum, 20 percent of the congregants will not be all that impressed with what their leadership does or with the direction of the church. It really does not matter what direction the church goes or what the leadership does; they will not be supportive. For many of them, this stance is their general outlook on life. Within this 20 percent, approximately 6 percent will actually be very troubling for the lead pastor and the leadership. Among them are the chronic complainers who believe if you do it their way everything would go just fine. So if a church has 100 adults attending, approximately 6 people will be causing a problem on a somewhat regular basis. This statistic is especially troublesome if the person is a large donor who uses giving to hold the leader hostage to his or her will.

In the middle of the continuum, we find the 60 percent of the congregants who follow based on whatever direction has the strongest message and energy behind it. If the top 20 percent are very enthusiastic about the ministry leadership and the direction of the church, the 60 percent will follow. They are the *following* sheep.

When a church votes for a pastor, my coaching advice is that a 94 percent vote is an A+. Why? Individuals in the bottom 6 percent will be contrarian by nature. They are typically negative and resistant, countering whatever direction is dominant. Some are so bold as to disclose that they did not cast a supportive vote because everyone else was voting for the pastor, and they wouldn't want a 100 percent vote to give the new pastor the idea he can do anything he wants! It seems inconceivable that some people actually think this way, but they do. It is oftentimes the same people who are among the first to get to know the new pastor and make sure he or she is "in the know" on how things should be changed (or stay the same)!

Though I do not have proof based on research, my belief based on my counseling/coaching experience is that this 20/60/20 principle applies in other people-helping vocations too. For example, no matter how effective a nonprofit CEO or college president is, about 6 percent of the employees will (at least privately) dissent from most of the leader's decisions. So if there are a hundred employees approximately six will not get on board with the plan and direction.

So how can this 20/60/20 principle be helpful? It helps one accept the reality that no matter how kind, respectful, and effective a leader may be, you will *always* have a certain percentage of people who will respond resistively or negatively. In other words, you can win most of the people most of the time if you do an excellent job. However, you will never win over all the people!

Confronting Incongruence

In the life of every good leader, you will need to confront an associate who is highly respected by others. The desire to guard against offending an associate is commensurate with the depth of the respect you feel toward your associate. It is very difficult to confront individuals on the team who are highly talented and respected for the character they project. Confronting someone you regard can often be more awkward than confronting those who are frequently out of line in their attitude and behaviors.

The strategy of *confronting incongruence* is where you clearly identify all that you respect in the person you need to confront. You identify their good character, attitude, and behavior, utilizing them as the plumb line and placing them up against their current poor attitude or behavior.

In the early years of developing a Christian-based psychological service, the need to confront a number of staff members who had rightly earned the respect of the team surfaced. Many of these very talented individuals were much more capable than me. They possessed the character qualities and gifts that I could only hope to attain sometime within my lifetime. Yet circumstances warranted the need to address attitudes or behaviors that did not fit their known characters.

Barry was one of our psychologists who exemplified a high capacity in his clinical skills and was exceptional in character. Barry was summoned to my office to deal with actions that would have been easy to ignore or excuse because of the gift he was for our team. It would have been easy to just assume, *"Oh well, that's just Barry. He doesn't mean any harm."* However, his behavior was a problem because the team enjoyed and respected Barry. He was setting a poor example for those younger and less-capable staff who looked up to him as an example to follow.

The time arrived for the confrontation. Barry was informed of how much we appreciated and respected him, noting several of his gifts and talents that many of us wished to emulate someday. Then I proceeded to point out a behavior that appeared incongruent with his level of professional stature.

Basically the confrontation pointed out all that we respected and the counterintuitive behavior that did not seem to fit his character. His behavior was like taking a piece of a jigsaw puzzle that was from a different box. I simply asked him to help me understand how his behavior and my high regard for him fit together. The psychologist friend simply replied, "I have a bad attitude, and I need to change it!"

Several hours later Barry came into my office, gave me a hug, and said, "That was the most respectful confrontation I have ever experienced. You can count on me to be an example to the other staff."

When confro,nting incongruence, never put a person down. Confronting incongruence is based on respect. You are putting the responsibility on that person to explain the incongruence between your respect for them and their bad behavior.

Over the years, this confronting incongruence has worked time and time again, almost without failure to attain fruitful and growth-producing outcomes for everyone involved.

Implementation

Now it is time to put into practice these paradigms, postures, and procedural strategies. But keep in mind that they are not intended to be a step-by-step solution to dealing with the challenges of working with difficult people and circumstances. They are the attitudes and practices that so many clients have taught me over the years. They have been found to be helpful and others have benefited greatly.

Sometimes a small change in our attitude, perspective, or behavior can produce tremendous fruit. Putting them into practice is much like a physical training program. Incremental steps are better than grand failure.

You can begin today by asking yourself: What is the one thing that you can do in each area that if you did it faithfully and consistently would make a significant difference in your work and private world? What paradigms, postures, or procedural strategies would be beneficial for you to put into practice?

To complete your Personal Insight Exercise, go to chapter 6 of the online workbook at FullStrength.org/AtFullStrength.

PART 3

Navigating Spiritual and Moral Challenges

Self-Deception and Moral Failure: "It Will Never Happen to Me!"

Far too many leaders who slide into moral failure have thoughts like this:

- *It will never happen to me!*
- *Moral failure is for the weak, but that's not me. I have my act together.*

Men and women who I've known and considered paragons of virtue have later sat in my office and confessed moral failure, sadly sabotaging everything they valued in life—their marriage, family, calling, reputation, and self-esteem. Woe to leaders who believe that it can't happen to them. While believing failure to be impossible, a strange sense of dissatisfaction begins to invade the leader's soul. Sinful thoughts begin to take root. Hiding behaviors begins to characterize their conduct, which sooner or later relaxes the restraints that once served as guardrails to keep healthy leaders on the leadership roadway of joyful service. Self-deception so easily wraps itself around the heart of a person, slowly cutting off the lifeblood of spiritual vitality.

Among the greatest fears of those who lead isn't something that can happen *to us*. Rather, it is something that can happen *within us*, cloaked in a self-preserving hiddenness that ultimately can destroy us. It flows from a sense of dissatisfaction in one's very soul.

The Crosshairs Research offers some helpful indicators that seem to attend situations where ministry leaders and other vocational caregivers succumb to career-disrupting or career-ending moral failure. In this chapter, we'll outline some of the patterns or indicators that accompany catastrophic moral failure.

The ABCs of Moral Failure

Is there a way to anticipate the pernicious moral drift that erodes a leader's mission, credibility, and relationships? The Crosshairs Research reveals five conditions that were present in all the men and woman who fell into the pit of moral failure. Understanding and watching for these conditions, should they emerge in your life, will serve as an early warning system that the conditions are right for a catastrophic decision and act to occur. By understanding and watching for these early warning signs, you can take preventive action to disrupt and destroy the conditions that commonly precede moral failure.

These conditions were identified in 94 percent of counseling clients who were part of the Crosshairs Research study pool. These clients were dismissed from their leadership positions due to moral failure that included such things as adultery, pornography consumption, theft, and other types of misconduct. When these five conditions are present at the same time, catastrophic moral failure is almost certain unless a major intervention occurs:

- ◉ **Accountability** is rejected or non-existent.
- ◉ **Blind** or naïve belief that it won't happen to me.
- ◉ **Commitment to work** takes precedence over commitments at home.
- ◉ **Devotional life** suffers with the only exception being moments of desperation.
- ◉ **Emotional energy** is invested in self-justification instead of self-evaluation.

Let's evaluate each of these five conditions in turn with the goal of converting each one into an early warning indicator.

Accountability

You experience a subtle drift or an intentional decision to move into a *hiddenness* and *self-preservation* mode. Self-preservation, by its very nature, diminishes any safe relationship that may exist in your circle of fellowship. A lack of accountability in your life is a declaration of independence, refusing to answer to anyone outside of yourself. If we refuse accountability from others, we probably refuse it from God as well. God designed us to live in community with one another, holding one another accountable, not as independent entities.

So it's important to ask yourself:

◉ Who has your ear?
◉ Who do you willingly allow to speak truth into your life?

Lack of accountability is the key indicator that the stage is set for moral failure. When leaders begin to ignore and disregard any form of accountability, they are opening the door for dark thoughts and musings to circulate. Confessing and discussing such thoughts with trusted others normally disempowers and neutralizes dangerous thoughts before they can take root in the mind. Pushing away all forms of accountability constraints is tantamount to giving yourself permission to allow dangerous ideas to enter the otherwise normal and healthy thought life of the leader. Sooner or later, spiritual enemies will activate some aspect of your old nature and a beachhead will be established where reinforcing negative thoughts will rush in and begin to invade and overwhelm your heart and mind.

Clear evidence that the enemy is beginning to win the battle for control of the mind and heart is found when hiding and avoiding behaviors begin to manifest themselves. A discerning accountability partner can sense when this behavior is beginning to activate and can lead you into exposing the dangerous thoughts that you're seeking to protect or hide. We often lack the courage to confront our own hiding behaviors and the dark thoughts we're trying to protect. Allowing others to help us become more fully aware of and take responsibility for these early warning behaviors can prevent catastrophic failure from occurring.

If we won't submit to accountability with trusted others in the family of God who are genuinely concerned about our wellbeing, then it follows that we will eventually refuse to submit to God. We are designed by God to live in community with trusted others. When we start to isolate and hide ourselves from our spouses, our families, and our fellowship of believers, then the stage is being set for moral failure to occur.

Take a moment and reflect on the following questions carefully:

- Do you have a trusted and available accountability partner with whom you meet regularly?
- Are you able to share honestly, expose, and dismantle the unwholesome thoughts that enter and want to take up long-term residence in your heart and mind?
- Do you have the courage to own and confess your hiding behaviors and remove the masks you've started to wear to prevent others from seeing the evolving you as you dance with dark and dangerous thoughts and imaginations?
- If you're not accountable to someone, what beliefs are keeping you from establishing such a relationship?

Blind Belief

As human beings living with an old or fallen nature, we have a tremendous vulnerability to self-deception. *Self-deception* is a denial of reality or a false or misguided interpretation of the forces at work in our lives that lead us to faulty conclusions about actions we may take.

Based on the profile of clients who have visited my office, self-deception is possible at any age or stage of life. The saddest scenario of all occurs when a leader who has persevered throughout a lifetime, succumbs to a catastrophic moral failure as their retirement season of life approaches. Just when the community should be celebrating a life well lived, the leader, if he or she doesn't handle his or her failure correctly, slinks out of town in shame and disgrace. Take heed; failure can occur to anyone at any time in one's career.

The forces of darkness lack all virtue, save one—they are patient. Just as a sniper can lie motionless day after day to accomplish his mission, our spiritual adversary and enemy waits patiently. Sometimes the wait is for thirty or forty years until the right set of circumstances are lined up to place us in the crosshairs and make a kill shot. The spiritual adversary waits patiently for the opportunity that will leave the most nefarious impact on the faith community.

Regularly talking things through with a trusted accountability partner can help you expose areas of thinking where you may be self-deceived and setting the stage for attack by the enemy. Even now, consider the following:

- Can you create a list of the reasons why you give yourself permission to believe or assume that failure will not happen to you? Where are these reasons flawed?
- What do you think will happen when another trusted friend helps you expose and understand the ways in which you allow yourself to be self-deceived?

Commitment to Work

This third condition results from the compulsion to meet outside expectations at the expense of marriage and family. The pressures in our hurry-sick culture are enormous for vocational people helpers, with many functioning at their limit with no margin for recovery. Nonprofit and ministry leaders feel that the financial pressures are relentless.

Added to the pressure of outside expectations are those we place on ourselves. The burden of expectations placed on us pale in significance to the burden of our own unhealthy, misguided need for approval. Disappointing others can be cruel, so we work feverishly in order to avoid disapproval at the expense of our most important relationships.

At these junctures, remember: You will likely not be working in the same context a decade from now. However, you do hope to have a relationship with your spouse and kids that is both enduring and endearing throughout your lifetime.

Devotional Life

This fourth condition toward moral failure takes place when the individual's spiritual feeding has deteriorated into a starvation diet. In counseling and coaching sessions with clergy and other ministry leaders, I frequently ask, "How is your own spiritual feeding?" Only on rare occasions is the response encouraging. Quite often, there is an awkwardly long silence. Much too frequently the response is, surprisingly, "No one has ever asked me that question before!" And this response is coming from those expected to lead others spiritually.

Unfortunately, the church is usually not the place where church workers are spiritually fed and nurtured. Spiritual leaders rarely have others who are willing to inquire about their spiritual nourishment. This is oftentimes due to their lack of willingness to invite or grant the permission to ask the deeply personal and challenging spiritual questions.

So let me ask:

◉ Who in your circle of relationships are you willing to give the permission to ask the tough spiritual questions?

- What are the questions that would be important to ask?
- Who has your spiritual welfare as their concern?
- Again, who do you willingly allow to speak truth into your life?

Emotional Energy

The final condition found in every autopsy of moral failure involves a subtle shift in emotions and attitudes from self-evaluating and being honest with yourself to self-justifying and rationalizing feelings and behaviors that allow you to continue to flirt with sinful, dangerous thoughts. This process continues to the point where your conscience becomes numb and anesthetized. Slowly over time you begin to shut down your early warning systems or simply learn to ignore them. In essence, you give yourself permission to become self-deceived.

Either as an element of our old natures or through the influence of active spiritual forces seeking to destroy us through lies and deceit, we lose our ability to see our situations rationally. We give ourselves permission to become insane (lose our sanity and sensibilities). Often we don't realize it is happening, because we are obsessed with some sinful objective that we believe will bring us some big payoff and improve our condition in life. I cannot find an instance in all human history where a person is better off after achieving a sinful objective. In all cases, regret and heartache is the ultimate reward for falling or failing into sinful conduct, no matter how enticing and alluring the object of self-gratification may appear.

Self-justification and self-deception go hand in hand. Nowhere is this truth more problematic than in cases of marital infidelity. Infidelity, when deeply analyzed, is not a search for a new partner that will fulfill my needs, but a *new self* that will be happier and more content with life after a long season of discontent and discouragement. In situations where marriage reconciliation occurs after vow violation, the offender often feels guilt or remorse over injuring his or her spouse but may not necessarily feel guilty about the illicit relationship itself, providing evidence that the underlying search for a new more respectable self is not resolved.

Every individual battles self-deception in one form or another; it's just a matter of where and to what degree. A wise or healthy person acknowledges this reality and lives in a state of vigilance, knowing that he or she is always vulnerable to a self-deception trap or scenario.

So how can you be more certain that you are moving away from an unhealthy self-justification toward an emotional and spiritually healthy self-evaluation? First, recognize several important indicators of unhealthy self-justifying. Also, recognize that you are always self-deceived— it is just a matter of where and to what degree. "The heart is deceitful above all things . . . who can understand it?" (Jer. 17:9).

Upon first consideration, full acceptance of your capacity for self-deception may seem unfair. But with further consideration, you will realize that it is actually a posture of self-respect. If you have any dignity at all, why wouldn't you want to know the truth about yourself that can eventually lead to growth and transformation?

To pursue God's highest and best in your life, you must first face the challenging truth about yourself. My experience as a coach and counselor has lead me to believe that confident and mature individuals really have no problem in believing that they are always self-deceived; it is just a matter of the degree.

Dr. Charles Ringma, in his book, *Dare to Journey—with Henri Nouwen*, describes the dilemma of self-deception in these words:

The internal pressure and societal constraints on us to be strong, self-sufficient, self-reliant and independent are enormous. We can easily begin to believe in ourselves so much that we begin to think we are invulnerable. It is easy to believe our own illusions, particularly when they are reinforced by others and held up as achievable ideals by our society.

While being responsible is important, being self-sufficient is an illusion. Leaders particularly feel the pressure to be strong and self-reliant. Not only do they find themselves in situations where they have to operate in this way, but others expect this of them as well. Thus leaders frequently find themselves in positions where they have to continue to give, but are not nourished themselves.[1]

Here's a stark truth: If we are unwilling to be accountable to another trusted person, then we are likely unwilling to be accountable to God. We are open and vulnerable to self-justifying beliefs and behaviors. Hiddenness is the hallmark condition for self-deception and self-justification.

A key clue that you are engaged in self-justifying behavior is the practice of blame shifting. *Blame shifting* involves attributing responsibility to or blaming others for your own unhealthy attitudes and behaviors. A contrasting and equally damaging practice is *blame absorbing,* where you place all the blame on yourself, ignoring or not dealing with unhealthy beliefs and behaviors in others. A manifestation of either extreme indicates that self-deception is occurring. Truth can only be discovered when you take ownership of your own attitudes and actions and address bad behaviors when manifested in others.

When we blame, we are relinquishing our God-given prerogative to choose who we want to be and how we want to live before God. We let others write the script of who we are becoming.

Here are some helpful self-reflection questions:

⦿ How and where am I expending energy in self-justifying rather than self-evaluating?
⦿ Who or what do I tend to blame rather than take responsibility for my beliefs and behaviors?
⦿ Where in my life do I tend to practice hiding behaviors, so people don't or won't see the real me?
⦿ What areas of my life have I allowed to be exposed without any form of accountability to trusted others who are concerned about my spiritual safety and wellbeing?

Five Guardrails from Moral Failure

Now let's look at the conditions or guardrails that contribute to our moral, spiritual, and relational wellbeing:

⦿ **Accountability** is intentional and preemptive.
⦿ **Belief** that moral failure *can* happen to me leads to intentionally taking precaution.
⦿ **Commitment** to develop and maintain key personal relationships.
⦿ **Devotional life** is intentional, strategic, and periodically reviewed.
⦿ **Emotional energy** is intentionally invested in self-evaluating matters of your thoughts, passions, word, and actions—enlisting the help of others as accountability partners.

In more than three decades of counseling, I have yet to meet a person who has fallen into disqualifying moral failure while having all five of these guardrails in place. In order to faithfully keep these guardrails in your life, there is an underlying theme—*intentionality!* Most people have good intent, but it is not the same as being intentional. These guardrails do not come naturally. However, when you cultivate them intentionally, they can become disciplines of the Christian life, deeply woven into the fabric of your reflexes.

A person who honestly, sincerely, and intentionally practices all five of these protective criteria will enjoy a blessed life free of the consequential pain that accompanies self-deception and moral failure. These ABC practices must become the disciplines of all leaders.

Over the years, we have collected numerous accountability questions that can serve as a personal and spiritual audit. They have been the gifts from many people and can serve to catalyze your endeavor to create your own list of accountability questions.

As you read through the following personal and spiritual questions, reflect: Which accountability questions are relevant and important for my current life situation? Where in my life might I need to be more intentional in order to grow and mature? Who do I willingly allow to speak truth into my life?

- Am I involved in relationships that reflect a healthy accountability?
- Am I content with whom I am becoming?
- Do I have a place of quiet reflection in my life?
- Is my spiritual nutrition the right diet for me? How might it need to change?
- Is my prayer life improving? How does it need to change?
- Is my humility genuine? Where in my life might I lack a teachable spirit?
- Where have I seen God's faithfulness in recent days?

◉ In what area of my life am I having difficulty trusting God, even though he is faithful?

◉ What actions in my life demonstrate a deeper trust in God?

◉ What areas of life tend to busy my mind and distract me from hearing the voice of God's Spirit?

To find an expanded list of accountability questions and to complete your Personal Insight Exercises for chapter 7, go to the online workbook at FullStrength.org/AtFullStrength.

Incongruence:
Pride, Humility, and Idolatry

The apostle John's parting words to the readers of his first epistle were an admonition to keep themselves from idols (see 1 John 5:21). As rendered in the New Living Translation, the verse reads as follows: "Dear children, keep away from anything that might take God's place in your hearts."

In the third verse of the great hymn, *Come Thou Fount of Every Blessing,* author Robert Robinson aptly describes a problem we all have as leaders and Christ followers:

> Oh, to grace how great a debtor
> daily I'm constrained to be!
> Let that goodness, like a fetter,
> bind my wandering heart to thee:
> prone to wander, Lord, I feel it,
> prone to leave the God I love;
> here's my heart, O take and seal it;
> seal it for thy courts above.[1]

Robert Robinson, at the age of twenty-two, seemed to know the struggle with idolatry when he wrote, "Prone to wander, Lord, I feel it, prone to leave the God I love." Robinson wasn't suggesting that we have a problem of abandoning the faith. However, his hymn does suggest a tendency for idols to find a way back onto the mantle of our hearts.

Several thousand years earlier, the prophet Jeremiah wrote God's words: "My people have committed two sins: They have forsaken me, the spring of living water, and have dug their own cisterns, broken cisterns that cannot hold water" (Jer. 2:13).

It seems counterintuitive that when we need God the most we have the strongest propensity toward counterfeits—broken wells that can hold no water. What should be our highest and best response to that deep thirst for God? It is captured in these words from the psalmist: "O God, you are my God; earnestly I seek you; my soul thirsts for you; my flesh faints for you, as in a dry and weary land where there is no water" (Ps. 63:1 ESV).

We cannot reach full maturity as followers of Christ until we first realize our propensity to be idolatrous, even as Christians in positions of influence. Anytime we shift from a posture of God-sufficiency to self-sufficiency, from reliance upon God to self-reliance, we are guilty of idolatry. Idolatry manifests itself in subtle ways in the life of busy ministry professionals. For growth and maturity to occur in spiritual leaders, we must discover and purge the idols from our lives.

I am absolutely convinced that nothing drains us of the spiritual vitality needed for lifelong ministry service more than idolatry and its close and ever-present companion, pride. Idolatry and pride are invasive forces that diminish our effectiveness and drain us of the spiritual power and resources that God puts at our disposal. To believe that we do not struggle with pride and idolatry is to be self-deceived. We must constantly pray the prayer of the Psalmist: "Search me, O God, and know my heart; test me and know my anxious thoughts. Point out anything in me that offends you, and lead me along the path of everlasting life" (Ps. 139:23–24 NLT).

The reformer John Calvin was famous for stating that the human heart is a "factory for idols." We churn out new idols as quickly as the old, irrelevant ones are thrown out. And after we have made new idols, our desire to worship and serve them is nearly irresistible. Even old idols seem to find their way back onto our mantle even though they have been tossed to the ground over and over.

Idolatry and pride drain us of the precious vitality essential for lifelong service. They are at the root of all that can render us ineffective and spiritually impotent. In this chapter, we'll focus on seeing and addressing the idols that worm their way into our hearts and our ministries.

Recognizing the Insidious Nature of Idolatry

How can you recognize idolatry in your life, especially when idolatry is so subtly seductive? Idolatry and pride are like an insidious disease that can go unrecognized for weeks, months, or even years. To examine your heart, start with these questions:

- Where does my heart go when I do not feel loved, respected, or appreciated?
- What are my distractions from God, the Spring of Living Water?

These questions deserve our attention because the answers can stand guard over our hearts.

In our image-managed and narcissistic culture, our lives can be defined by incongruences, consisting of a *front stage* and *backstage* that are worlds apart. Vocational people helpers such as clergy, missionaries, and nonprofit leaders feel an intense pressure to present a certain front-stage persona designed never to disappoint. At the same time, the backstage reality at home can be ugly and incongruent.

A poem written in 1897 by E.A. Robinson and titled, *Richard Cory,* captures the illusion of the front stage and tension between it and the backstage:

Whenever Richard Cory went down town,
We people on the pavement looked at him:
He was a gentleman from sole to crown,
Clean favored, and imperially slim.
And he was always quietly arrayed,
And he was always human when he talked;
But still he fluttered pulses when he said,
"Good-Morning," and he glittered when he walked.

And he was rich—yes, richer than a king—
And admirably schooled in every grace:
In fine, we thought that he was everything
To make us wish that we were in his place.

So on we worked, and waited for the light,
And went without the meat, and cursed the bread;
And Richard Cory, one calm summer night,
Went home and put a bullet through his head.[2]

Numbered among the disappointments of life is the discovery that people we respect and admire have been found to be living double lives. What they purported to be and who they actually were, were not the same person. Their lives were characterized by incongruence—a front stage and backstage that seem totally different. We are left deeply disappointed and disillusioned.

Before the age of thirty, I personally knew more than a dozen spiritual mentors and leaders who had derailed their ministries by falling into disqualifying moral failure. It was these deeply disappointing experiences that God used to direct me to graduate school in counseling, because I wanted to play a part in curbing the number of wrecks I had witnessed in my younger years. God has given me a passion to restore fallen leaders nonjudgmentally, but more importantly to be an agent of preemption and prevention, helping leaders to become and remain aligned, congruent, and faithful servants throughout their lifetime of ministry leadership.

In our image-managed culture, it can be difficult to spot insincerity or prideful motives in ministry leaders. In Romans 12:9, Paul reminds us that our love must be sincere, without pretense or hypocrisy. In Hebrews 10:22, we are instructed to enter God's presence with sincere hearts. If we cannot stand before God and people with sincere hearts, then we must make the effort to confront and expose that which causes us to live pretend leadership lives. God desires that we represent him as men and women of sincerity, integrity, and authenticity, not cracked vessels that have been patched with painted wax to hide the flaw in our characters.

There is a theory that the word *sincere* comes from the Latin *sincere* and means to be "without wax."[3] In New Testament times, an artist might sculpt a statue for display in a wealthy person's garden or courtyard. The artist would advertise his creation as "sincere" (without wax). Less scrupulous artists might fill a crack that occurred during sculpting with wax to hide the flaw, then try and pass off their piece of art as flawless. The real artist would boldly display his work in the hot noonday sun as proof that it was without wax. God desires for his leaders to be sincere, without wax. Only as we deal with the idols and pride in our lives can God sculpt us into flawless leaders, with no cracks puttied in with wax and painted over with hypocrisy.

Adversity has a way of revealing the flaws in a person's life. When our hearts are full of sincerity, then we will endure the heat of adversity and remain a leader full of integrity. Let it be so in your life.

Understanding the Relationship between Pride and Idolatry

Pride and idolatry are integrally related in that they are both *self-preserving* in nature. Pride and idolatry insist that we value someone or something more than God. They move us away from the Spring of Living Water and toward broken wells unable to hold life-giving water. They force a life of incongruence, with a front stage and backstage—a life characterized by counterfeits rather than God's highest and best.

An obscure passage in the Bible addresses this dynamic of pride and idolatry. In the book of Jude, the Bible warns us about "the way of Cain" (see Jude 11).

But what is the way of Cain?

- **It is to worship God with impure motives.** Cain brought his offering to the Lord, but he did not bring it in *faith*. A gift brought with the wrong motives means nothing to God.
- **It is to have a heart filled with envy and jealousy.** There are and always will be people who will have more impact and be more effective than we are. If we idolize them, however, we will seek something other than God's best for our lives.
- **It is to lie to God and others about what you have done.** In other words, Cain's life was marked with incongruence and hiddenness. Cain had his front stage and backstage. However, in time, the truth came to light when Cain murdered his brother Abel. Even while Abel's blood flowed upon the ground, Cain asked, "Am I my brother's keeper?"

What does this have to do with those who serve in vocations of ministry and people helping? We must be careful not to walk in the way of Cain.

Instead, walk in the way of Abel. Hebrews 11:4 states, "By faith Abel brought God a better offering than Cain" for one simple reason—it was brought in faith. The way of Abel leads to blessing.

Incongruence, pride, and idolatry bring depletion to our lives. They give a false sense of being filled up, but ultimately they deplete us of the rich benefits of God's blessing. By contrast, a life of congruence and integrity brings vitality. Among the best descriptions of a life of congruence and integrity was presented by the apostle Paul in his letter to the Colossians.

So that you may **live a life worthy** of the Lord and please him in every way: **bearing fruit** in every good work, **growing in the knowledge** of God, **being strengthened** with all power according to his glorious might so that you may have great endurance and patience, and **giving joyful thanks** to the Father, who has qualified you to share in the inheritance of his holy people in the kingdom of light. (Col. 1:10–12; emphasis added)

The apostle Paul described the spiritual essence of congruence and vitality. The expression "live a life worthy" in the original text uses the word *axios* or "axle the high calling." But why would he choose the word *axle*?

During that time period, the four wheels of a cart would turn on the axles but without bearings. So if a person put a mark on all four wheels and traveled several miles down a road, the marks would remain in the same position in relationship to one another. What Paul is indicating is that the wheels and axles would turn in concert with one another.

So what does it mean to "axle the high calling"? In this seventy-eight word run-on sentence, Paul described the wheels that are to turn in concert with the high calling of Jesus Christ:

- **Our words and actions:** "bearing fruit in every good work"
- **Our thoughts:** "growing in the knowledge of God"

⦿ **Our passions and heart of gratitude:** "being strengthened with all power according to his glorious might . . . joyfully giving thanks to the Father"

⦿ **Our source of strength:** "Father, who has qualified you to share in the inheritance"

The life of congruence and integrity means that these aspects of our existence all turn in concert with the high calling qualified by our source of strength.

Dismantling Our Idols

Based on my career of counseling ministry leaders, following is a list of common things that I have observed that often reach the status of idols in the lives of busy ministry and caregiving professionals. I'll start with the list, then address each one in turn.

⦿ Allowing self-preservation to dictate decisions and behaviors
⦿ Being driven to performance rather than drawn by God's Spirit
⦿ Measuring work based on worldly success rather than faithfulness
⦿ Permitting myself to become burned out or depleted
⦿ Allowing my word and ways to take precedence over God's Word and ways
⦿ Feeling the need to speak into the lives of others
⦿ Blaming others for my emotions and behaviors
⦿ Seeking the approval, admiration, or adoration of others
⦿ Being consumed by compulsions and addictions[4]

Let's dig deeper into each one of these conditions. Remember that each condition has the possibility to form idolatry in a person's life.

Self–Preservation

A colleague once shared with me that "the person who is humble cannot be humiliated." Yet, the natural response to adversity is pride, and the very essence of pride is *self-preservation*. A posture of self-preservation always diminishes a relationship. When it is birthed out of pride, it dictates our decisions and actions.

The twentieth-century German theologian, Karl Barth, asserted this about pride in the face of adversity: "The root and origin of sin is the arrogance in which man wants to be his own and his neighbor's judge."[5]

You must face at least five essential truths in order to remove the idol of self-preserving pride from the mantle of your heart. These same essential truths can move a heart toward humility as it relates to adversity.

1. Life is difficult no matter our social status or resources.
2. I am not as important as I would like to think I am.
3. It is not about me.
4. Control is an illusion, and I am not the one who is in control.
5. Our God is self-existent and all-powerful—I am not!

Driven to Performance

A person who is *driven* is motivated by the fundamental need for security, contentment, significance, or control. These and other drivers influence the behavior of all human beings. The challenge for every Christ follower is to make sure that our efforts to fulfill these human needs are done in accord with God's design for healthy human living. When we attempt to fulfill these needs outside of God's design for healthy human living, such behaviors take on the status of idols that begin to control the allegiance and focus of our hearts and minds.

Dr. Paul Tripp presents a series of questions that can be extremely helpful in discerning whether you are driven for self-gain or drawn in service for God's glory:

- ◉ The *absence* of *what* causes you to want to give up or quit?
- ◉ The *pursuit* of *what* leads you to feel overburdened and overwhelmed?
- ◉ The *fear* of *what* makes you tentative and timid rather than courageous and hopeful?
- ◉ The *craving* for *what* makes you burn the candle at both ends until you have little left?
- ◉ The *need* for *what* robs ministry of its joy?
- ◉ The *desire* for *what* creates tensions between ministry and family?[6]

If you have the tendency to be driven by your own will rather than drawn by God's Spirit, pause and deeply reflect so you fully understand the forces at work driving or controlling your behavior. How would your life be different if you allowed God's Spirit to draw and lead you in your service to him as your Lord? Has your drive and will to succeed become an idol in your life?

Work

Every human wants to be successful in life. In worldly terms, it's much more rewarding than failure. In God's economy, however, we often grow and advance based on what we learn from our failures because the lessons of failure (doing it our way) teach us much about living a life of faith (doing it God's way).

A great paradox of Christianity is that we grow and harvest eternal rewards, not based on what we can achieve by our own human, success-driven efforts, but by our faithfulness in understanding, aligning, and living our lives in accord with the truths outlined in Scripture—all facilitated by the sanctifying work of the Holy Spirit.

Many of us Christians were brought up believing that faithfulness is equivalent to obedience or conformity to a regimen of dos and don'ts. We were taught the more we conformed, the more we would be judged as being faithful. We were taught this definition of faithfulness in our homes, schools, and churches—it's an embedded and controlling belief. This notion about faithfulness is inadequate and misleading. The formula—more right behavior plus less wrong behavior equals godliness—has done more to stunt our spiritual growth (success) than perhaps any other belief. Living our life according to this formula is not what pleases God, because we are in essence living life (succeeding or not) in our own strength.

Hebrews 11:6 reveals the simple but powerful truth about what really pleases God, and it contains a much deeper and richer explanation of the nature of biblical faithfulness: "And without faith it is impossible to please *Him,* for he who comes to God must believe that He is and *that* He is a rewarder of those who seek Him" (NASB).

To understand the essential teaching of this verse, substitute the word *trust* for the word *faith.* More than anything, God's desire is that we learn to trust him and what he reveals as truth, as the means by which the Holy Spirit will bring *success* into our lives. Faithfulness is not living in your strength in accord with dos and don'ts; faith is learning to believe in and trust God in every domain or aspect of your life. You trust God and do it his way when you come to believe that living in accord with the truths he has revealed in Scripture is the only way to experience a successful, healthy, joy-filled life—a life that pleases God. It pleases God because you honor him by believing him and his instructions for how to live the life he intends for you and relying upon him to meet all your needs in the course of living a faith- or trust-driven life.

Here are some helpful diagnostic questions:

- In what areas of my life am I not fully trusting God? (i.e., vocation, marriage, children, finances, relationships, and leadership)
- What is causing me to believe that God is not trustworthy in any of these or other areas of my life?
- If I began to surrender control (reliance on myself) in my quest for success in any area of my life and began trusting God for success in that area, how would that transform how I live day-to-day?

◉ Is God pleased with the progress I'm making in trusting him? If not, what changes do I need to make to remove the idol of trusting myself to achieve kingdom success?

Nowhere in the Bible does it indicate that we are called to *succeed*. However, we are called to *faithfulness* time and time again. In Hebrews 11, of those who are listed in the Hall of Faith, only a few would have been considered successful at the time. Success is good, but faithfulness is a higher principle, based on God's Word.

Toward the end of Hebrews 11, the author described the lives of more than a dozen heroes of faith starting each story with the expression "by faith." Some were successful despite a life of incredible adversity. Others would not have been considered successful. The chapter concludes with those who did not receive this side of heaven what was promised to them. Their lives would be considered a tragedy.

··

There were others who were tortured, refusing to be released so that they might gain an even better resurrection. Some faced jeers and flogging, and even chains and imprisonment. They were put to death by stoning; they were sawed in two; they were killed by the sword. They went about in sheepskins and goatskins, destitute, persecuted and mistreated—the world was not worthy of them. They wandered in deserts and mountains, living in caves and in holes in the ground. These were all commended for their faith, yet none of them received what had been promised, since God had planned something better for us so that only together with us would they be made perfect. (Heb. 11:35–40)

··

What higher principle is evidenced in your attitudes, choices, and actions: success or faithfulness?

Burnout

Why is burnout so common among those who serve in vocations of ministry and nonprofit? What is unique to these vocations that results in such a dramatic dropout rate? Consider these reasons taken from hundreds of cases encountered throughout the years:

- The unrealistic or unreasonable expectations placed on them, by themselves or others, resulting in a chronic state of exhaustion.
- An unwillingness to let go of many of the unrealistic or unreasonable expectations.
- The 24/7 mentality that won't allow some people helpers to turn off their work, at least in their minds. Even on their days off, they are waiting for that next call or email that spells crisis that could wait a few days. Thus, they never truly relax.

Not all burnout is idolatrous. Many of us have had to face potent and persistent stress that can result in becoming weary in the soul. Health issues contribute to chronic states of depletion. You can find many exceptions to this statement of burnout being potentially idolatrous. However, I suggest that you *consider* the possibility that your burnout and depletion may be a result of trying to do too much.

Trying to do too much without leaving some margin in your life, all in an attempt to achieve some unrealistic expectation of super-human performance, is a sure way to diminish your vitality in the long run. Such behavior is an unacceptable sacrifice in the eyes of the Lord. God himself took time to rest after his creative work, and he has established a rhythm of rest and work as necessary to healthy living.

Pride

Idolatry has its roots in the sin of pride. The paradox about pride is that it's about self-preservation, but in the end, it always accomplishes the opposite. Nothing can rob us of precious vitality more than the sin of pride. Pride presents the delusion that we will be filled up, but it eventually leaves us empty, with an even deeper craving for something to fulfill us.

Pride Paradigms

Let's look at just a few of the pride paradigms that lead to idolatry:

- "I am right! Or at least more right than you."
- "I have my story straight! What is your problem?"
- "My theology is clearly the plumb line by which all others are measured."

From time to time, I encounter a client (usually clergy) who feels compelled to vet my theology. What is interesting is that it is usually a client who is in a heap of trouble! Rarely is it a person who is actually doing reasonably well. Most clients, though very interested in right theology, usually come to counseling or coaching with three questions in their hearts and minds:

1. Do you care, and are you confidential?
2. Can you really help me?
3. Can I afford it?

Occasionally, though, a client wants to make sure that my theology is fully aligned with his or her "correct" theology. I really don't mind, if this will increase the client's comfort or allow me to make a good referral. But rarely is that their motive for the vetting.

On one occasion, a member of the clergy came to his appointment wanting to see whether I was worthy theologically to counsel him. My response took him by surprise: "Your wife is about to leave you. Your teenager is going off the rails morally. Your previous church fired you. You are on the bubble in your current position. Why would I be interested in your theology? How's your theology working out for you?"

Humility Paradigms

Being a *student of life* rather than the expert who can bring wisdom has helped several leaders adjust their way of thinking and help their maturing process. By taking a teachable stance, we can embrace the following humility paradigms:

- ◉ "My perceptions are always incomplete, it is a matter of degree and where."
- ◉ "My theology is always in error, it is a matter of degree and where."
- ◉ "I am always in error, it is a matter of degree and where."[7]

I cannot emphasize enough how significantly these paradigms can contribute to a person's growth, maturing, and wisdom. They exemplify a teachable spirit, recognizing that this side of heaven our perception is always flawed to some degree.

Speaking into the Lives of Others

Incredible freedom and vitality come when we fully realize that we do not have to be the go-to answer person. It is acceptable to say, "I really don't know."

Marcos is a brilliant surgeon, a leader in his field, who sought me out for coaching. He is a person who deserved my respect based on his performance and character. As we developed our friendship, he revealed several things about himself that increased my respect for him because of his willingness to be vulnerable. Marcos is a man who others look up to and admire. But Marcos, who was in a leadership position, wanted someone to be honest with him and stop patronizing him based on his positional power. He was refreshingly open to candid feedback.

On one occasion, we ran into each other at a community luncheon. We reconnected briefly, and he asked if he could join me at my table. It was an honor. After lunch this good man said to me, "I really don't know what to do in those social situations! I don't know how to talk about sports, family, or politics." This brilliant man set his coaching goals for things like learning how to small talk, how to play with his kids, and how to enter a social situation without feeling awkward. I felt a genuine empathy for this brilliant, loving, and godly man who didn't know how to live out some of the basics of life. He took me on as a coach, and we went on an incredibly rewarding journey into the everyday simplicity of relating, which he began to experience for the first time in his midlife.

So many people felt compelled to speak into Marcos' awkwardness. The wounding kept happening over and over, driving him further away from confidence in the simple things of life. Well-intentioned people hurt him time and time again.

Marcos' experience made me wonder how many times I have possibly wounded others with a compulsive need to speak truth into their lives with a terrible sense of timing and context. When we do not consider the timing, the context, and the receptivity of others, we may be speaking into their lives out of our own idolatry.

Because those who feel called to serve and minister to others have the desire to be genuinely helpful, it is easy for us to speak out of our own need rather than the need of the other person. When we speak truth or serve others in the way we believe we need to, they sometimes dismiss our advice or help. When we assume others do not love or respect us because they did not take our advice, it may be a problem of idolatry.

We have all known individuals who seemingly *must* tell us what to do. It is easy to assume this is control or manipulation. But sometimes such behavior simply demonstrates that they lack the skills to express their insecurity in a more appropriate way.

Blame Shifting

When you place all the blame on others (blame shift) concerning the challenging circumstances in life, you miss the truth about yourself. You discover the truth only when you are willing to take ownership of your own attitudes and actions. When you blame others, you relinquish your God-given prerogative to choose who you want to be and how you want to live before God. You let others write the script of who you are becoming.

This truth was clearly evidenced in the idolatry of Aaron as the High Priest under Moses. Moses returned from the mountain with the Ten Commandments in his arms, and the first thing he saw was people celebrating a golden calf as the god that brought the Hebrew people out of slavery (see Ex. 32). The thought is disturbing, although we don't have to think too hard to find similar situations in our current culture.

How did Aaron as high priest deal with it? Just like a lot of ministry workers and other people helpers, he blamed others. Aaron blamed his congregation: "Moses, don't be mad at me. These people are set on doing evil. All I did was collect their gold and threw it into the fire. And what do you know, a golden calf popped out!" What a lame excuse! Does it sound as foolish when I make excuses and blame others or the situation for my dilemmas?

When you blame others and circumstances for your poor choices, attitudes, and behaviors you may be in danger of being idolatrous.

Approval of Others

Vocational people helpers of all types have to deal with unreasonable and unrealistic expectations placed upon them by those they serve. This is especially true for those who serve in ministry. Working with people who are experiencing struggles can be very draining. It can be quite difficult not to take home all the anger, frustration, and sadness seen in the work setting.

Despite all the ludicrous expectations placed on ministry workers and vocational people helpers, being a *pleaser* continues to rob leaders of precious vitality that can be used to advance God's kingdom. The deep need for significance in the forms of approval, admiration, respect, or being liked by others, can derail us from God's highest and best. Sometimes out of the need to feel significant we make a fool's bargain! In trying to keep others happy, we sacrifice what matters most. If we do not prioritize our lives, someone else will.

Entire books have been written on the subject of being a pleaser. Yet it continues to be a nagging issue. The need to please seems to be a result of our desire to have a truly positive impact on others. However, we must guard our hearts from the idolatry of wanting to please. The apostle Paul responded to the issue with these words to the Galatians:

Am I now trying to win the **approval** of human beings, or of God? Or am I trying to **please** people? If I were still trying to please people, I would not be a servant of Christ. (Gal. 1:10, emphasis added)

Accepting that we are not perfect and giving up on the idea that perfection is a viable way to escape negative feedback from others leads to deep freedom. You will never please everyone no matter how hard you try.

Giving up on pleasing everyone is not only a good idea—it is the only sane choice. Aim to please the Lord without dismissing the feedback of others. Their views, even when erroneous, are still potentially helpful information. Their views are input, but do not have to leave an imprint in your heart.

Compulsions and Addictions

Since the beginning of time, men and women have been in search of ways to fill their deepest longings. The human brain's pleasure centers have not changed in any significant way. Each restless heart beats so imperfectly. Vocational people helpers are not an exception.

Entire books can be written on the problem and challenge of addictions for even those who serve in vocations of people helping. I won't spend much time on this topic here except to say that compulsions and addictions are a serious problem among vocational people helpers and ministry professionals.

Addictions have been a problem among God's people even since the earliest times. In the Old Testament there was a young king of Judah, named Josiah, who was revered for his commitment to honor the one True God in heaven. He was also known for his tenacity in destroying the Asherah poles (see 2 Kings 23).

The Asherah pole was a sacred pole used in the worship of the pagan goddess Asherah. The Asherah pole was often mentioned in the Old Testament as one of the ways the Israelites sinned against the Lord and worshiped other gods.

The first mention of an Asherah pole is in the Old Testament book of Exodus. God instructed the Israelites to break down their altars, smash their sacred stones, and cut down their Asherah poles. King Josiah, before the age of twenty, made sure the Asherah poles were destroyed. But why were they such an issue? And what is the current-day equivalent?

The Asherah poles were phallic symbols. They were the pornography of the day. Sexuality is deeply rooted in the pleasure centers of the brain. We are sexual beings and our spiritual adversary wants to distort God's creation and God's beautiful intent for our sexuality and intimacy in any way possible. Pornography is Satan's gauntlet in our current culture designed to destroy the basic unit of the marriage and family. Most of the pressures on women in our culture revolve around the perfect body—referred to as *body objectification.*

Even if I were not a Christian, I would still have a personal disdain for pornography, because research indicates that it creates a significant disconnect in marriage and the family. It destroys the relational connection between husband and wife, father and children. Businesses overtly communicate to women through marketing that they are objects of lust. *If you do not look like the advertisement, you don't measure up. If you don't buy our product, you are not sexy.* Eating disorders are the new psychological scourge of the age. In previous generations, conditions like anorexia rarely existed. They did not appear until the 1960s and later when "thin was in."

Our spiritual adversary's creative strategy to derail God's beautiful intent features shame-inducing compulsions and addictions! Anything that would make a man or woman feel good now and demolished later is the desire and plan of the adversary. Each restless heart beats so imperfectly, but God can raise us up to be more than we could possibly hope or imagine this side of heaven. You must take a moment and ask: What are the Asherah poles that must be taken down in your life?

Getting Back to the Spring of Living Water

We need to realize that by looking any place other than our Creator for our security, significance, and sense of control, we are attempting to make it through life independent of the Sustainer of life. Independence from God means we must be dependent upon our idolatry—counterfeit means to attain security, significance, and a sense of control. What we often fail to recognize is that God created us dependent upon the Spring of Living Water just like the deer returns to the brook several times each day. We have confused the gifts with the Giver. Apart from God, no amount of security, significance, or control will ever satisfy our thirsty hearts permanently.

Anything good this side of heaven that can temporarily meet our need for security, significance, and control is a blessing from God. King Solomon points us to the source when he penned these words: "Remember your Creator in the days of your youth, before the days of trouble come and the years approach, when you will say, 'I find no pleasure in them'" (Ecc. 12:1).

It is immensely important to discover God's blessings *in the journey* instead of anticipating that it is somewhere in the future, yet to be experienced. Consider this journey through life as best described in a short story by Robert J. Hastings called "The Station".

Tucked away in our subconscious minds is an idyllic vision. We see ourselves on a long, long trip that almost spans the continent. We're traveling by passenger train, and out the windows we drink in the passing scene of cars on nearby highways, of children waving at a crossing, of cattle grazing on a distant hillside, of smoke pouring from a power plant, of row upon row of corn and wheat, of flatlands and valleys, of mountains and rolling hills, of biting winter and blazing summer and cavorting spring and docile fall.

But uppermost in our minds is the final destination. On a certain day at a certain hour we will pull into the station. There will be bands playing, and flags waving. And once we get there so many wonderful dreams will come true. So many wishes will be fulfilled and so many pieces of our lives finally will be neatly fitted together like a completed jigsaw puzzle. How restlessly we pace the aisles, damning the minutes for loitering . . . waiting, waiting, waiting, for the station.

However, sooner or later we must realize there is no one station, no one place to arrive at once and for all. The true joy of life is the trip. The station is only a dream. It constantly outdistances us.

"When we reach the station, that will be it!" we cry. Translated it means, "When I'm 18, that will be it! When I buy a new 450 SL Mercedes Benz, that will be it! When I put the last kid through college, that will be it! When I have paid off the mortgage, that will be it! When I win a promotion, that will be it! When I reach the age of retirement, that will be it! I shall live happily ever after!"

Unfortunately, once we get it, then it disappears. The station somehow hides itself at the end of an endless track.

"Relish the moment" is a good motto, especially when coupled with Psalm 118:24: "This is the day which the Lord hath made; we will rejoice and be glad in it." It isn't the burdens of today that drive men mad. Rather, it is regret over yesterday or fear of tomorrow. Regret and fear are twin thieves who would rob us of today.

So, stop pacing the aisles and counting the miles. Instead, climb more mountains, eat more ice cream, go barefoot oftener, swim more rivers, watch more sunsets, laugh more and cry less. Life must be lived as we go along. The station will come soon enough.[8]

If you cannot recognize God's work in the moments of your life, you are not likely to recognize it in the future. Count the blessing in the midst of adversity. A heart of gratitude will lead you back to the Spring of Living Water.

To move toward and remain close to the Spring of Living Water, the Bible instructs us on these courses of action.

Let us **draw near** to God with a sincere heart and with the full assurance that faith brings . . . Let us **hold unswervingly to the hope** we profess, for he who promised is faithful. And **let us consider** how we may spur one another on toward love and good deeds. (Heb. 10:22–24, emphasis added)

You must first *draw near to God* (v. 22). The opposite is running to someone or something other than God. You must forsake even the good for Christ. It is not based on your work but rather, the work of Christ. You must draw near *intentionally* and *faithfully*.

Second, you must *hold fast to our hope* (v. 23), to God's saving and sustaining grace. So much competes for our time and energy. Hold fast intentionally and faithfully. Hold fast to the declaration captured in this old hymn written in 1834 by the English clergy, Edward Mote:

My hope is built on nothing less than Jesus' blood and righteousness;

I dare not trust the sweetest frame, but wholly lean on Jesus' name.

> On Christ, the solid rock, I stand; all other ground is sinking sand.
>
> All other ground is sinking sand.[9]

....

Finally, *let us consider* how we can build up one another (v. 24), knowing one another and helping each other become vital for the cause of Christ. Who needs encouragement? Everyone!

To complete your Personal Insight Exercise, go to chapter 8 of the online workbook at FullStrength.org/AtFullStrength.

Mistakes, Failures, and Other Disappointments

James and Harley discovered that mistakes can be opportunities in disguise. Harley's soap factory, founded by his father, supplied the Union Army during the Civil War. After the war ended, Harley and his cousin James needed a unique idea to keep the business flourishing. They thought that a scented, pure-white soap affordable to the common man might do the job. However, it was the "mistake" of an employee that later caused the business to boom. On one particular day, an employee went to lunch and forgot to turn off the mixing machine. Not wanting to discard the batch of white solution, he poured it into the hardening frames anyway. The mistake resulted in "floating soap." Customers were enthusiastic. No more fishing for the soap in murky bath water. Harley named this scented, white soap "Ivory," an idea taken from a biblical phrase: "out of the ivory palaces" (Ps. 45:8 KJV). Oh, I almost forgot to mention the men's last names. They were none other than Procter and Gamble.

To Err Is Human

We all make mistakes. We all experience failure when success was expected. How we manage the trailing disappointment that follows in the wake of mistakes and failures is an important life and leadership competency.

Getting stuck in a doom loop of mentally rehearsing and agonizing over your mistakes and failures unnecessarily drains your vitality and draws you away from thriving and flourishing in leadership.

Pause for a moment and think about how you typically react when you make a mistake or experience unexpected failure. Do you become angry and display your anger in the presence of others (throw an adult tantrum)? Do you go silent and seethe inside? Do you retreat and go into hiding, avoiding others because of shame? Do you look for someone else to blame? Reflect on and write down one sentence that characterizes your reactive pattern to mistakes and failures. Then ask yourself: *Is this the reactive pattern that I want to characterize my response to the inevitable mistakes and failures I will periodically face in my life journey?*

Take a moment and write down a one-sentence description outlining how you'd like to respond as a mature leader to mistakes and failure. Post this aspirational goal where you will see it daily. With every future mistake or failure, do a postmortem and ask yourself how well you performed against the response pattern you set as your goal.

Two Perspectives

Let's consider two perspectives on how you might think about and react to life's mistakes and failures. The first is to view yourself as inadequate, less that what you should be, less than other people in the same situation would be. This type of self-reflection is illegitimate and self-destructive. It diminishes and depletes your energy and effectiveness. It diminishes or derails your leadership and relational effectiveness.

The second perspective is to view yourself as involved in God's work, taking risk, striving on the path to success and accomplishment for kingdom purposes. A mistake or failure represents a temporary, albeit unpleasant or in some cases deeply painful, detour. With God, detours are not dead-ends; they are an unexpected disruption to your plans.

These are times when God allows you to be delayed and rerouted through unknown territory, with the goal of once again bringing you back on course toward your desired destination. How you respond to these detours brought on by mistakes or failures strengthens or weakens you.

You can view your mistakes as obstacles and respond with anger or frustration, or you can view them as opportunities by which God can teach you new things that produce a growing reservoir of wisdom in your heart and mind. A learner's perspective protects your mental, emotional, relational, and spiritual resources. It supports resiliency, keeping you productively moving forward. Mistakes or failures are rarely fatal. However, your attitude toward them *can* be fatal, or at least disabling and disruptive, to your growth and leadership effectiveness.

The Origin of Your Response Pattern

We acquire our response patterns to mistakes and failures at an early age in our homes and in elementary school. If your parents harshly punished you for mistakes or failures, you learned to feel shame and hide. You came to believe that you were inadequate or subpar as a person during times when your behavior wasn't perfect. In extreme cases of poor parenting, you came to believe that you were inadequate or subpar as a person.

In elementary school, if your classroom behavior and your home-work wasn't perfect, you were labeled as a lazy slacker, an unmotivated misfit, or worse yet, dull or unintelligent. Depending on the shaping influences of your early growing-up years, you developed a consistent response pattern to mistakes and failure.

To grow in your effectiveness and leadership skills, you must learn to understand and take control of your response pattern and come to view mistakes and failures for what they really are—the inevitable experience of being human. In fact, down through all time, the people who are remembered as "making history" are the ones who developed a different response mechanism to mistakes and failures.

You must learn to think of mistakes and failures differently. Fortunately, you can find great examples of people who just didn't get this "failure as evil or something to be avoided at all cost" perspective.

Consider, for example, history makers such as Orville and Wilbur Wright or Thomas Edison. Such people viewed mistakes and failures through a different and empowering lens. To these people, mistakes and failures were opportunities to grow and to learn.

Orville and Wilbur Wright, who in December of 1903 took flight for the first time at Kitty Hawk in the Carolinas, didn't get it. Neither of them had a high school diploma. They did not experience only a few failures and mistakes in the adventure of human flight; they experienced hundreds. These two bicycle builders were thought of by many as having a "few loose screws." They had no government funding, but rather, utilized the funds of their bicycle company in Dayton, Ohio. Even with photographs, most people did not believe they took flight for the first time. It wasn't until five years later that the American people and government took them seriously, and then, only after the French military was ready to pay good money for the famous flying machine.

Consider the hyperactive Thomas Edison who changed the way we live with the light bulb after more than 10,000 failed attempts. This famous inventor Thomas Edison was once heard saying that, "Successful people are those willing to endure more failed attempts." Thomas Edison had a file cabinet of successes and a room full of failed attempts. But to Mr. Edison, the recording of those failed attempts was of great value. His team learned vast amounts from those many files of documented failures.

Your attitude toward failed attempts makes all the difference. All learning occurs by means of mistakes and failures. Consider a child learning to walk or a youngster learning to dribble a basketball—to learn what works, we often first must learn what doesn't work.

Consider these notable individuals once referred to as failures taken from my personal collection of stories and illustrations over the decades. They are illustrations I frequently refer to in order to encourage clients from different walks of life. So often we think that others with similar talents had it easier or got a lucky break. But it simply isn't true. Here are just a few illustrations:

- **Sports:** Football coaching legend Vince Lombardi was deemed by one sports announcer as possessing minimal football knowledge and lacking motivation.
- **Medicine:** Florence Nightingale's parents were horrified at her decision to do such degrading work with the poor and sick during wartime. Physicians rejected her. But by the time she died, she had won worldwide respect and revolutionized the way hospitals were operated.
- **Literary Field:** A newspaper once fired Walt Disney because he lacked creativity.
- **Visionary:** In her teen years, Joni Erickson Tada made an ill-fated dive into shallow water that left her paralyzed from the neck down. She has become a champion for the advancement of those who struggle with disability.
- **Artist:** Little Sparky failed every subject in the eighth grade. He was a klutz in sports and socially awkward. He never went out on a date in high school for fear of being turned down. His peers described him with one word—loser! An aspiring artist, he and his cartoon strips were turned down by the Disney Corporation. However, his character eventually captured the hearts of millions around the world. The little boy who could never get his kite to fly is none other than the renowned Charles Schultz, creator of the beloved cartoon strip, *Peanuts*, with the central figure Charlie Brown.
- **Inventor:** A major newspaper in the 1800s stated that Mr. Nobel was a Swedish inventor of dynamite that could kill more people in a single blast than anything ever known to man. Today he is

known around the world as the inventor and founder of the coveted Nobel Peace Prize.

Even one of basketball's greatest players of all times, Michael Jordan, once said: "I've missed more than 9,000 shots in my career. I've lost almost 300 games. Twenty-six times, I've been trusted to take the game-winning shot and missed. I've failed over and over and over again in my life. And that is why I succeed."[1]

Respected seminary president and author, Chuck Swindoll wrote,

The remarkable thing is we have a choice everyday regarding the attitude we will embrace for that day. We cannot change our past . . . we cannot change the fact that people will act in a certain way. We cannot change the inevitable. The only thing we can do is play on the one string we have, and that is our attitude. I am convinced that life is 10% what happens to me and 90% of how I react to it. And so it is with you . . . we are in charge of our attitudes.[2]

We are all faced with opportunities brilliantly disguised as impossible situations.

The longer I live, the more I become convinced that people who can succeed at overcoming obstacles are those who seem to possess a higher tolerance for personal failure than the average person. I've always been attracted to human-interest stories of those who have overcome incredible obstacles. Some people have discovered that mistakes have a positive side as well. Where some people see barriers that are impenetrable, others see them as obstacles to be conquered.

As a leader, how you handle your own personal mistakes and failures can have a profound and transforming impact on others who support and serve alongside you. Great leaders are those who have a higher-than-normal tolerance for personal failure. This kind of leadership inspires others to remain resilient and persevere, knowing that the Holy Spirit is present and teaching you in the unknown terrain you encounter on your detour experiences.

Life confronts us with a series of lessons that are learned though painful mistakes and disappointments. How you choose to deal with "Mistakes and Disappointments 101" has a significant impact on your character and vitality. If God allowed you to look at the last chapter of your life first, you would probably respond much differently to all that which should have never been—your mistakes and disappointments.

Types of Mistakes and Failures

As you reflect on mistakes and failures, know that they usually fall into one of the following categories:

- **Inexperience-based mistakes:** Your intent is good, but your knowledge, timing, or methods are lacking.
- **Panic or fear-based mistakes:** You impulsively act or react without fully analyzing the situation and possible outcomes of your actions.
- **Curiosity-based mistakes:** You are attracted to new or different things without properly reflecting on possible outcomes or thinking about the consequences. This is sometimes the cause of moral failure.
- **Sloth-based mistakes:** Either through weariness or laziness, you fail to attend to an important time-based issue that produces a failure outcome.
- **Blind-spot mistakes:** Mistakes that result from being unaware of a missing positive personality attribute necessary to maintain healthy relationships.

⊙ **Worldliness mistakes:** Sinful actions contrary to God's Word or the leading of the Holy Spirit, typically oriented toward one of three worldly cravings: physical pleasure, materialism, or pride of achievement (see 1 John 2:16).

It will be helpful to identify whether you have a pattern of recurring mistakes and failures in any of these categories. If you do, you should consider obtaining the aid of a coach or a counselor to help you dismantle your response pattern and transplant a new one. Your effectiveness, to a lesser or greater degree, will be impacted by your willingness and ability to seek and gain victory over the weak area from which recurring mistakes or failures occur.

Five Unhealthy Reactions Regarding Mistakes and Disappointments

There are ways of dealing with disappointment and mistakes that can diminish our vitality even more than the initial impact. Let's explore some unhealthy ways of responding that can rob us of vitality. Later, we will take a close look at healthy ways of responding that can actually help us recover our vitality.

Self-flagellation

You take yourself to the "whipping post" and emotionally beat yourself up for making the mistake. You overtly punish yourself, often in public, when you make a mistake or experience failure. Punishment might be physical, but more than likely it will take some form of verbalized self-criticism for being less than perfect.

By going public, perhaps you think you're acknowledging to nearby witnesses that you know that you made a mistake worthy of punishment;

in other words, you're preemptively letting others know that you know that you were bad or wrong to forestall that message coming from them.

Perspective Distortion

You overblow the degree or permanence of mistakes and failure, thinking you'll never be able to right your world again. Questions like, "What can be learned from this?" or "What action you can take now to achieve the best outcome under the circumstances?" never come to mind.

Personalization

You think, "Because I made a mistake, I am a mistake or failure as a person." This pattern of thinking may be embedded from family of origin issues. Counseling may be helpful to expose and dismantle the hidden belief system undergirding a response pattern like this. To overcome this pattern, a believer must come to understand and embrace their new identity in Christ Jesus.

Worry

You become a prisoner to overblown or undue concerns such that your thoughts enter a doom loop (hamster wheel) of disabling concern, thinking your mistake or failure may have irreparably injured another person. How many nights have you laid in bed with your mind running laps around the same worrisome thought over and over without any positive end to it?

Consider getting out a journal and writing your thoughts on paper. This will accomplish two things. First, getting it down in writing helps in the process of acquiring greater objectivity concerning our troubles. Second, it sometimes stops the treadmill thinking in your mind that keeps you awake at night. God has provided tools to neutralize or dissolve worry, but the person with the *worry* response pattern lacks knowledge of the tools or how to use them to find peace.

Emotion Lancing

You use sarcasm, cynicism, whining, or negative verbalizations to lance your emotions, without realizing that you have just "flung your monkey" onto the backs of others, leaving them repulsed by having to endure your immature responses to mistakes or failures.

Six Healthy Responses to Mistakes and Disappointments

Here's a list of alternative, much healthier, ways to manage mistakes and failures.

Learning Experience

A mature person realizes that he cannot "un-ring" a mistake or failure bell. He instead transitions into learning mode and asks, "What can I learn from this experience? What wisdom can I gain from this unpleasant event? How can I repair and strengthen any relational damage that may have occurred?"

Others' Perspective

If you observed this experience happen to someone else, what feelings would you have for the other person? This type of analysis brings the whole matter into perspective. Depending on the scope and severity of the problems that your mistake or failure causes your or others, you can develop a reality-based action plan to manage and repair the damage and unintended consequences.

Do-over Preparation

Here you take the learnings gleaned from the experience and develop a step-by-step action plan for how you will react to a similar mistake or failure in the future to prevent damage amplification caused by an ineffective or unhealthy response pattern. From time to time, review and rehearse your new action plan to keep it top of mind and ready for deployment.

Believe God

Here you remind yourself that God is never through with you, and that he works all things together for your good (even your mistakes and failures). With God the best is always yet to come, even on your worst day. That's the whole essence of sanctification: God is at work in us through every circumstance in life (good and bad) transforming us more and more in our journey to be, live, and think like Jesus. For God, your mistakes and failures can be some of your most teachable moments.

Trust God

Your faith (trust) is what pleases God (see Heb. 11:6). Here you learn to rely upon his promises. He promised he would never leave or forsake you. Your faith and trust motivate you not to give in or give up in the face of mistakes and failures. God fully understands the overwhelming power of temptation. He's always there to help in times of need and to restore you to feeling and knowing his love when you fail.

Embrace God's Love

Just as children troubled by a mistake or failure turn toward loving parents for consolation and comfort, your loving God (your perfect Father) wants you to turn to him for consolation and comfort following mistakes and failures. It's only as you experience the love of God that true healing and growth can occur.

When You Feel Hopeless About Your Mistakes

Some individuals do not place much value on themselves, mainly because they have made poor choices that they feel are permanent. However, there is good news: Your value is not based on what you think of yourself, but rather, how much God loves and values you.

To understand your value, you must begin to see yourself through God's eyes. That begins with understanding the very foundation of your value: God loves you, not because you have value; but rather, you have value because God loves you. Nothing you do can cause God to love you more. Nothing you do can cause him to love you less.

The problem is that in your own strength you are either incapable or you refuse to see yourself from God's perspective. When you see yourself as having no value, your argument is not only with yourself, but also with God. You are, in a sense, saying to God, "You made a foolish investment!"

Vincent VanGogh was an artist that lived in the late 1800s. VanGogh struggled with mental illness throughout his entire adult life. Much of his stormy life involved extensive and ongoing hospitalization in asylums for the chronically mentally ill. On one occasion, during an episode of rage, Vincent cut off the bottom of his ear and sent it to his ex-girlfriend as an act of revenge. Vincent eventually ended his life by placing a gun to his head. VanGogh, who sold only one painting during his entire life, died a pauper.

In the mid 1980s, one of VanGogh's works of art, called *Irises,* made it to the auction block in Paris, France. The painting was a still life of blue irises in a white water pitcher. *Irises* sold in the auction for a mind-boggling $53 million dollars. If one is baffled by the selling price of *Irises,* consider the fact that another one of VanGogh's paintings, his portrait of Dr. Gochet, sold one hundred years after VanGogh's death for a historical landmark price of $83.7 million dollars. These staggering sales left even those who deeply appreciate fine art stunned and baffled. What made the paintings so valuable? Nothing about the life of Vincent VanGogh appeared to be worth $83 million dollars. Then what could it possibly be?

These paintings were worth millions, because it was what one man was willing to pay to claim the painting as his own. It would belong to no other person.

If God was willing to sacrifice the life of his only Son on our behalf to claim us as his own, then who do we think we are to have no self-regard or to view another human as having no value? If we do so, we are saying to God, "You made a foolish investment." The world can influence your self-esteem but it cannot declare your value. Your value has already been established. The price tag has been written. The redemption has been made with the high price of Jesus' death on the cross. God has established you as valuable even in your sinfulness. "But God demonstrates his own love for us in this: While we were still sinners, Christ died for us" (Rom. 5:8).

Even if we, in and of ourselves, did not have any intrinsic value—we would have imputed value, because God values us. He not only values us, but also loves us unconditionally. There is nothing we can do to earn or deserve his love. There is nothing we can do to diminish his love. All we need to do is accept his love by embracing his free gift of salvation.

Your value is not in what you can contribute, in your appearance, or in the status you have in the eyes of this world. Your value is in what one was willing to pay to redeem you as his very own. You cannot escape the world's scourge on self-esteem, but your value remains as declared by Christ's sacrifice.

It seems to be human nature to view some individuals as having little value. However, you cannot continue to see someone in the same light once you have come to the realization that this person is one for whom Christ died.

Personal Responses to Mistakes and Disappointments

So how do you respond to the mistakes and disappointments that come your way? Is your response one that can maintain your personal vitality, or do you react in such a way that it robs you of vitality? Pause for a moment and take inventory of both the healthy and unhealthy ways that you respond or react to mistakes and disappointments. Consider:

- How do you react to mistakes and disappointments in ways that might rob you of vitality (based on the unhealthy reactions listed)?
- What would be a healthy response that you need to adopt as a way of dealing with mistakes and disappointments (based on the healthy responses listed)?

People who succeed are those ordinary people who learn powerful lessons from failed attempts and disappointments. They can find the hidden opportunity in the most disparaging circumstances of life. They put their trust in the Lord and step out in faith against what seems to be impossible odds.

So, as one who wants to have a positive and transformational impact on others, how you respond to mistakes and failures is a matter of spiritual maturity. Has the Holy Spirit done his sanctifying work and trained you to respond in healthy ways to mistakes and failures of others as well as your own? Have you learned how to thrive and flourish in the aftermath of mistakes or failures? If not, we urge you to seek out others who can help you grow and mature in this important area of your life.

To complete your Personal Insight Exercise for chapter 9 in the online workbook, go to: FullStrength.org/AtFullStrength.

PART 4

Navigating Emotional and Directional Challenges

Danger:
The Challenge of Anger

*Speak when you are angry and you will make
the BEST speech you will ever regret!*

—AMBROSE BIERCE

Everyone struggles with the emotion of anger. During an office visit, I once had a pastor who was struggling with anger ask me, "Is it okay for me to curse in here?" This pastor was dealing with anger over how people were treating him, while at the  same time expecting him to remain calm and collected in the face of personal attacks. Smiling and being patient with the most obnoxious and demanding people was taxing this pastor beyond his limits.

Those who serve in people-helping vocations can be more at risk because they continually deal with the physical, emotional, and spiritual problems of others. They experience a pressure to display an acceptable emotional posturing even if it is totally incongruent with what one is justifiably feeling at the time. This is occasionally referred to as *emotional labor.*

If anger is allowed to simmer over a long period of time, it often develops into physical ailments and health issues or spews out and harms innocent bystanders such as a spouse or children.

How to Approach Anger Effectively

One of the greatest and most dangerous vitality drainers is unresolved anger. Anger, when not dealt with effectively, will seek its own expression in the same four ways as stress addressed in chapter 3:

1. People explode with harsh verbal or physical expressions.
2. People experience somatization whereby negative physical conditions or illnesses occur.
3. People turn to underhanded behaviors, such as becoming negative, cynical, gossipy, or exhibiting other passive-aggressive behaviors.
4. People punish themselves in their anger believing themselves to be wrong in some way and worthy of punishment.

In order to manage and navigate the high seas of anger, it's critical that you face up to what's going on and admit or confess that you are angry. Suppressing anger or denying that it's influencing or controlling your emotions only compounds and lengthens the period of time that damage or harm to yourself or others can occur.

Only as you acknowledge your anger and gain a more realistic view of its activity in your life can you gain control and make it a force for good. Anger is a signal, like a flashing light on our car dashboard. It reveals something of great importance in the life of the person displaying anger. In some or many cases, the angry person may not understand or be fully aware of the issues that have activated the anger.

When you are trying to help yourself or others deal with anger, your main task is to discover and understand the concerns or issues that drive the angry response or behavior. The Bible contains many references to God's anger—which is a righteous form of anger. However, in most cases, anger paves the way for sinful responses to occur. We tend to embellish and distort facts when we are angry, in an effort to justify our grievance. While angry, it is easy to give our spiritual enemy a foothold that can be exploited for greater harm. "Don't sin by letting anger control you. Don't let the sun go down while you are still angry, for anger gives a foothold to the devil" (Eph. 4:26–27 NLT).

Anger, when allowed to fester, produces a form of spiritual alchemy, whereby we give ourselves permission to transmute feelings and speculations into "facts" that we use to rationalize and justify inappropriate behaviors. When we are angry, we often say things that don't represent our actual beliefs; we can say harmful words that we don't really mean.

In the political realm, anger is used to justify various sorts of political activism that oftentimes are not squarely centered on facts. Theologian Howard Thurman, who was a frequent source of inspiration to Dr. Martin Luther King Jr., stated concerning anger:

It is particularly relevant because hostility tends to keep up the illusion of self-importance and pride. There are many people who would feel cheated if suddenly they were deprived of the ego definition that their suffering gives them.[1]

The Anatomy of Anger

In order to navigate the anger you experience effectively, you need to understand fully the anatomy of anger. But first, you have to admit that you are experiencing anger. It does not help to be dishonest with yourself about the anger hidden below the surface of your front stage (public self). Being honest with yourself precedes your discovering effective ways to navigate the anger that stems from offenses and injustices.

Jessica Shaver addresses this issue with this poem titled "Anger at God":

I told God I was Angry
I thought He'd be surprised.

I thought I'd keep hostility
quite cleverly disguised.

I told the Lord I hated Him
I told Him that I hurt.

I told Him that He isn't fair,
He's treated me like dirt.

I told God I was Angry, but I'm the one surprised.

What I've known all along,
He said, you've finally realized.

At last you have admitted what's really in your heart.
Dishonesty, not anger, was keeping us apart.

Even when you hate Me I don't stop loving you.
Before you can receive that love
you must confess what's true.

In telling Me the anger you genuinely feel,
it loses power over you, permitting you to heal.

I told God I was sorry and He's forgiven me.
The truth that I was angry has finally set me free.[2]

You have to admit to feeling angry before you can be free of its negative impact. In many Christian circles, coming clean about the anger we feel is seen as unacceptable. When we gain a more realistic view of anger, only then can it become a force for good.

Anger is a signal—one worth paying attention to. Ignoring anger is like clipping the wires to the dashboard lights of your car. You lose your capacity to assess your situation. Anger means that something matters to you. We never get angry about things that do not matter to us. There are, however, those times when a person becomes angry but is confused about the exact nature of their concern.

After you have admitted you feel anger, you now can begin to deal with the offense in a healthy, God-honoring manner. To adequately assess the situation, we must understand the progression of anger. Let's take a closer look.

Anger	Resentment	Bitterness & Rage	Murder

The Progression of Anger

Anger operates along a scale of escalating intensity—we progress from anger to resentment to bitterness and rage and then finally to murder in the most extreme manifestation of anger.

Anger always involves a physiological reaction to a perceived or real threat. Biochemical processes activate and move us into a posture of preparation to deal with what we believe is an impending threat. As anger begins to take control, people report different physical responses. Some report their hearts start to pound, their legs feel like rubber, their ears become hot, their neck muscles tighten, or they feel tightness in their chests. Regardless of the manifestation—physical responses like this can be used to alert an aware person that the tide of anger is rising.

If you do not manage and deal with anger in a timely and healthy manner, it will progress or escalate to the second stage: resentment.

Resentment functions like a slow cooker, allowing your feelings to marinate and simmer slowly over time. You may lie awake at night thinking about the different retorts you might have made to put a person in his place after an anger-generating offense that occurred earlier in the day. As resentment springs to life, it desires one thing—to get even. Nelson Mandela, quoting a first-century historian, was reported as saying: "Resentment is like drinking poison and then hoping it will kill your enemies."

Resentment unchecked turns to bitterness and rage, which is the third stage of anger. Bitterness is like a malignant cancer; it grows and slowly destroys the person from within. Bitterness offers no curative benefit, yet people progress to and can live in this state for extended periods of their lives. The irony in many if not most cases is that the alleged offender is completely unaware that they are the object or focus of someone's bitterness.

Bitterness essentially reveals that the person has an unforgiving spirit, a matter of great importance and weight in the Scriptures. Given what Jesus has forgiven in our own lives, if someone lacks the capacity to forgive others, it calls into question whether he or she is a genuine follower of Jesus. Bitterness and resentment neutralize our talents and spiritual gifting, rendering us impotent or useless in service to God.

Leaders approaching burnout must be cautious, because anger leading to resentment leading to bitterness can quietly invade their hearts. After eight years of intense ministry service, one couple visited me as a requirement of their sabbatical. I helped them discover that their exhaustion was self-inflicted, due to the attempts to please each and every person in the church. While they maintained a positive front-stage demeanor, a growing resentment began to simmer backstage over their exhaustion caused by their own unhealthy people-pleasing behaviors. They were not being proactive in protecting and preserving their own wellbeing. Two verses became particularly meaningful for this couple as they experienced healing from their resentment and growing bitterness.

Yes, this anguish was good for me, for you have rescued me from death and forgiven all my sins. (Isa. 38:17 NLT)

And I will give you a new heart, and I will put a new spirit in you. I will take out your stony, stubborn heart and give you a tender, responsive heart. (Ezek. 36:26 NLT)

The final stage of anger is murder or death. In the most extreme cases, anger can lead to causing physical death, such as when Cain slew Abel out of a jealous rage or when Moses slew the Egyptian supervisor who was abusing Jewish laborers. But murder can be a metaphor for a figurative slaying as well. We can allow escalated anger to "murder" a marriage or destroy a child's self-esteem.

How to Identify What Drives Your Anger

To steer through the roiling seas of anger effectively, you must begin to identify and comes to terms with the underlying emotions that are driving your anger. Anger is a secondary emotion. Think of anger as an iceberg. What others experience when we are angry is that which is observed above the waterline. Angry words and actions elicit defensiveness in others, and they want to distance themselves from the anger that can be unnerving. However, when we can identify the emotion that is beneath the surface and causing the anger, it is much easier to process the anger and to engage others.

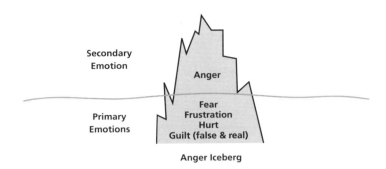

Anger Iceberg

The four prime suspects for the underlying emotion are: fear, frustration, hurt, and guilt, whether false or real. Let's look more in depth at each of these emotions.

Fear

We become afraid when we feel that our physical lives or our personal identity are being threatened such that we might be destroyed. God has endowed us with an innate desire to want to preserve our wellbeing.

The simplest way to disrupt and defeat anger arising from fear is to publicly confess your fear—first to yourself, then to others. By admitting that, "I'm feeling fearful in this situation," you invite others, including the Holy Spirit, to move in to help you address your need. Confession can transform others from adversaries to allies, for no normal, otherwise healthy person wants to be the cause of another person's pain or suffering.

Frustration

This prime emotion is perhaps the most difficult to manage, because it typically does not elicit empathy from others when acknowledged or confessed, most likely because the cause of frustration is often shrouded in mystery. Frustration occurs when you become thwarted from achieving a goal, desire, or expectation. When you perceive that others are the cause or obstacle that is keeping you from your goal, you can become angry with that person or persons.

The most effective way to manage frustration is to communicate your desire or goal clearly, assuming it is a worthy goal and not intrinsically selfish or sinful, and then humbly recruit assistance from other people to help you achieve your goal. Generally speaking, normal, healthy people enjoy helping others achieve something worthwhile, as long as it doesn't come unfairly at their own expense.

A special warning is required at this point: As a leader, you should always seek for the best answer to an issue, not necessarily *your* answer to that issue. Further, if you become angry because you are unable to obtain selfish or sinful outcomes, your anger is wholly unjustified, and you are the problem. Healing from your anger must take a spiritual path, involving confession and bringing your life into alignment with God's truths. Otherwise, you are traveling a path that ensures resentment, bitterness, and "death" as your destination.

Hurt

As with fear, others may be quick to rally to your aid when they learn that the underlying cause of your expressed anger is hurt. Telling people that what they said or did hurt your feelings will in most cases lead to healthy discussion and an outcome that defeats the secondary emotion of your anger. If another person does not positively engage with you to address the causes of their hurtful conduct, that's a signal that it's time to set and enforce protective boundaries with that person.

The tricky part about hurt as a primary emotion is that in some cases your motives or needs may be unduly selfish or perhaps even sinful. For spiritual growth to occur, it's very important that you take the time yourself, or with the aid of a trusted friend or advisor, to expose the underlying motive causing you to feel hurt or pain. If the underlying cause is selfish or sinful, then an action plan to replace a wrong motive with a godly motive is required. You may be able to accomplish this on your own, but working with an accountability partner will generally be more effective. For health and growth to occur you must "be transformed by the renewing your mind" (Rom. 12:2) in this area of your conduct.

Guilt

Unlike shame, which for the Christian is always unhealthy, guilt can be a healthy emotion as it serves as an early warning system that you have potentially done something that may have hurt another person. To defeat the anger that can sometimes emerge from intense feelings of guilt—you must pause and take the time to identify precisely the issue that is causing you to feel guilty. As part of this analysis, you must confirm whether the guilt is false or real. Our spiritual enemy delights in causing us to feel guilty for no justifiable reason.

After you have identified real guilt, you must go to the person and confess that you are feeling guilty about something you have said or done that might have hurt them and then apologize if your behavior has indeed caused them hurt or pain. In the vast majority of cases, restoration of the relationship will immediately occur, and the underlying cause of your anger will be soundly defeated. If the person does not or will not respond in a spirit of forgiveness and reconciliation, then they are not behaving as a Christian should behave. In that case, you need to step back and begin to view and relate to that person as in need of hearing the gospel and experiencing the forgiveness that Christ has made possible by his death and resurrection.

The Triggers and Underlying Themes of Anger

To learn how to master and overcome unhealthy anger in your life, reflect on the situations that emotionally "pull the trigger" or "push your buttons" and send you into a damaging and nonproductive state of anger. As best you can, make a list of the common or recurring times in your life when you tend to become angry. As you think about these triggering events, ask yourself:

- ◉ What about this situation caused me to feel threatened?
- ◉ What circumstances around this situation caused me to be offended?
- ◉ Do I feel anger when . . . ?
- ◉ I feel fear when . . .
- ◉ I feel frustration when . . .
- ◉ I feel hurt when . . .
- ◉ I feel guilt when . . .

If you can learn to understand your triggering circumstances, then you've taken a big step to gain control over your anger when the triggering events occur.

Following is a list of common anger triggers. This chart may help you identify what is behind your anger. If you know your triggers and can identify the underlying themes, then you can choose your response, instead of just reacting! This is like a soldier safely navigating through a field of landmines with a map.

Anger Triggers and Underlying Themes

___ Someone says or tells you that you did something wrong.
___ You hear or learn that another person is speaking ill of you.
___ Your spouse says that you haven't been doing enough at home.
___ You are getting stuck in traffic and running late.
___ You are late or being delayed for something important.
___ Someone interrupts you.

___ You are already overwhelmed and the responsibilities keep coming.

___ You want something but can't obtain it when you want it.

___ Someone tries to tell you how to run your life.

___ An employee doesn't respect your authority.

___ Someone doesn't respond to your request or demand.

___ Other: _____

Of the thousands of potential triggers, what do you suppose is the story behind your triggers? What is it in your history that may have created them?

What might be the underlying themes? Here is a list that might assist you in clarifying your underlying themes:

___ Disrespected	___ Devalued	___ Unloved
___ Dismissed	___ Inconvenienced	___ Unkind
___ Manipulated	___ Incompetence	___ Overlooked
___ Others: _____		

···

To find an expanded list of triggers and themes and to complete your Personal Insight Exercise for chapter 10, go to the online workbook at FullStrength.org/AtFullStrength.

How to Express Anger in a Productive Way

As you become aware when an anger trigger is pulled and you understand the underlying theme that's part of your anger pattern, then you can begin to harness and express your anger in a way that supports healthy outcomes. While you have no control over how another party reacts, you can handle the situation in a respectful manner without attacking or diminishing others.

Here's an anger-management protocol that you can learn and practice as you relate to others who pull one of your anger triggers:

When you (describe the person's triggering behavior without impugning the person),

I feel (describe your underlying emotion—hurt, fearful, frustrated, guilty),

Because (describe the impact on you; share underlying themes).

It would be helpful if you could (describe the behavior that you expect),

Then (describe the fruitful and positive outcome desired).

When Anger Does Not Go Away

What should you do when you are captured by an anger that simply will not go away? Seek help! Try as you will, you will experience times when you cannot unravel and neutralize an ongoing feeling of anger. If allowed to persist, this anger will take a heavy toll on your health and degrade your ability to remain in a thriving and flourishing posture. Your productivity will be diminished, and you're likely to cause emotional harm to others.

Unrelenting anger may be bound up in some past life trauma that you don't fully understand, or it may be endogenous or physiologically based. Though rare, it's possible that medications may be required to stabilize a condition that leaves you in a constant state of anger or some other destabilizing mood. It's heartening to watch the old stigmas and taboos around mental health issues recede and people become proactive as they care for themselves or others.

Consider biological factors as it pertains to anger. For example, some men, because of testosterone, can be easily frustrated, irritable, and angry when depressed. We think of depression as being sad and low in mood. However, some men experience an agitated depression, which can make them grumpy. Once a man's anger is aroused due to a real or perceived threat, testosterone pushes the delete button on another hormone called oxytocin. *Oxytocin* is referred to as the "tend and befriend" hormone. This hormone causes people to be nurturing. When men become angry, they experience a surge of adrenalin, followed by a rise in testosterone, which can deplete their systems of oxytocin.

If someone were to break into your home and threaten your family, this hormonal system would go into effect. Women often want to protect and calm the children, even when they are fearful themselves. Men often surge with adrenaline and testosterone, which deletes oxytocin, leaving them ready to draw their weapons and protect their families. This system is very functional in a violent culture. However, in a more civilized culture, the hormonal response needs to be toned down.

Men who are chronically agitated and women who are hostile during certain cycles of life can benefit from antidepressant medications that can take the edge off these imbalances. As a counselor, I am not necessarily pro-medication. But for the person who experiences anger that is severe or chronic, you must consider several questions: First, is there any harm in considering a trial of medical intervention to balance your brain chemistry? Second, are you more effective for the cause of Christ on the medication or off the medication?

This side of heaven, in a sin-filled world, we all eventually have something wrong with our biological system that may be helped by medication.

A Word Concerning Unmet Expectations

It's important to note the link between anger and expectation. As a general rule, *all* strong emotional reactions are interwoven and connected to our expectations. These expectations may not always be consciously realized. We only get angry concerning things that matter to us. In fact, we rarely expend emotional energy on things that do not matter to us.

Your *emotional triggers* are tied to *underlying expectations*. If you become angry over something trite or insignificant, it is likely symbolic of an unmet expectation. This is why married couples seem to fight over some of the strangest things. The matter they're arguing over is likely not the *real issue*. The underlying issues generally involve themes such as respect, consideration, love, and caring.

When in the counseling office a person is asked to consider whether his or her anger might be based on the desire to control, the question is usually met with resistance and defensiveness. However, we all have a basic need for control in our lives. The way we express our need for control can vary in intensity and modality. Regardless of how it manifests, our need for control has a strong influence on all our lives. Anything that makes us feel helpless, lacking fundamental control over our circumstances or relationships, can trigger a strong emotional reaction.

Let's take a closer look at a strategy that will help you manage your life well without leaving others feeling controlled by your anger. In the words of psychologist Richard Carlson, "Don't sweat the small stuff. And most of it is small stuff."

Stephen Covey, in his book *First Things First*, sets forth a strategy to manage time and priorities. This strategy to manage anger is based on the same concept.[3]

We all have issues and concerns in our lives—our Circle of Concerns. Within this Circle of Concerns are the many challenges we face in life.

Some of these concerns we can manage. Others fall totally outside of our capacity to manage or even influence. When we confuse the difference between our Circle of Concerns and our Circle of Control, it results in anxiety, discouragement, frustration, and anger.

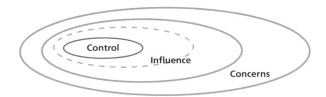

Using this circle concept, here's an exercise you can do to help decipher your expectations: Think of all the current concerns in your life. Every concern has importance or you wouldn't think of it as a concern. You can place all these concerns in one of three circles. Where you place them impacts the toll on your emotional state and energy.

Write down all the concerns that are on your heart and mind at the current time. Then place them in one of three circles: *Circle of Control, Circle of Influence, or Circle of Concerns.* This will help you rank them, which can reduce your stress surrounding the concerns.

When we place a concern over which we have no control in our Circle of Control, we expend mental, emotional, relational, and physical energy that will lead to nothing but further frustration. In the process, we often create further challenges for ourselves and for others, all the time wasting precious energy that could be better spent elsewhere in our lives.

The only kind of control for which the Bible advocates is self-control—and that can be an uphill marathon. When we increase our Circle of Control, it comes out of our influence real estate. In other words, it diminishes our capacity to influence others and our circumstances. The more we strive for control, the more we increase the likelihood of a strong emotional reaction when the expectations aren't met. A significant aspect of managing anger is learning to manage expectations.

You have a decision when encountering difficult challenges. You can choose to influence lovingly or you can resort to control. It is wise to remember that control, for the most part, is an illusion. When you are emotionally flooded, it usually requires an intentional act of the will to choose influence over your need to control. When you choose to use your Circle of Influence, rather than control, you increase your imputed authority. You make it easier for others to trust you.

Your highest and best choice is where you choose to place your trust. Will you trust in the One who loves you deeply and is more concerned for you than anyone else is, including yourself? When God is working through our circumstances, he is under no obligation to meet our expectations. Nor is he obligated to explain to us what he is wanting to birth in our lives. Remember this: God is absolutely dependable, yet totally unpredictable.

To complete your Personal Insight Exercise for chapter 10, go to the online workbook at FullStrength.org/AtFullStrength.

Depression and Worry Sickness

I once heard a very appropriate analogy describing the similarities between ministry and people-helping vocations and deep-sea divers. The deep-sea diver goes to extreme depths in search of various forms of rewarding experiences. But every deep-sea diver understands the incredible

> **USE CAUTION WHEN DIVING**
> **SERIOUS OR FATAL INJURY MAY RESULT**

pressure that is exerted on his body in each diving venture. At sea level, the air around us has a pressure of 14.7 psi (pounds per square inch) referred to as one atmosphere. This is considered the normal pressure for the human body. Because water is so heavy compared to air, it does not take much water to exert a lot of pressure. At thirty-three feet below the surface, the pressure on the body doubles and the diver's lungs contract to half their normal size. When a diver resurfaces, the air expands and the lungs return to normal size.

If a diver remains under water too long, nitrogen from the air will dissolve into his body. If he swims to the surface too rapidly, it is like uncorking a bottle of soda—gas is released. This is referred to as the bends (decompression sickness). It can be very painful and is potentially fatal. To avoid the effects of quick decompression, the diver must rise slowly, making intermittent decompression stops on the way up to the surface to let the gas out slowly.

As a safeguard, divers are equipped with a depth gauge and oxygen gauge. At all times the diver monitors the pressure gauges, carefully calculating how long he or she can remain at depth without severe consequences. Oxygen levels are monitored, as well, ensuring enough oxygen supply remains to be able to safely return to the surface. Failure to do so can result in permanent damage to the body, including the brain, lungs, and neurological system. Those who experience the bends may never dive again, or they could possibly lose their lives.

Those of us who believe serving others is our calling and mission want to invest *deeply* into the cause. But there is a fundamental difference between deep-sea divers and ministry leaders and other people helpers: We do not possess a depth gauge to calculate the risk of diving into the cause. We have no oxygen gauge to aid us in knowing when and how fast we must return to the surface. If we get lost in the deep waters of serving, we may experience the bends upon surfacing for those much-needed sources of renewal. Many vocational people helpers seem to run out of oxygen without much warning. They surface too late and too fast.

We received a call again last week. A ministry leader and friend announced his resignation. No moral failure. No severe crisis at the church. No major family problems. No sickness. He was simply burned out. That's how he described it. He said he had gotten to the point that he was having trouble putting one foot in front of the other.

When he arrived at my office, his hands were trembling. The depression was overwhelming. He could not focus on anything of importance. This minister was convinced that he was no longer capable of running the long race of ministry. So he had quit without another job in sight. In our counseling time together we discovered that he had numerous early warning signs that his vitality and resilience were rapidly declining.

We just wished he had called a few weeks earlier, which could have prevented a lot of shock and heartache for his spouse and church family. The dive was deep for many years, and now he suffered from the *ministry bends,* believing he was no longer fit to minister to others.

It seems that hardly a week passes that we do not hear another story of a ministry or nonprofit worker who reached the end of the rope and quit the work they once considered a calling.

Early Warning Signs

What are your early warning signs (EWS) indicating that you are losing your resiliency? What are your earliest warning signs of diminishing vitality? Is it in the physical domain with low energy or sleep difficulties? Is it in your attitude or relationships? To get started, write down your EWS in each of these aspects of life:

- ◉ **Physical:** Where in your body do you first see the impact of stress? (Example: You experience sleeping difficulties.)
- ◉ **Mental Attitude:** What is the shift in your general outlook? (Example: You are irritable or oversensitive.)
- ◉ **Relational Dynamics:** How are your closer relationships impacted by your diminishing vitality? (Example: Your family senses that you are distant or self-absorbed.)
- ◉ **Spiritual Life:** What happens to your prayer life and spiritual feeding? (Example: Your prayer life becomes nonexistent except in moments of desperation.)

The Four Directions of the Heart

Have you stopped to think about what happens in your heart when life is not treating you well? Take a moment, and consider these questions:

- ◉ *Where does your heart go* when you do not feel loved, respected, or appreciated?

◉ The *absence of what c*auses you to want to give up?
◉ The *fear of what* makes you tentative rather than courageous?
◉ The *need for what* robs you of joy in your work and life?

These dynamics and others like them can cause our hearts to move away from the Spring of Living Water. Remember the words God through the prophet Jeremiah who said, "My people have committed two sins: They have forsaken me, the spring of living water, and have dug their own cisterns, broken cisterns that cannot hold water" (Jer. 2:13). A closer examination of these directions can be very helpful if we are to gain and maintain the vitality essential for lifelong service that honors God.

When life does not treat you well, your heart might go in four fundamental directions. They are:

◉ Fear
◉ Faltering
◉ Frustration
◉ Foolishness

It is important to identify your tendencies. After reading the following sections, identify your primary and secondary heart directions that seem most common for you.

Fear

The fear malady takes the form of anxiety, worry, hurry, panic, or urgency. While not all fear-based decisions are bad decisions, fear keeps us from discovering and pursuing God's best for us. Faith is required to please God (Heb. 11:6), but to the extent that fear begins to emerge in the heart of a pastor, faith begins to recede in a corresponding amount. Fear-based decisions are risk adverse, hesitant, and reluctant decisions—hardly the posture God intends for his people.

Faltering

The faltering malady takes the leader to the land of the Big Ds: discouragement, doubt, despair, distress, downcast, and depression. When you falter and become hesitant, you lose energy and vitality. Even worse, you lose the passion and confidence of those who want to follow you.

Frustration

Frustration is what you experience when your expectations are thwarted no matter how hard you try. When the goal remains frustrated, you can become angry, agitated, aggravated, or controlling.

Foolishness

While you may find it easy to admit that at times you are fearful, faltering, and frustrated, it's harder to admit that you at times have foolish attitudes and behaviors. The book of Proverbs in the Old Testament describes the fool who lives in a pattern of foolishness. Some patterns of foolishness are very clear, such as addictions, idolatry, and compulsions. However, others are more subtle, such as procrastination or, on the opposite extreme, the tendency to make hasty decisions that lack forethought. The self-talk associated with foolishness is very self-justifying.

What is your heart direction when life is not meeting your expectations? Try to identify your primary and secondary direction. Fearfulness and behaving foolishly are rarely my challenge. However, faltering (becoming discouraged)

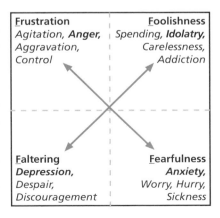

Frustration
Agitation, **Anger,** Aggravation, Control

Foolishness
Spending, **Idolatry,** Carelessness, Addiction

Faltering
Depression, Despair, Discouragement

Fearfulness
Anxiety, Worry, Hurry, Sickness

followed by frustrated (angry) are my nemeses. What is the tendency of your heart? Note it on the chart with an arrow. Then ask what it would look like for you to go to the Stream of Living Water instead of a broken cistern.

The Big Bad D—Depression

Among the big challenges for vocational people helpers is having to navigate those emotional challenges that are referred to as the *Big Bad Ds*—depression, discouragement, doubt, despair, disappointment, and downcast. Nothing is worse than faltering while having to stand in front of a congregation, classroom, or counseling client day after day.

Depression, with its many disappointments and losses, is very real. No one is immune to it. The fact that medications for depression are at the top of the charts in revenue indicates the impact of stress in the developed world.

Many admirable historical and public figures, known by their character and/or contribution to the world, suffered from depression. They include US President Abraham Lincoln, church reformer Martin Luther, champion for those with disabilities Joni Erickson Tada, painter Vincent VanGogh, Princess Diana, musician Ludwig Van Beethoven, preacher John Wesley, Bible teacher Charles Spurgeon, Prime Minister Sir Winston Churchill, and civil rights leader Martin Luther King Jr.

The word *depression* is not found anywhere in the Bible. However, you can find many words, especially in the book of Psalms, that are descriptive of depression. In fact, more than 50 different emotions are identified in the Psalms. Some are positive, such as joy, and others are more adverse emotions such as downcast. You only have to open your Bible to the book of Psalms and begin reading. Within a few minutes a description of depression can be found in verses like the following:

I waited patiently for the LORD; he turned to me and heard my cry. He lifted me out of the slimy pit, out of the mud and mire. (Ps. 40:1–2)

My tears have been my food day and night, while people say to me all day long, "Where is your God?" (Ps. 42:3)

My soul is downcast within me. (Ps. 42:6)

Restore to me the joy of your salvation and grant me a willing spirit, to sustain me. (Ps. 51:12)

You are God my stronghold. Why have you rejected me? Why must I go about mourning, oppressed by the enemy? (Ps. 43:2)

Other Accounts of Depression in the Bible

There are numerous accounts of the Big Ds of depression, despair and discouragement throughout the Bible. Here are just a few:

- A "thick and dreadful darkness came over" Abraham (Gen. 15:12).
- Moses asked God to blot him out of the book of life (Ex. 32:32–33).
- The prophet Jeremiah was considered the "weeping prophet" and wished he had never been born (Jer. 15—20).
- David wept until he had no strength remaining (1 Sam. 30:3–4).

The Main Symptoms of Depression

Though the symptoms used to diagnose depression are the same in men and women, the presentation may be different. Men may present as more agitated and possibly angry. Women may present as being sad and tearful. Though this chapter is focused more on a spiritual perspective and helpful strategies to manage depression, be aware of the main symptoms:

- ◉ Fatigue as a slowing down of physical movements, speech, and thought processes
- ◉ Sleep problems, such as insomnia, waking up very early in the morning, or excessive sleeping
- ◉ Somatic symptoms, such as various body aches or intestinal disturbances
- ◉ Irritability, anger, or hostility, especially in men
- ◉ Women tend to be more down, sad, blue, or experience a low mood
- ◉ Difficulty concentrating or remembering important details
- ◉ Difficulty making decisions
- ◉ Feeling a sense of guilt, worthlessness, and helplessness
- ◉ Feeling of hopelessness and/or pessimism
- ◉ Loss of interest in activities once pleasurable
- ◉ Overeating or appetite loss
- ◉ Suicidal ideation

Fundamentally, depression is a *lack of resiliency*. You don't have enough internal energy mentally, emotionally, and spiritually to help you bounce back when confronted with the losses you experience from time to time. You need something to regain your resiliency. It may be rest or a need to communicate something that is bothersome. You may need to exercise or change your diet. Depression may be related to a deficit in your biochemistry calling for the utilization of medical intervention. Whatever the case, depression is basically a lack of resiliency.

Sometimes we use the word picture of a basketball. For a basketball to function properly, there has to be an adequate amount of inflation exerted against the skin of the ball to give it resiliency—or to bounce. Inadequate inflation results in a lack of resiliency.

The Two Main Forms of Depression

Though there are technically many types of depression, for the sake of a clear understanding, we'll look at two forms of depression.

Exogenous (External) Depression

Exogenous depression is a reactive type—the depression is about how you are reacting to an event in your environment. Reactive depression can happen throughout each day in small and insignificant ways. You perceive a loss and feel discouraged or disappointed for a short period. However, most of us bounce back in a matter of minutes or hours. You can have a reactive depression that can last for weeks when you encounter a major loss, such as the death of a loved one, dealing with major illness, or the loss of a job.

Endogenous (Internal) Depression

Endogenous depression is a biochemical type—your brain chemistry is actually out of balance. This biochemical depression can be brought on by a number of precipitating factors. It can have its onset as result of a physical illness or a traumatic event. It can be caused by your having to deal with a reactive depression that seems to have no apparent solution in sight. Some forms of depression actually have a genetic basis and can be inherited.

A Healthy Spiritual Perspective on Depression

Among the hallmark lectures on depression was one presented by the famous preacher Charles Spurgeon in 1856. This was the birth year of Sigmund Freud, an Austrian neurologist and the atheistic father of psychoanalysis. Spurgeon's insight was approximately one hundred years before its time as it related to effective treatment of depression. Below are excerpts from this famous lecture that Spurgeon delivered to seminary students in order to have them well informed concerning the depression they were likely to encounter as clergy.

When a Preacher is Downcast

Fits of depression come over the most of us. Cheerful as we may be, we must at intervals be cast down. The strong are not always vigorous, the wise not always ready, the brave not always courageous, and the joyous not always happy.

There may be here and there men of iron to whom wear and tear work no perceptible detriment, but surely the rust frets even these; and as for ordinary men, the Lord knows and makes them to know that they are but dust.

God's Preachers Are Still Frail Humanity
Moreover, most of us are in some way or other unsound physically.

Certain bodily maladies, especially those connected with the digestive organs, the liver and the spleen, are the fruitful fountains of despondency; and let a man strive as he may against their influence, there will be hours and circumstances in which they will for a while overcome him.

As to mental maladies, is any man altogether sane? Are we not all a little off the balance?

Some minds appear to have a gloomy tinge essential to their very individuality. Of them it may be said, "Melancholy marked (them) for her own"; fine minds withal and ruled by noblest principles, but yet they are most prone to forget the silver lining and to remember only the cloud.

Preachers, by Lack of Exercise and Recreation, Tend to Melancholy

There can be little doubt that sedentary habits have a tendency to create despondency in some constitutions.

He [a man] will make his study a prison and his books the warders of a gaol, while Nature lies outside his window calling him to health and beckoning him to joy.

A day's breathing of fresh air upon the hills or a few hours' ramble in the beech woods' umbrageous calm, would sweep the cobwebs out of the brain of scores of our toiling ministers who are now but half alive. A mouthful of sea air, or a stiff walk in the wind's face, would not give grace to the soul, but it would yield oxygen to the body, which is next best.

God Allows Fainting After Great Victories Lest We Should Be "Exalted Above Measure"

Men cannot bear unalloyed happiness. Even good men are not yet fit to have "their brows with laurel and with myrtle bound" without enduring secret humiliation to keep them in their proper places.

Failure to Take Regular Periods of Vacation and Rest Promotes Fainting and Weariness

To tug the oar from day to day, like a galley slave who knows no holidays, suits not mortal men. Mill streams go on and on forever, but we must have our pauses and our intervals.

Who can help being out of breath when the race is continued without intermission? Even beasts of burden must be turned out to grass occasionally. The very sea pauses at ebb and flood. Earth keeps the Sabbath of the wintry months. And man, even when exalted to be God's ambassador, must rest or faint; must trim his lamp or let it burn low; must recruit his vigor or grow prematurely old. It is wisdom to take occasional furlough.

In the long run, we shall do more by sometimes doing less.

The Inevitable Blows of Betrayal, Slander, Criticism Depress God's Best Preachers

Constant dripping wears away stones, and the bravest minds feel the fret of repeated afflictions.

Accumulated distresses increase each other's weight, play into each other's hands and, like bands of robbers, ruthlessly destroy our comfort.

One affords himself no pity when in this case, because it seems so unreasonable, even sinful, to be troubled without manifest cause. Yet troubled the man is, even in the very depths of his spirit. If those who laugh at such melancholy did but feel the grief of it for one hour, their laughter would be sobered into compassion.

God Allows a Minister's Troubles for His Glory
Such mature men as some elderly preachers are, could scarcely have been produced if they had not been emptied from vessel to vessel and made to see their own emptiness and the vanity of all things round about them.

Glory be to God for the furnace, the hammer and the file. Heaven shall be all the fuller of bliss because we have been filled with anguish here below; and earth shall be better tilled because of our training in the school of adversity.[1]

God's Response to Elijah's Depression

An entirely important and pertinent question for any pastor or people-helping professional is this question: "How does God himself view and respond to depression?" The story of Elijah's depression provides a helpful start in answer to this question.

Elijah, a prophet of God, fell victim to depression. His suicidal thoughts and behaviors are documented for us in 1 Kings 19. Responding to Jezebel's venomous death threat in verses 3 and 4 we read:

Elijah was afraid and ran for his life. When he came to Beersheba in Judah, he left his servant there, while he himself went a day's journey into the wilderness. He came to a broom bush, sat down under it and prayed that he might die. "I have had enough, LORD," he said. "Take my life; I am no better than my ancestors."

Though speculative, we can imagine the events in Elijah's life that positioned him to enter a state of deep depression. He was hated and persecuted by the false religious leaders in the kingdom, especially after he had commanded that they be rounded up and killed in the Kishon Valley (1 Kings 18:40). The people of the land had been scorning and denouncing him for years, saying he was the reason that rain was withheld from the land. He was exhausted from battling the false prophets, then running with "special strength" ahead of King Ahab (who was traveling by chariot) to beat Ahab to the entrance of Jezreel. Finally, Jezebel told Elijah that he would be dead within twenty-four hours.

Elijah was spiritually, emotionally, relationally, physically, and intellectually exhausted, which is the perfect womb for the birth of depression. He was suffering mission fatigue. His faith in God had been put to the ultimate test against 450 prophets of Baal and 400 prophets of Asherah (financed by Jezebel) atop Mount Carmel (see 1 Kings 18). Ministry leader, be warned: Following any great kingdom event or achievement, the stage is set for a faltering experience to occur. It's a good time to retreat immediately and allow your vitality reserves to be restored and replenished, lest you fall victim to a faltering experience. When you achieve a vision goal, it's very easy to lose your sense of divine direction, because you don't yet know how the Lord wants to lead you in your next steps. After any great achievement, it's as if your brain says, "I've had it! We are going to take a break whether you like it or not!"

There were other factors too that created a context for Elijah's depression. Slowly over time, Elijah had allowed himself to become isolated, thinking that he was the last prophet standing up for the Most High. His last act was to abandon his servant before moving on alone into the wilderness (19:3). Later, God had to remind him that there were 7,000 others who had not bowed the knee to Baal (19:18).

Every leader must understand and expect that, as a consequence of taking strong stands for God's truth, people who are deemed friends and who provide relational comfort, may begin to peel away, fearing man (worldly social pressure), rather than fearing God. Steps must be taken to build enduring friendships with people that will survive the rigors of strong ministry leadership. Isolation and loneliness are two of the greatest threats every pastor must battle.

In 1 Kings 19:9–10, anger or agitation was a part of Elijah's response in his exhausted state:

....

And the word of the LORD came to him, "What are you doing here, Elijah?' He replied, "I have been very zealous for the LORD God Almighty. The Israelites have rejected your covenant, torn down your altars, and put your prophets to death with the sword. I am the only one left, and now they are trying to kill me, too."

....

So here's the picture of a depressed Elijah—he's all alone, having lost faith in others; running and hiding in fear; spiritually, emotionally, relationally, physically, and intellectually depleted; and believing that his calling and purpose are lost. His attitude is negative and cynical. Elijah is the classic picture of a depressed person.

How does God deal with Elijah's depression? God *ministers* to Elijah through the various domains of life: emotional, physical, mental, spiritual, and relational. Let's closely examine how God responded to the depression of Elijah.

The Physical

God dealt with Elijah in the physical dimension first by giving him a restful sleep: "Then he lay down under the bush and fell asleep" (1 Kings 19:5). Elijah was exhausted from all the activity of dealing with the prophets of Baal. Physical fatigue and the lack of rest can eventually result in depression. It is the organic brain staging a strike on the level of activity.

A second way that God dealt with Elijah in the physical realm was by providing proper nourishment and nutrition.

All at once an angel touched him and said, "Get up and eat." He looked around, and there by his head was some bread baked over hot coals, and a jar of water. He ate and drank and then lay down again. (1 Kings 19:5–6)

The food and drink you consume contribute significantly to your mood. Over-consumption of sugars, gluten-based foods, and stimulants will temporarily manipulate your mood, but with a residual effect that results in depletion of your various energies. Research suggests that a poor diet often correlates with poor mood. Also, skipping meals has a negative impact on your mood.

The third way God dealt in the physical area of life is through physical touch. "All at once an angel touched him," the Bible says (1 Kings 19:5). Significant research in the modern medical and psychological fields

Depression and Worry Sickness

strongly suggests that appropriate touch has a powerful role in our overall emotional vitality.

The final physical way that God helps Elijah through his depression is through exercise. "So he got up and ate and drank. Strengthened by that food, he traveled forty days and forty nights until he reached Horeb" (1 Kings 19:8). Exercise produces endorphins in the body. Endorphins affect the level of serotonin and dopamine, brain hormones that serve as the fuels for our cognitive and emotional stamina as well as resiliency. In fact, exercise is the most effective, quickest-acting, God-given, natural antidepressant available to us.

A number of other physical aspects can affect mood stability. They are referred to as God's antidepressants. They affect the serotonin in the brain that contributes to your sense of wellbeing and include:

- **Natural Light:** Exposure to natural light on the skin and the retina of the eyes affects the levels of melatonin in our body, as well as the level of Vitamin D, which is essential for mood health. Lack of exposure to natural light causes some people to experience Seasonal Affective Disorder (SAD), a low-grade depression that seems to persist in the time of the year that there are days with less daylight.
- **Hugs:** Being hugged by someone you want to receive hugs from actually releases endorphins into your body, increasing your mood stability.
- **Exercise:** Regular exercise, twenty minutes or more, three times a week can contribute greatly to mood improvement. It causes the quickest release of endorphins into the bloodstream giving an immediate antidepressant effect.
- **Sexual Intimacy:** Sexual intimacy in the context that God intended it causes the strongest, natural release of endorphins into the body.
- **Laughing:** Recent research has shown that laughter has an antidepressant effect. It is God's mood stabilizer. Several thousand years ago, the Bible, in Proverbs, spoke of laughter being like medicine.

◉ **Worshipful Prayer:** A number of studies, even secular-based ones, indicate that prayer has a positive impact in the process of healing emotionally and physically.

◉ **Uplifting Music:** Daniel Amen, MD, in his book, *Change Your Brain, Change Your Life,* writes about his research utilizing the SPECT Scan on the human brain and found that music has a powerful impact. Some music can cause agitation or a depressed mood. However, uplifting music, including worship music, can have a profoundly positive impact on our brain chemistry.[2]

◉ **Diet, Sleep, and Exercise:** Some well-intentioned men and women in leadership positions in ministry and other caregiving vocations can make the error of minimizing the impact physical condition has on depression. The default setting that assumes depression is purely spiritual or psychological overlooks the biological component. To be healthy, your body needs a nutritionally healthy diet, adequate sleep, and regular physical conditioning.

Find the expanded version of God's antidepressants in appendix D, chapter 11 of the online workbook, by going to FullStrength.org/ AtFullStrength.

Nutritional and Body Health

Research in the past several decades has linked a significant number of biomedical conditions to depression. For instance, low thyroid, testosterone, or Vitamin D contributes significantly to depression. Diabetes, seizure conditions, and Parkinson's disease are also major contributors to depression. In fact, for some individuals, a depression is the first symptom of these serious medical conditions.

It will help to expand on a few facts concerning nutrition as it pertains to brain balance and emotional health. We are fortunate to live at a time when nutrition supplements can contribute significantly to our quality of life, including emotional vitality. Unfortunately, most people overlook this entire aspect of personal vitality. But for those with some curiosity, here are a few tips on nutritional supplements as they relate to a more positive mental-emotional vitality:

St. John's Wort is the most studied herb of all time with more than two-dozen double-blind studies around the world. The active ingredient is *hypericum perforatum* (which means "above the ghost"). Hundreds of years ago, this flower was used to supposedly ward off an evil spirit. What it was actually doing was acting on the brain and the body to help digestion, act as an antiviral, anti-inflammatory, and support thyroid function.

Vitamin D is useful in the treatment of mild and moderate depression. Most people who live in areas of the world that have seasons likely have low levels of vitamin D due to the lack of natural sunlight on the skin. This lack of light increases the potential for endogenous depression that some refer to as the *winter blues* or *cabin fever*.

Testosterone supplementation can be very helpful for aging men if the male hormone levels are found to be low. This supplementation has to be done through a physician. Low testosterone is a major contributor to male depression, fatigue, and irritability.

5–hydroxytryptophan (5–HTP) is an amino acid found in low amounts in foods like turkey and bananas. 5-HTP is the molecule the body uses to make serotonin, a molecule that helps elevate mood by giving the body more of the raw materials it needs to make more serotonin. 5-HTP is best used with a person who is experiencing both depression and anxiety. It is also effective in helping individuals who suffer from insomnia-based depression and anxiety.

Anti–Inflammatory Foods and Supplements can also be helpful for many people. In recent years, research has indicated that some depressions may be connected with inflammation of the brain. Our bodies, including our brain tissues, experience inflammation. This inflammation is similar to what you experience when you get a wood splinter in your skin. In just a few hours, it becomes inflamed.

There are indications that the organic brain can experience inflammation influenced by a wide range of factors. The main inflammatory of the brain is in our diet such as gluten, sugars, and yeasts. In fact, gluten is terrible for the brain even if a person is not sensitive to gluten.

There are foods you may enjoy that have an anti-inflammatory effect. Omega-3 fish oils are among the best. You can find them as a supplement to foods or consume them directly. You can find some oils these days that do not have the fishy aftertaste.

A Word Concerning the Use of Medications

Many clients ask for my opinion as it relates to psychotropic medications for depression. Oftentimes, these questions come from those who have strong reservations concerning psychotropic medications. Personally, my position is neither pro-meds nor anti-meds. My counsel is in the form of another question: "Are you more effective for the cause of Christ on the medication or without it?" Medication does not eliminate spiritual or relational problems. However, it has been my experience over the decades that some of us do better on the medication.

Think again of a basketball without the proper inflation—it has no ability to bounce. With the return of resiliency comes vitality in many areas of life. It is interesting that the same individuals who are resistant to psychotropic medication have no problem taking insulin, anti-seizure meds, or thyroid medication. All these medications, when used properly, can improve a person's overall wellbeing psychologically.

The Mental

After God had dealt with Elijah in the physical realm, he challenged Elijah's thinking pattern—the mental realm. Elijah, like many who suffer with depression, needed a change in his perspective and attitude. The Lord challenged Elijah two times: "What are you doing here, Elijah?" (1 Kings 19:9, 13).

The point God was making is evident in the emphasis placed on the word *here*. "What are you doing *here*?" Elijah was not where God wanted him. Elijah needed to reframe his thinking, because he was absorbed in self-pity and making poor choices.

When struggling with mood-related problems, it is easy to become involved in stinking thinking or ANTS (Automatic Negative Thoughts). Elijah, like many prophets of the Old Testament, had strong tendencies toward bouts of melancholy. Being negative in your self-talk is certain to exacerbate an already problematic mood. It is difficult to determine, as a professional counselor, whether a person's self-talk aggravates the depression or if the depression is fueling the negative self-talk. What we do know for certain is that negative self-talk and depression tend have a parasitic relationship.

Anything that can help us see a dark situation from a different vantage point can be beneficial. Here are a few strategies we've alluded to before that can help you step outside your otherwise melancholy default perspective:

- ◉ **Imagine that you are an observer of the same situation.** If these same circumstances were being encountered by someone else in your position, how would you view it differently?
- ◉ **Ask a wise friend in what ways they might see the same circumstances differently.** The idea is not to get them to agree or disagree with your perspective on the difficulty you are facing. What you want to accomplish is to identify a different perspective on the same situation.
- ◉ **Imagine looking back on the same events and situations from the vantage point of a future time.** In what way will the same situation look differently several months from now or even a year from now?

The Spiritual

Only after dealing with Elijah's physical needs and mental needs did God begin the process of dealing with the spiritual realm. God revealed himself to Elijah in a very powerful way, by letting Elijah see behind the scenes and giving him insight into the situation spiritually. The Lord said, "Go out and stand on the mountain in the presence of the LORD, for the LORD is about to pass by" (1 Kings 19:11).

God then showed Elijah how his assessment of the situation was quite different from God's assessment. Elijah's assessment was made evident in his angry statement, "I have been very zealous for the LORD God Almighty. The Israelites have rejected your covenant, torn down your altars, and put your prophets to death with the sword. I am the only one left, and now they are trying to kill me too" (v. 10).

Notice how differently God viewed the situation, "I reserve seven thousand in Israel—all whose knees have not bowed down to Baal and whose mouths have not kissed him" (v. 18).

There was a huge discrepancy between how God and Elijah saw the same events. Elijah was assuming a martyr or victim posture.

The Mission

God later revealed to Elijah a new purpose—a significant work to accomplish. God gave Elijah a mission and a legacy. The Lord said to him:

Go back the way you came, and go to the Desert of Damascus. When you get there, anoint Hazael king over Aram. Also, anoint Jehu son of Nimshi king over Israel, and anoint Elisha son of Shaphat from Abel Meholah to succeed you as prophet. (1 Kings 19:15–16)

A person, when suffering with depression, can lose a sense of purpose and direction in life. This is why expending effort on developing a personal mission statement is helpful in keeping you on course when life seems difficult and you don't have the emotional vitality essential to fight the battles that lay ahead.

Clarity of your call, mission, and vision can help you maintain personal vitality necessary as you navigate the more challenging chapters of your life.

There are a number of good books that can assist a person in developing a personal mission statement. You can find a list of these books and authors in appendix D of chapter 11 of the online workbook, by going to FullStrength.org/AtFullStrength.

The Relational

Depression is typically related to some form of perceived or real loss, and some depressions manifest in the form of grieving. Life this side of heaven is filled with necessary endings, often considered difficult losses. Anytime we confront a loss (perceived or real), it can result in a sense of deep disappointment, despair, discouragement, and ultimately, depression. Elijah had lost many relationships as he pursued with a sense of duty the mission God had assigned. It is likely that Elijah was grieving the loss of relationships due to abandonment and betrayal.

Elijah, a man of God, became so discouraged that he wished to die—suicidal ideation. Finally, God encouraged Elijah with a new and close friend—addressing the social-relational realm. The Bible states that "Elijah went from there and found Elisha . . . Elijah went up to him and threw his cloak around him . . . Then he set out to follow Elijah and became his servant" (1 Kings 19:19–21).

The two men remained close friends for life, bringing to Elijah a relationship marked by open communication, shared purpose and vision, emotional support, and moments of laughter. Very little in life is more meaningful during periods of depression than a trusted friend with whom you can confide. Honest and open communication with someone who is trustworthy is a significant ingredient in the recipe of renewed vitality.

You can find a number of good books on depression and grief in appendix D of chapter 12 in the online workbook at FullStrength.org/AtFullStrength.

Anxiety, Fear, and Worry Sickness

Now it is time to take a close look at *worry sickness*. It is interesting that among all the emotions known to man, fear and worry are among the few for which the Bible has clear instructions: "Be not afraid," "Do not worry," and "Do not be anxious."

The King James Version of the Bible contains at least seventy-four instances of "fear not" and twenty-nine instances of "do not be afraid." The New American Standard Bible has four instances of "fear not," fifty-seven instances of "do not fear," and forty-six instances of "do not be afraid." Yet one "fear not" from Jesus should be sufficient.

There are no references in the Bible that say, "do not be depressed," nor does it state that we should not be angry. In fact, it says, "Be angry and do not sin" (Eph. 4:26 ESV).

When life is not treating you well, you have a bent toward a particular heart direction. Some people move toward frustration (anger), foolishness, or depression. However, some of us tend to move in the direction of fear (anxiety and worry). For most of us, we tend to fall off one side of the fence or the other. We tend toward either depression or fear. My tendency is to move toward depression. However, some individuals seem to experience both at the same time, alternating between states of depression and the anxiety spectrums.

Fear, worry, and anxiety are rooted deep in our need to control and make life conform to our expectations. We all have rules in our heads about how life "should be." But we don't think of them as *our* rules; we think of them as *the* rules. So the desire to have life meet the expectation of our rules drives our hearts in the direction of fear, anxiety, and worry.

Worry actually means "to strangle or give pain."

Worry is the kind of fruitless, mental treadmill activity that keeps our thoughts tumbling over and over but fails to result in action that could solve the problem. Worry and fear are twin thieves of our joy that can rob a person of a rewarding future. It actually has its roots in our need to control circumstances, maybe even our destiny.

Jesus said that worry concerning our future is pointless and destructive. "Can any one of you by worrying add a single hour to your life?" (Matt. 6:27).

The apostle Paul offered this strategy concerning worry:

....

Rejoice in the Lord always. I will say it again: Rejoice! Do not be anxious about anything, but in every situation, by prayer and petition, with thanksgiving, present your requests to God. And the peace of God, which transcends all understanding, will guard your hearts and your minds. (Phil. 4:4, 6–7)

....

These verses give us clear instruction on how to deal with our fear, anxiety, and worry:

Rejoice in the Lord + Do not be anxious + Keep praying + Give thanks = Peace that defies logic will guard (sentinel) your heart and mind.

These instructions call for a willful act of obedience. It is intentional and not based on your emotions. It places your loving Father in heaven at the center of your concerns. God is absolutely dependable, yet totally unpredictable.

So what does control have to do with fear and worry? When you strive to control others and circumstances, you eventually experience three emotions: fear, anger, and worry. Attempts to control that result in these emotions demonstrate a lack of trust in God and a failure to understand his plans and provisions for your life. It is the outcome of what happens when God's children try to live their lives independent of God. Unless some intervention takes place, a person will become trapped in a cycle of control and worry.

Control eventually produces a fear of loss or failure to achieve. This fear gives rise to worry. Instead of trusting God, you may become angry and strive to take control of circumstances.

Dr. Les Carter, in his book *Imperative People*, says this about those who struggle with the need to control:

....

People who worry are not merely concerned about their present and future circumstances; they have a mental agenda of the way things must occur. The worrier's mind is so captivated by what ought or ought not to be, that he can only respond with duress and despair when situations displease him.[3]

....

"Despite our best efforts," asserts psychologist Larry Crabb, "life never gets quite good enough. Our standards are never met."[4]

The creation of the illusion is rooted in our deepest longings to be satisfied and complete—a dynamic that will not fully take place this side of heaven—to possess security, significance, and control. The illusion is fueled by each person's private impression of how he or she thinks life should be. It is like peering into a mirror to see an ideal image of life. But how a life really appears falls far short of that ideal. When your sense of how life *should be* is taken to an extreme, it gives birth to an illusion.

Life's illusions are often based on *false assumptions*, lies that we believe and have adopted on an emotional level. It includes illusions or lies, such as:

- I must be perfect.
- I must be approved of (accepted) by certain others to feel good about myself.
- I must have everyone's love and approval.
- I must not disappoint or upset others.
- Life should be fair.
- It won't happen to me.
- It is my responsibility to change my marriage partner.
- I'm not responsible for my reactions. It is your fault I feel this way!
- When I fail, I am unworthy of love or respect from others.
- Because I am a good person, God will protect me from pain and suffering.
- The grass is greener over . . .

John Garner captures the deception of what is referred to as the "If only syndrome": "If [comforts and pleasures of good living were enough], Americans who have been able to indulge their whims on a scale unprecedented in history would be deliriously happy. They would be telling one another of their unparalleled serenity and bliss instead of trading tranquilizer prescriptions."[5]

Coming to the realization that your foundational needs will not be fully met this side of heaven helps you become proactive in preventing unnecessary pain and disappointment. According to Peter and Paul, we are "foreigners and exiles" in this world, "but our citizenship is in heaven" (1 Pet. 2:11; Phil. 3:20). With this perspective, it becomes easier to determine whether your efforts are worth the emotional, physical, mental, and spiritual energy required to achieve the desired results. Failing to realize that these needs will not be fully met this side of heaven can actually drain your reservoir of vitality in your attempt to fill it.

But what can we do about our anxiety, fear, and worry? These emotions are not very fuel-efficient. They use up a great deal of emotional, physical, mental, and spiritual energy. This energy could be otherwise used toward something purposeful and fruitful if we could at least decrease or eliminate the irrational anxieties and fears. In the following sections, I share some suggestions on how to combat these emotional responses.

Stomping Out the ANTs in Your Brain

Strong emotions are generally preceded by *expectations* combined with *self-talk*. And the things you say to yourself play a significant role in how you experience life. Anxiety, fear, and worry are no exception. A significant amount of these emotions are anticipatory and the script is written with your expectations and the internal script of your self-talk.

Psychiatrist Daniel Amen, MD, in *Change Your Brain, Change Your Life,* refers to the self-talk and expectations in counterproductive situations as ANTs—or Automatic Negative Thoughts. Amen asserts that you must learn to stomp out the ANTs in your brain. What are these ANTs that cause anxiety, fear, and worry?

ANTs are cynical, gloomy, and complaining thoughts that just seem to keep marching in all by themselves.

ANTs can cause people to be depressed and fatalistic. . . .
This kind of thinking makes for a self-fulfilling prophecy.[6]

Amen goes on to present this summary of the ANT species:

- *Always/never* thinking: using extreme words like *always*, *never*, *no one*, *everyone*, *every time*, and *everything*.
- Focusing on the negative: seeing only the bad in a situation.
- Fortune-telling: predicting the worst possible outcome to a situation.
- Mind reading: believing that you know what others are thinking, even though they haven't told you.
- Thinking with your feelings: believing negative feelings without ever questioning them.
- Guilt beating: thinking in words like *should*, *must*, *ought*, and *have to*.
- Labeling: attaching a negative label to yourself or to someone else.
- Personalizing: investing innocuous events with personal meaning.
- Blaming: blaming someone else for your own problems.[7]

How do you stomp on the self-defeating ANTs in your brain? Call them for what they are—self-defeating distortions. When you are experiencing anxiety, fear, or worry, ask yourself, "What is my expectation in this situation? Is my expectation reasonable? Is it realistic?"

Identify the ANT in your brain, and then ask, "Is it really true? If so, just how true is it?" Then consider what the alternative might be.

Learning to Price Tag Your Concerns

The energy we expend on a concern is in direct proportion to the value we place on it. We do not really become angry, worrisome, or discouraged over something that does not matter to us. The inverse is true as well. The higher the value we place on a concern, the greater the energy expended. Those of us who tend toward a heart direction of anxiety, fear, and worry may move this direction because we tend to put a *high* price tag on *all* our life concerns.

Most people have had a garage or yard sale at some time in their lives. You set out personal items you no longer value and price each item to sell. Why? You want to sell it, rather than haul it away to the local charity. Items you once spent good money on because they brought some level of satisfaction or contentment are sold at a rock-bottom prices.

The same principle applies to our concerns that bring so much fear, worry, and anxiety. The depletion of our precious energy is expended in direct proportion to the emotional price tag we assign to the concern. Some concerns *should* have a high price tag. They are worthy of the attention. However, when we place a $1,000 price tag on a concern that should be reduced to a $100, $10, or $1 price tag, we are expending energy that would be better directed toward more fruitful endeavors.

Sometimes in workshops I joke that people worry about things that God does not even think about. This mental state results from placing a high price tag on all of your concerns. *Price tagging* is a strategy that allows you to "take captive every thought" (2 Cor. 10:5), and in so doing, become a better steward of your precious energies.

Can you think of concerns that you have priced too high and allowed to waste your energies? Try this Emotional Price-Tagging Exercise. List your current concerns and estimate the price tag you've placed on each one. Then, for each one establish a new, realistic price tag.

Emotional Price-Tagging Exercise

Current Concern	Current Emotional Price Tag	New Realistic Price Tag
1.		
2.		
3.		

Each and every time you reduce the price tag on a concern, you are reserving energy that can be expended productively, rather than used up on the treadmill of worry. You do not have an unlimited supply of energy. Being the highest and best steward of your God-given energy resources sometimes begins with a willful decision to choose how much we want to expend on a particular concern. Giving the same value to all concerns is like saying that everything you own has equal value.

I once heard Billy Graham tell a story that drives home the point of price tagging our concerns. On the night of April 14, 1912, the Titanic crashed into an iceberg in the Atlantic and sank, causing a tremendous loss of life. Among the stories of the disaster was one about a woman who had her place in one of the lifeboats. She asked if she could return to her stateroom for something, and she was given just three minutes or she would miss the lowering of the lifeboat to the ocean surface.

As the woman ran through the corridors of the ship, she stepped over money and jewels littering the floor that had been dropped by the panicked passengers. In her own room, the woman ignored her jewelry and instead grabbed a bag of fruit. She then quickly returned to her seat in the lifeboat. Just several hours earlier, it would have been ludicrous to think she would have placed such high value on the bag of fruits while precious jewelry was strewn on the floor in her room. In the moment of crisis, she quickly changed the price tags on all that was previously important to her.

Do you have some concerns that it would be beneficial to change the price tag on in order to be a better steward of your mental, emotional, and spiritual energies? Changing one price tag may make all the difference in your overall vitality and perspective.

To complete your Personal Insight Exercise for chapter 11, go to the online workbook at FullStrength.org/AtFullStrength.

Call, Mission, Vision, and Values

In the early morning of February 20, 1942, Lieutenant Commander Butch O'Hare's squadron flew off the deck of the aircraft carrier *Lexington* on another mission in the South Pacific theatre of war. Once airborne, Butch noticed that his gauges indicated that he was low in fuel, meaning that a crew member had apparently failed to top off his fuel tank. When his flight leader learned that Butch would not have enough fuel to complete his mission, he ordered Butch to return to the carrier, so he dropped out of formation and circled back to the carrier group.

What Butch saw in the distance sickened him to the core of his being. A squadron of bombers were heading straight toward the carrier group. With the fighter squadron out on their mission, the carrier would be nearly defenseless. Butch could not reach his squadron leader in time to ensure the safety of the American fleet, nor was he able to warn the fleet of the approaching danger.

Realizing he must do something to divert the enemy bombers from attacking the fleet, and now believing that this would likely be his final flight, Butch decided to go after the bombers like a small bird assertively attacking a falcon. With his wing-mounted fifty-caliber guns, he charged in and attacked the bombers, taking them by surprise. Weaving and diving, he broke their formation as he kept firing at every bomber he could get in his gun sights. When his ammunition ran out, Butch dove at the planes, trying to clip off a wing or tail with the body of his plane, in a desperate attempt to disable as many bombers as possible. With the attack formation disrupted and several bombers damaged, the bombers retreated.

Relieved to survive against impossible odds, he then faced the challenge of making it back to the *Lexington* with a fuel gauge sitting on empty. To his relief, he made it back and safety landed his badly damaged fighter plane. Butch's plane-mounted camera told the amazing story of his heroism, downing five enemy bombers and disrupting the planned attack on the fleet. Butch became the US Navy's first Ace of World War II, as well as the first naval aviator to be given the Congressional Medal of Honor. A year later, Butch was killed in aerial combat at the young age of twenty-nine. Today, Chicago's O'Hare Airport proudly bears Butch's name in tribute to their hometown hero. Between terminals one and two, you can find a memorial erected in his honor.

Each of us has circumstances and influences that shape our personal stories. Butch grew up in Chicago in a family with nearly unlimited resources. Butch's father was a lawyer who withheld nothing from his beloved son. Butch grew up in a mansion and estate that was so large that it filled an entire Chicago city block. Live-in butlers, maids, and cooks were available to serve the residents twenty-four hours a day. Butch had the finest clothes, attended good schools, and enjoyed every opportunity that only the wealthy could afford. Nothing was withheld that was in his father's ability to provide. There were however two things that his father did not provide—a role model of integrity and a good name.

Butch's father was known as "Easy Eddie." Eddie was a gifted lawyer with skills that served clients willing to pay Eddie's exorbitant fees. He was the lawyer for the notorious mobster Big Al Capone, who was involved in everything illegal from bootlegging to prostitution to extortion to murder. The cunning legal maneuverings of Easy Eddie kept Al Capone out of jail on many occasions.

However, Easy Eddie had one virtuous soft spot. Though he was entangled in organized crime, Eddie deeply loved his son Butch and wanted to teach him right from wrong. He wanted Butch to rise above the association with the sordid life of crime that characterized his own life. He deeply desired for Butch to grow up to be a better man than he was. To fulfill this desire for his son, Eddie made the decision to sacrifice the legacy of wealth he could have bestowed on his son, preferring instead to leave Butch a restored family name.

Eddie chose to right the wrongs of his shady life by going to the authorities and exposing the truth about Al Capone and the activities of the mob. He opted to be an example of integrity to his son and to clear the O'Hare name. Eddie made the difficult decision to testify in a court of law against Capone with full knowledge that it would likely mean his death sentence. Within a year of the court hearings, Edward O'Hare was gunned down on a lonely Chicago street in a blaze of a sawed-off shot gun. He paid the highest price possible to leave the legacy of a good name for his beloved son.

Today when we hear the name O'Hare, we think of the massive airport that serves as a reminder of a true national hero, a brave son shaped by the courage of his father who, in the end, chose to do the right thing.[1]

The story of Butch O'Hare's heroism wonderfully illustrates the topic of call, mission, vision, and values that we want to discuss in the remainder of this chapter.

- ◉ O'Hare's **call** was to preserve the freedoms of a nation under attack.
- ◉ As a gifted pilot, his **mission** was to execute air sorties against the enemy to protect his nation from being conquered and subjugated.
- ◉ His **vision** was to preserve the freedoms enjoyed by his beloved nation and carry out his call and mission even if it meant losing his life as a young pilot. Butch knew the risks undertaken by pilots flying the South Pacific.

⦿ Finally, his **values** (principles) were rooted in patriotism, bravery, and a deep desire to defend freedom at any cost.

These four concepts—call, mission, vision, and values—are the anchor points for anyone in leadership, and particularly for anyone involved in ministry and the people-serving professions. The more clarity and conviction you have around these four concepts, the greater your capacity to stay the course and finish the race that God has called you to run.

Let's take a closer look at these core concepts that can help us navigate the forces and pressures that conspire to blow us off course in our service to God. If you find yourself adrift at this moment in your ministry work, I hope that this discussion will help guide you back on course. These four concepts serve as a map and a compass to guide you on the journey that God has ordained for your life.

The Call

Your effectiveness and your ability to the stay the course of your life journey begins with God's call on your life. You do not (or should not) choose God's call—you discover it. Rough seas always exist for pastors who try to choose their call, doing so without a clear sense of calling and gifting by God. When God calls you to serve in his body, he provides you with the gifts, talents, and abilities needed to serve him in a joyful and natural way. The more clarity and conviction you can have around this calling, the greater your ability to persevere during the inevitable storms of life.

The idea of *call* derives from the Greco-Latin word *vocatio,* from which we get the English word *vocation*. Though commonly used in a nonreligious context, the meaning of the term *vocation* has its origin in Christianity. Before the sixteenth century, *vocatio* was understood as an action by God toward an individual. The Roman Catholic Church recognized marriage, celibacy, religious, and ordained life as the four main vocations. The reformer John Calvin emphasized that we have a divine calling that could include most secular occupations. Martin Luther, as well, made reference to the *vocatio* or the calling.[2]

For these reformers, the *vocatio* was used in the deepest sense of the word. To use it about one's career or job would be to diminish its true meaning. The calling was about an individual's deep purpose and way of life. So in the truest sense of the word, we cannot be terminated or retired from our *vocatio*. No organization can take it away from us. In fact, we can be on our deathbeds and still be responding to our call. How we live and die can serve as a testament to it. The idea of vocation is central to the Christian belief that God has created each person with gifts and talents oriented toward specific purposes and a way of life.

Your call is of God and not derived from you. God, whose purposes will prevail, is very serious about his call on the lives of his children: As the apostle Paul asserted, "God's gifts and his call are irrevocable" (Rom. 11:29).

Jacques Ellul, in his book *The Judgment of Jonah,* has this to say concerning the call from God:

Jonah teaches us that this storm, whose physical causes are the same as those of all other storms, is there only for Jonah and because of Jonah. It has other effects. It sweeps the coasts, disperses fish, cause ships to flounder. But its purpose is to smash inflexible Jonah. Thus the elements and many men, especially the sailors, are engaged in the adventure of Jonah with him and because of him. One sees here the weight and seriousness of vocation. God thinks his choice is so important, and takes the one elected so seriously, that he brings nature into play to see that this man fulfills his vocation.[3]

You must not confuse your call with your job or career. Your job and career can fit within your call, but it does not define it. The word *career* comes from the Latin word *carraria* or *carrus* meaning racecourse or racetrack for wheeled vehicles. In the ancient Roman Empire, we might go to the *carraria* for entertainment. The *carraria* was their version of NASCAR. In oval arenas across the empire, horse-drawn chariots would race with maddening intensity until it became difficult to discern who was winning and losing from all the dust and life-threatening chariot collisions. These races were referred to as "the career."[4] You may feel that your job is a dust-filled, bloody, life-threatening race at times, but this is still not your calling.

The call goes to the heart of who you are and who, upon deep reflection, you feel God has called you to be. To help articulate your call, draw a heart on a sheet of paper and place a blank line inside. Do not put what you *do* on the blank. Focus on the specific purpose for your existence. It is usually broad and not specific. A person can work in *any* field and carry out God's call. Reflect on the following question, then write and rewrite your answer as needed until you have a statement that represents your call. "I, *[your name]*, exist to honor God for the purpose of *[fill in the blank]*."

If you have become disillusioned with your job or career, this exercise can help clarify your calling, from which your direction and vitality is derived. To have and own the answer to the question above is critical to understanding your call.

What is such an important part of your Christian faith journey that at some gut level you feel that it defines you? What do you feel compelled by God to be? What causes you to feel purpose in life, and what shapes the forces of your character? You can quit or be terminated from your current job or career, but the underlying sense of who you were meant to be and what you were meant to do continues in your life.

No human can dismiss you from your call; it comes from God. You can find comfort in the spiritual reality that nothing can remove God's call on your life. If you have lost your way or sense of direction, our prayer is that this exercise to understand your call can bring your life back on course, full of energy and vitality to fulfill that which God has equipped and desires you to be and do.

The Mission

The word *mission* is descended from the thirteenth-century French word *mittere* meaning a "sending abroad." It began with Jesuits who referred to the *mittere*—or mission—as sending the Holy Spirit into the world. Therefore, the origin of a cause having a mission statement is deeply spiritual in nature.[5] So when an organization refers to their *mission statement*, there may not be the awareness that it is a deeply religious word.

It's important to understand the difference between *call* and *mission*. You can gain and maintain vitality when you have clarity on both your call and your mission. Mission (your current assignment) speaks to what you do to fulfill your call. To help understand the essence of mission, draw or outline your hand then write the following:

"I, *[your name]*, exist to honor God for the purpose of *[fill in the blank with what you are about]*, as evidenced by *[what you do]*."

For example, my own call and mission would look like this:

"I, Denny, exist to honor God for the purpose of helping others navigate the challenges before them to the extent that they invite me to do so, as evidenced by counseling, coaching, conducting seminars and workshops, and providing work team assessments."

Your call is imparted by God and can be fulfilled through a variety of activities and vocational contexts. Your mission activities can change over time and with the seasons or chapters of life. You can live out the heart of your call in secular or ministry occupations. Across your lifetime, God may involve you in many different missions or assignments, all of which in one way or another should be involved in helping you fulfill God's call on your life.

So how can knowing the difference between call and mission contribute to our overall vitality and effectiveness? You could be working in a ministry or nonprofit venture that has to close its doors. Or maybe you are terminated or laid off from your work. This is a disruption on your mission, not your call. The call is your heart's anchor, but the mission is the boat that can be tossed in the storms of life.

The Vision

The word *vision* comes from the thirteenth-century Anglo-French word *visioun*, meaning something seen in the imagination or in the supernatural. Now we know that call, mission, and vision are all originally deeply spiritual terms.[6]

Vision is what helps you look into or toward the future to confirm that you are staying true to your call. As you envision the future, you are creatively listening or reflecting on the mission work that can best serve God's kingdom interests and the call he has uniquely imprinted into your heart. Envisioning can fuel us with energy and enthusiasm. You rally the spiritual, emotional, relational, physical, intellectual, and financial domains of your wellbeing in service to the inspiration of vision. If you are in a leadership role, vision casting is what enables you to inspire and motivate others under your leadership and influence to activate their callings and bring them into alignment around a shared vision. When this happens in your congregation and community, exciting things can happen in service to the advancement of God's kingdom.

There will also be times of struggle, confusion, and stress in your mission activities. Just like when you have to travel long distances by air, land, or sea, your travel plans can be disrupted or even derailed by forces outside your control.

I've had the privilege of leading teams of counselors on mission trips in various places around the world to strengthen and support local ministry leaders in other countries. During these trips, I often witness the stress of team members when our mission plans are disrupted or encounter unanticipated hardships. Culture shock, language barriers, long flight delays, missing a flight connection—these can fill team members with stress and concern. When assurances around the purpose and destination of the mission are cloudy or uncertain, people can lose their energy and focus; worry and anxiety can set in.

It's important to understand that you will experience the same kind of stress in the mission journeys you undertake in fulfillment of your call. Maintaining focus on your call, mission, and vision can bring peace and quickly restore confidence as you learn to endure, and maybe even enjoy, such hardships for the new experiences and lessons that they teach us.

Developing a clear vision of a hopeful future can sometimes be a difficult task. God has designed us as human beings to thrive and flourish in community. Considering this divine design, engaging others in the process of shaping and defining your vision can be a helpful activity. Here are some coaching questions that I like to use in coaching or counseling engagements to help clients get a clearer perspective on a vision for their future:

◉ What kind of life scenario or job endeavor would get you up early, keep you up late, and cause you to live life with enthusiasm, passion, and purpose?

- ◉ If you knew you could not fail, what endeavor would you undertake for God?
- ◉ If resource limitations were not a constraint, what would you do to fulfill your call?

Along with the heart and hand you've drawn on your blank piece of paper, draw an eye. Using the eye as a metaphor for vision, please add the following phrases to the exercise.

"I, *[your name]*, exist to honor God for the purpose of *[fill in the blank with what you are about]*, as evidenced by *[what you do]*." "What I see for my future is *[your dream or aspiration]*."

Just as you would share a photo album of a past vacation with a friend, imagine that you are showing a photo of your vision as it would be in reality five years from now. What would be in your vision photo? What would you be doing? Who might be participating with you? If you were sharing your vision photo album of your future, what images would you be sharing? This future photo album exercise may be helpful as you think about what your future vision in service to God could and should look like.

Consider this question: What is the one thing that I can do (that I am not currently doing) that if I did it faithfully and consistently would make all the difference in my life?

Think about this question as it pertains to the vision for your future. Here is another exercise, questions adapted from Gary Keller's *The One Thing* that may be helpful:

- ◉ What is the one thing that I *aspire* to achieve *someday*?
- ◉ Based on my *someday aspiration*, what is the one thing I can do in the *next three years*?
- ◉ Based on my *three-year goal*, what is the one thing I can do in the *next year*?

◉ Based on my *one-year goal*, what is the one thing I can do in the *next month*?

◉ Based on my *monthly goal*, what is the one thing I can do *this week*?

◉ Based on my *weekly goal*, what is the one thing I can do that will eventually make all the difference?[7]

The Values and Principles

Spiritual energy and vitality also spring from your personal values and principles. Your values serve as a plumb line telling you that you're living life by the standards you have set for yourself. They are your moral compass, directing your decisions and actions. When you violate your values and principles, the incongruence depletes your energy and diminishes your vitality.

If you are truly a principled person with deeply held values, your conscience activates a warning when you contemplate a decision or action that violates your principles. Over time, if you consistently ignore the warnings of your conscience, you will develop a seared conscience—your conscience sensors are no longer able to warn you that you are about to act against your convictions. Another possible explanation, when you act contrary to expressed values, is that you do not actually possess what you profess as your principles. Such people in essence are hypocrites; your actions speak louder than your words.

Integrity is living life such that your passions, feelings, thoughts, words, and actions are all congruent. The person you are when you are on the front stage of life is the same person you are when you step backstage. Your family, friends, and colleagues don't have to wonder who you are from day-to-day and interaction to interaction. There is not an observable difference in thought, word, or deed between your onstage and offstage lives.

Following is a partial list of some of the benefits of living life with clarified and prioritized values:

- ◉ You make better decisions, faster.
- ◉ Difficult decisions require less mental and emotional energy.
- ◉ You experience a higher level of personal contentment and fulfillment.
- ◉ You have a lower level of stress and frustration in complex and difficult situations.

The order in which you rank your values makes a world of difference to the process of making wise decisions. When a pastor values a mighty reputation based on congregational size above the spiritual flourishing of individual members in the congregation, his decision-making processes are conflicted. In almost all such cases, the pastor's professed values and priorities do not align with his decisions and actions. Taking the time to clarify your values and principles, and prioritizing them by importance to ensure that higher value actions are taken over lower value actions, is essential to living a congruent life of integrity.

To discover your values and principles, you can simply complete this sentence twenty to thirty times until you have a list of things that are important to you in your life journey:

What is really important to me is *[fill in the blank]*.

After you make your list, ask this question: If I had to choose, which item on the list is *most* important to me? Which is second most? Third most? And so on.

To help illustrate this exercise, see my personal list of guiding principles or values in appendix A of the online workbook.

I encourage you to make your own list and record your values and principles in a written document that you place somewhere in sight of your work area for periodic review, reflection, and ongoing refinement. To deepen the impact and importance of this exercise, share your list with a trusted colleague, and ask your friend to conduct an informal audit of your behavior to confirm that your day-to-day actions align with your stated values.

To complete the larger exercise outlined in this chapter, we have added a fourth image and question to the exercise. It is the image of a stomach. Why? Because when you violate your values, the place you feel it is in the pit of your stomach. It's that sick feeling of having made the wrong choice.

> **"I, *[your name]*, exist to honor God for the purpose of *[fill in the blank with what you are about]*, as evidenced by *[what you do]*."**
> **"What I see for my future is *[your dream or aspiration]*."**
> **"What am I truly about at the core of my being?"**

Gaining clarity on your call, mission, vision, and values is important as you navigate the challenges and opportunities of this short life. If you want to leave a mark on the world, you must live a life of intentionality. In biblical terms, life is a mist that quickly evaporates with the rising sun. Spiritual history is sprinkled with people who have had a profound effect on the world around them largely because they were individuals with a clear call, mission, vision, and values.

Consider the following analysis. Let's say you lived to the age of sixty-five. Here's how you spent your life:

- Four full years as a baby and toddler
- Twenty-five full years sleeping (one-third of your life)
- Three full years on chores (two to three hours a week)
- Three full years on hygiene (some of us could use a little more)
- Five full years on eating (some of us could do a little less)
- Four full years on education (if a college graduate)

- Four full years on the toilet (if we are the non-reading type)
- Three full years watching TV and wasting time on the internet (if only three hours a week)
- Four full years travelling to and from work and activities (three hours a week)
- Six months waiting in lines (if we do not go to theme parks)
- Six months opening and throwing away junk mail
- Fourteen full years working from age twenty to sixty-five (I hope you like your job)

Keep in mind we have not factored in health problems, time spent on worry, battling kid issues, and your car breaking down. Considering all the above, you may have a total of five to six years to pursue your heart's desire.

Ask any elderly person, and they are likely to advise you that "life is short" or "time passes so quickly." Considering the time allocation of a normal lifetime of seventy-five years, invest your time and energy in those things that really count.

It's worth repeating that clarity in your call, mission, vision, and values provides you with a clear direction, energy for the journey, and resources that can help sustain you on your journey. Those who are true followers of Christ and have clarity around these four concepts live and die differently than do most people.

In an older survey of men and women age ninety-four and older, the survey participants were asked this question: "What do you wish you had done differently in your life?" Expecting the respondents to include comments such as "make more money," "pursue a different career," "travel more," or "live in another location," the survey sponsor was surprised by the responses.

Three nearly equal response themes dominated the survey results. No other comments were even close. The top three responses were:

⊙ I wish I had invested more time and energy in my family.

⊙ I wish I had taken more (positive) risks in relationships and built deeper friendships.

⊙ I wish I had been more committed to causes greater than myself.

If you don't want to end your life wishing that your life journey had been different, then it's essential to master the exercises outlined in this chapter. Being proactive in the areas of call, mission, vision, and values is essential to gain and sustain the energy and vitality needed to make the life journey you desire before God to make.

To complete your Personal Insight Exercise for chapter 12, go to the online workbook at FullStrength.org/AtFullStrength.

13

All Aboard the Principle Train

Yet when I surveyed all that my hands had done and what I had toiled to achieve, everything was meaningless, a chasing after the wind; nothing was gained under the sun.
—ECCLESIASTES 2:11

There are many in the world who are dying for a piece of bread but there are many more dying for a little love. The poverty in the West is a different kind of poverty—it is not only a poverty of loneliness but also of spirituality. There's a hunger for love, as there is a hunger for God.
—MOTHER TERESA OF CALCUTTA[1]

How would you complete these sentences?

- "If only . . ."
- "I could be happy if . . ."
- "It would make me very happy if they would . . ."

We all struggle with the "if only" syndrome this side of heaven. This mistaken belief that happiness can be found in another opportunity or possession somewhere out there in your future or in the meeting of your expectations is only an illusion. The human drive to entertain illusions contributes to the magnitude of success in the advertising industry. TV, newspapers, and magazines all subtly promise that once we own certain products, we have arrived. Because of the deep yearning to be satisfied, people unknowingly continue to buy into the illusion behind the "if only" syndrome.

"Despite our best efforts . . . ," asserts psychologist Larry Crabb, "Life never gets quite good enough. Our standards are never met."[2]

Famed NCAA basketball coach John Wooden said the following about expectations:

We seek happiness in the wrong places and in the wrong form. The primary cause of unhappiness is simply wanting too much, overemphasizing the material things. Happiness begins where selfishness ends.[3]

The creation of this illusion of a more permanent happiness is rooted in our deepest longings to be satisfied and complete—something that will not fully take place this side of heaven. The illusion is fueled by each person's private impression of how he or she thinks life should be. When our expectations are met, we are happy. Life's illusions are often based on false assumptions, lies that we believe and have adopted on an emotional level.

Donald McCullough, in his book *Waking From The American Dream*, tells the tragic story of seven men who thought they had it all and could hang on to it all, only to discover that finding happiness is an illusion.

....

In 1923, some of the world's most powerful men met at the Edgewater Beach Hotel in Chicago. Collectively, they controlled more wealth than the entire United States Treasury, and for years the media had held them up as examples of success.

Who were they? Charles Schwab, president of the world's largest independent steel company; Arthur Cutten, the greatest wheat speculator of his day; Richard Whitney, president of the New York Stock Exchange; Albert Fall, a member of the President's Cabinet; Jesse Livermore, the greatest bear on Wall Street; Leon Fraser, president of the International Bank of Settlement; and Ivar Kruegger, head of the world's largest monopoly. What happened to them? Schwab and Cutten both died broke; Whitney spent years of his life in Sing Sing Penitentiary; Fall spent years in prison but was released so he could die at home; and the others—Livermore, Fraser, and Kruegger, committed suicide.[4]

....

Nothing will drain a person of his emotional resources and vitality more quickly than deep-seated, unresolved negative emotions. For genuine growth and maturity to occur, we must discover and dismantle those areas in our lives where we are self-deceived. If we are controlled by negative emotions that we typically hide or cover up in our interactions with God and others, it is guaranteed to affect our health and vitality destructively.

It's helpful to regard negative emotions as clues, or an early warning signal, that an important dimension of your life is not functioning in a healthy manner. Your ability to objectively assess life situations is compromised when you are under the influence of negative emotions. Negative emotions can function like a two-edged sword, they can prompt you to *trust* other people or your own instincts when these sources of influence are not trustworthy, and they can influence you to *avoid trusting* other people and your own instincts when they should be trusted.

When governed by negative, tainted, or faulty emotions that put you into self-centered, self-preservation mode, your personal relationships are diminished, along with your personal vitality and optimism for life.

Many of us were raised in a home and church context that caused us to believe that our feelings are not to be trusted. This pressure to deny or stuff feelings away created an unintended behavioral consequence: Our only option was to employ hiding and mask-wearing behaviors and unhealthy "sin management" strategies rather than deal with our emotions in a productive way that resulted in growth and maturity.

In contemporary culture, the pendulum has shifted sides. Emotions now are allowed to be the deciding factor in how we live and govern our decision-making process and behaviors. If it feels right, just do it. In this shift, emotions have been placed in the driver's seat of our lives. The casualty of this shift is the loss of a culturally accepted moral compass. The last verse in the book of Judges describes our current culture perfectly: "In those days Israel had no king; all the people did whatever seemed right in their own eyes" (Judg. 21:25 NLT).

Chasing After the Wind

In today's culture, the pursuit of temporal happiness, a euphemism for self-gratification, is the cruelest of illusions negatively impacting a vital life experience. In simple terms, pursuit of temporal happiness is the wrong goal. In raw and blunt terms, the apostle Paul put his finger on the problem. Speaking of those who pursue the best life has to offer to achieve happiness, in contrast to the human wellbeing teaching of

Jesus, Paul says, "They are headed for destruction. Their god is their appetite, they brag about shameful things, and they think only about this life here on earth" (Phil. 3:19 NLT).

In contrast, Scripture sets forth faith, hope, love, and joy as the virtues of life we should pursue to live a fulfilled life, one that will bring us the riches and gratification that God desires for us in relationship with him.

The Westminster catechism asks this question: "What is man's chief end?" Its answer is, "Man's chief end is to glorify God and enjoy him forever." God desires for us to find joy in our relationship with him, living life in such a way that we glorify him by trusting (living in accord with) the truth principles he has communicated and recorded for us in Holy Scripture.

After a lifetime of chasing the wind, King Solomon made his final report on what he had learned about the proper way to live our lives. "That's the whole story. Here now is my final conclusion: Fear God and obey his commands, for this is everyone's duty" (Eccl. 12:13 NLT).

Here's a helpful paraphrase of King Solomon's summary statement: When you've tried everything else in life to find happiness and fulfillment, you will find that honoring God by trusting and living in accord with what he has revealed about finding meaning and value in life will be the only path that will bring you a joyful life experience.

Putting Emotions Where They Belong

You may find it peculiar that someone who has spent most of his career in a psychological field would write in such way concerning our emotions and feelings. In fact, you may have already formed the opinion that I dismiss emotions, relegating them to a position of insignificance. To take this position would run counter of what the Bible indicates concerning emotions. More than fifty different emotions are identified in the book of Psalms alone. Many Psalms reference the emotions of a passionate God.

Imagine God without passions. Could such a view be reconciled with the Bible? As early as Genesis 6, we find strong emotion in God concerning the sinfulness of man. The Bible states: "his heart was deeply troubled" (v. 6). In fact, the Bible frequently ascribes the changing of emotions in God. God was said to be grieved (see Ps. 78:40), angry (see Deut. 1:37), pleased (see 1 Kings 3:10), joyful (see Zeph. 3:17), and moved by pity (see Judg. 2:18).

It would be unwise to dismiss the role of emotions altogether. However, it is equally unwise to allow emotions to have center stage in your life. Those who navigate through life based on their emotions are most certain to encounter relational or moral derailments with greater frequency than those who navigate based on principles.

So what is the appropriate role for your emotions? To answer this question as a counselor and coach, I like to use a word picture of a train. The locomotive represents your principles and the coal tender your attitudes. The freight and passenger cars represent your behaviors, including words and actions. Finally, the caboose represents your emotions.

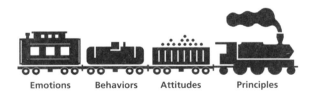

Emotions   Behaviors   Attitudes   Principles

Navigating life's many emotional challenges is especially complicated for the vocational people helpers and ministry workers for at least three reasons:

◉ Those in vocational people-helping professions are by virtue of their profession likely to be drawn into highly-charged and emotionally complex situations to help others resolve their issues.

- By nature, those drawn toward people-helping vocations tend to navigate more by their own emotional instincts and intuitions (with their hearts), rather than with their head (thinking). This tendency is validated by research studies and could be a complicating factor in people-helping situations.
- An automatic expectation exists that pastors, church staff, and other people helpers by virtue of their professions are by nature more emotionally and relationally intelligent than others. Parishioners or clients expect that those in trusted people-helping roles should have special gifts or capacities to intuitively grasp what others are feeling. This may or may not be the case.

Using the metaphor of the train, let's take a deeper look at the role emotions play as we navigate the challenges that lie before us.

The Caboose of Emotions

In the good old days of train travel, the caboose was a manned rail car coupled to the end of the train. The crew in the caboose was responsible for track switching and hooking and unhooking cars (shunting). The caboose occupants in the upper windows had a vantage point across the length of the train to make sure everything was operating smoothly. The crew could alert the engine staff of shifting loads or overheating axles (hotspots). The caboose crew would fire warning shots to disrupt and hopefully prevent robbers from capturing and taking over the train.

Even though it played an important role, the caboose never had responsibility for driving the train. It served as a watchtower protecting the passengers and cargo. Your emotions function in a similar way. They alert you when things are not in order and when your passage through your relational life is encountering potential risks that could result in a derailment or disruption of your ability to have a healthy relationship with others.

The Boxcars of Our Behavior

The *boxcar* represents your behaviors (words and actions). Your behavioral patterns are deeply embedded (ingrained) and are difficult, though not impossible, to change. They largely function on autopilot; that is, you react with words or actions before you even think about what you should say or do.

For pastors, church staff, and others in people-helping professions, some or much of your work involves discipling (coaching and counseling) others to be transformed in their behaviors to enjoy greater effectiveness in relationships and life's journey. This frequently involves issues dealing with relationships, the launching pad for most emotions.

Habituated behaviors are the most challenging to address. It involves *unlearning* and *relearning*, a topic addressed in Scripture by the "put off" and "put on" passages found in the Epistles. Here's an important principle in managing behavioral change: Incremental success is better than grand failure. Changing undesirable habituated behaviors is like losing weight or getting into shape—it takes time and intentionality.

Your repeated thoughts and actions activate and train different portions of the brain. As these behaviors are continuously repeated and become habituated, neural pathways are groomed in your brain until the behavior becomes second nature—you do the behavior without thinking about it any longer. In fact, it now becomes difficult to do anything but the habituated behavior without slowly creating new neural pathways that support healthier and more positive behaviors.

Scripture and research point the same direction when it comes to breaking a bad habit. The old undesirable behavior must be replaced with a new desirable behavior in its place. Reliable research reveals that it takes over one hundred days (111 days to be precise) of consistent behavioral conformity for the new behavior to overcome and replace the old undesirable behavior. It takes another nearly one hundred days (93 days to be precise) of staying the course to solidify abiding confidence that the desired behavioral response pattern is locked in.

The Coal Tender of Your Attitude

There is encouraging news concerning your capacity to change. The caboose represents your emotions and the boxcars represent your behaviors. In the same way, the coal tender represents your attitudes.

The easiest thing to change about a *bad situation* is a *bad attitude*. A good attitude is the fuel for much of what you do and accomplish. Emotions are often the last things that change when you are faced with difficult challenges. Behaviors are deeply entrenched. However, you can change your attitude with a choice to do so. Earlier, we explored the Lens Exercise that can help us make the necessary change in attitude.

A proverb in the Old Testament of the Bible states, "For as he thinketh in his heart, so is he" (Prov. 23:7 KJV). We need to learn to stomp out our ANTs (Automatic Negative Thoughts) by confronting these patterned thoughts that only defeat us. If the pattern of your internal dialogue is mostly negative it may be time to seek outside help. A negative or bad attitude will only bring you down. A positive and good attitude will often give you all the lift you need. Sometimes the only difference between a good day and a bad day is your attitude.

Here are a few tips to shake free from a bad attitude:

- Be honest with yourself by admitting that you have a bad attitude, rather than self-justifying it.
- Get some rest or exercise. Both contribute significantly to a healthier brain balance.
- Explore the expectation behind the bad attitude. Would others around you whom you consider to be wise find your expectations reasonable and realistic? What is it that you want?
- Consider the long-term consequences of your bad attitude. Nothing good ever comes out of a bad attitude.
- Cultivate the attitude of gratitude while focusing on the good things in your life.

The Locomotive of Principles

The last part of the train is the *locomotive*, which represents our *principles*. If you let emotions guide your life, you are headed for a derailment of some kind. It is not *will* it happen, but rather, *when* it will happen. However, when life is guided by principles, it is more likely to stay on track. The problem lies in the reality that most people, including ministry professionals, do not have clear principles. When asked in coaching or counseling, the reply is usually something like, "Follow Jesus" or "Honor God." But what does that look like in the day-to-day grind of marriage, family, and work?

The Bible instructs us in Romans 12:2, "Do not conform to the pattern of this world, but be transformed by the renewing of your mind. Then you will be able to test and approve what God's will is—his good, pleasing and perfect will." Unfortunately, many ministry leaders look much like the world. The mind is not renewing. They do not have a clear set of principles, but only rules to guide them on their journey. Having clear principles means that you want to be a certain way because you choose to, not because you have to. You have an intentional choice to be a kind person, especially when the other person does not deserve the kindness. It is based on the "one another" principle found in the Bible. You can find more than fifty references to it in the New Testament alone. They are initiated most effectively when done under the power of God's Spirit. Here are just a few:

- ◉ "Be at peace with each other" (Mark 9:50).
- ◉ "Love one another" (multiple references in John).
- ◉ "Honor one another" (Rom. 12:10).
- ◉ "Live in harmony with one another" (Rom. 12:16).
- ◉ "Be patient, bearing with one another in love" (Eph. 4:2).
- ◉ "Be kind and compassionate to one another" (Eph. 4:32).
- ◉ "Encourage one another" (1 Thess. 5:11).

Principles serve as a moral compass. When you live a principle-driven life, oftentimes your decisions are already made for you. You can navigate life with significantly more clarity when you are guided by personally chosen principles from Holy Scripture. When you navigate based on emotions, you're constantly battling fog never quite sure what lies ahead in your path. Emotion-based living causes you to experience chronic stress and expend energy at a reckless pace. Principles preserve, and even renew, your energy resources.

Engraving Your Principles into Your Life

What do you think of when you hear someone referred to as a person of character? The word *character* finds its origin in the ancient classical Greek language. It comes from the noun *charakter* and refers to a distinctive mark or impression, an engraving tool or the person who does the engraving. It is derived from the Greek verb *charassein* meaning "to engrave."

The trade language was Greek throughout the Roman Empire in the first century. If a person owned a business and needed a sign, that person would hire a *charakter* or engraver. He would bring his character or engraving tool and would labor for hours etching into a block of stone the name of your family or business. The stone would bear the name or emblem and preserve it beyond the lifetime of the business owner.

What do you want engraved in the hearts of your children? What do you want to be your lasting impression? What kind of mark or engraving do you want to leave as a legacy? What do you aspire to be the defining character qualities evidenced in your day-to-day life?

The answers to these questions are etched into your life by your guiding principles. Have you clearly defined the principles that you want to define your life? Start to make a list of guiding principles. Don't be concerned if they aren't perfectly suited. You can alter them through the process of prayer and dialogue with others.

Tom, a trusted friend, has posted in his office a list of principles that guide his life. Tom is thought of as a man of high character. Tom shared with me that the principles were those of a mentor who served in World War II. As a young soldier, grateful to be returning from the devastation of the war, he wrote down the principles while aboard the ship bringing the soldier home. That same soldier, known for integrity in his community as a business leader, used these principles to guide his life with the power of God's Spirit.

You will leave an impression. But more than likely, you want it to be more than the etchings on a tombstone. Whether your legacy is positive or negative is up to you. What do you desire to etch into future generations and the world around you? Many of us remember our past relatives such as grandparents. They have left indelible marks on us, some of which we are quite unaware of. Some have spent years trying to recover from a negative legacy and are hoping to pass on something good to their children and grandchildren.

Think about the immigrants who move to a new place to escape the oppression they face in their own homeland. Many of them live in poverty and do tedious jobs to provide a better future for their children. They are willing to make the sacrifice on behalf of those they love.

Engraving a positive legacy does not happen accidentally. It takes place when your intentionality is carved out by clear guiding principles. Would you consider writing out some principles? Don't be concerned about wording them just right. You can clean it up later. Shape them through concentrated prayer and dialogue with others you consider wise.

Guiding Principles for Life

Your guiding principles can help you thrive and flourish during the difficult times of life. They sustain and energize your soul, helping you persevere when others give up and compromise their convictions. Consider adopting the following principles for your life:

On Attitude

I will . . .

- Choose to exercise my God-given spiritual freedom and prerogative to not take offense at the foolishness of others (see Prov. 19:11).
- Choose what kind of person I will *be* with the help of God's Spirit and not allow circumstances or others to write the script for my life. Life is 10 percent circumstances and 90 percent attitude (see Eph. 1; 5:1).

On Behavior and Relating

I will . . .

- Be kind to others because it is who I want to be especially around those who need it but do not deserve it (see Eph. 4:32; 1 Thess. 5:15–16).
- Treat others as I wish to be treated (see all the "one another" references; Luke 6:31).

On Priorities

I will . . .

- Make prayer the first option, not an afterthought or an act of desperation (see Eph. 6:18; Phil. 4:4–8).
- Set my mind on things above and view life through an eternal lens (see Col. 3:2).

On Stewardship

I will . . .

◉ Remember and consider God's many blessings. All that is good in me and all that I think I possess actually belong to God and are on loan to me. This includes my assets, opportunities, relationships, possibilities, and capacities (see Ps. 89:11).

◉ Be generous. In doing, so I will be emulating my Father in heaven, the Giver of all good things (see 2 Cor. 9:6–8).

On Valuing

I will . . .

◉ Demonstrate regard for the value of others, because their value is derived from the sacrifice Christ made on their behalf (see Rom. 5:8; Eph. 2:10).

◉ Choose to bookend each day by letting my wife know that I love her, even if I am working outside the country. The day will eventually come when these words will be my final message to her this side of heaven (see 1 Cor. 13:13; Eph. 5:21).

◉ Be genuinely invested in the vitality and success of others. I will choose to intentionally invest in their success.

◉ Be grateful and express it regularly. Gratitude is among the greatest of all the virtues and the parent of all other virtues.

In the remaining chapters of this book, we will explore ways we can gain and maintain the vitality essential for lifelong effective service to our community and in doing so, honor God. We will discover how to develop our own personal and professional strategic plan to gain and maintain vitality throughout the changing chapters of life.

To complete your Personal Insight Exercise for chapter 13, go to the online workbook at FullStrength.org/AtFullStrength.

PART 5

Navigating toward Gaining and Maintaining Vitality

Developing a
Strategic Plan for Vitality

Throughout *At Full Strength*, we have explored strategies that allow us to navigate effectively the difficult challenges on the road before us. These strategies are effective only when we have the adequate energy to sustain and propel us forward. When our energy reserves are depleted, it's like having a reliable vehicle and a GPS, but no fuel.

Traveling on a long journey requires an adequate amount of energy in our tank and refueling stations along the route. Most of us have run out of fuel in our vehicle at some time in our life, usually in the most awkward of places and at the most inconvenient times.

So it is with the journey of life. We run out of vitality in awkward circumstances and at the most challenging of times. In the Crosshairs Research, we discovered four outcomes of these low times:

1. **A Loss of Resiliency:** Like a ball that has lost its inflation, you experience a diminished ability to bounce back from difficult circumstances.
2. **A Loss of Satisfaction:** The activities that once brought reward have become mundane and routine. It seems to take an inordinate amount of energy just to complete even simple tasks and responsibilities.
3. **A Loss of Vitality:** The spiritual, emotional, relational, and mental energies seem to be at an all-time low.
4. **A Loss of Vision:** The landscape of the future has become blurry, maybe even dark.

I know from personal experience that it's possible to reach a state where your personal reservoir of vitality is empty. During this season of life, my compassion, creativity, and energy for life flat-lined. I had nothing but a gooey sludge on the bottom of my vitality reservoir. My life of calling and service to others became a routine. I lost my ability to engage with genuine care with the clients who visited my office.

To address my plight and the fear that accompanied it, I began to relinquish many of the responsibilities that made it impossible for me to recover and replenish my vitality reservoir on a regular basis. A friend suggested that a sabbatical getaway was warranted, but the thought of a sabbatical unnerved me. However, something had to be done to rekindle my enthusiasm to continue to honor God with his calling on my life. The concept of enthusiasm, with its Greek origins of *en theos* (in God), was missing from my life.

This extended October 2002 citation from my personal journal describes my state at its lowest point:

....

This idea of a sabbatical came as result of a three-pronged stimulus: First, I have been experiencing an inner agitation that becomes stirred over each new summoning for help by another. Second, there was fatigue that seemed relentless and ever-present. Third, the deep passion/vision for my work has seemed to encounter one obstacle after another, and there is a need for a fresh perspective.

I've been very tired lately, which really is not unusual in itself. As a counselor people continue to stop me in parking lots, at church, in grocery stores, even while jogging. The conversations would always start the same way, "There's something I've wanted to discuss with you!" I have never really noticed how frequent and ongoing this occurred until my reservoir of vitality hit empty. There seems to be no escape from the "stress fractures" that continue to drain away the vitality that once seemed so plentiful.

This tiredness was as such that vacations just aren't able to fix—a weariness of spirit, an inner depletion. I've sensed a spiritual core to my fatigue and have been looking for a spiritual solution. In recent months there has been a sense of a deep need to be alone, to have solitude—a spiritual desperation for a wilderness experience.

Repeated attempts for solitude have been interrupted with phone calls, being cornered in parking lots, in a church hallway while trying to make a hasty exit, and in coffee shops by people desperate to unburden themselves of deep hurts they carry with them. Dietrich Bonhoeffer, in his book *Life Together*, referred to this as the "ministry of interruptions." Generally, I do not mind being summoned as a "trusted advisor." I have not forgotten that it is an imputed role of honor when others invite me to help them navigate the challenges before them. However, in recent months, while my energy ebbs away I find this summoning for assistance has been causing me to feel like a once-sturdy oak tree that has been uprooted with my roots groping heavenward for some kind of vitality.

In an attempt to resist doing more, I have stepped down from many responsibilities at church, removed myself from board positions, only to find a minimal relief. In all the Bible God did not give anyone an easy job and that is not my expectation. But in observing the patterns in the life of Jesus we can see that there were many attempts at solitude in order to renew his vitality even as the Son of God. There are many obstacles to the practice of solitude . . . there are too many reasons not to be alone . . . especially for those who are deeply invested in others. I know it must begin by carefully planning solitude into life and can no longer rely on my spontaneity to meet the need for solitude.[1]

The board at our counseling center graciously granted me a sabbatical. Before the sabbatical could be scheduled, a medical leave intruded into my life. My lack of sustained self-care over a long period of time resulted in my collapse with transport to the hospital emergency room. I had lost all feeling and ability to function on the right side of my body. As I became aware of my condition, fear swept over me like a tidal wave. Even with my precious wife and dear friends at my bedside, I began to feel an overwhelming sense of aloneness. What was once picture-perfect health changed in a moment of time.

Over the next few months, I made several trips to the Indiana University Medical Center to obtain an exact diagnosis of my neurological condition. The physicians began a treatment regimen for seizures, including the use of anti-Parkinson's medications. The physical activities that had once brought joy to my life, including jogging with my son, came to an end. God was forcing me to walk with him around a bend in the road, and I had no ability to see what was around the bend. My future was uncertain, and I was shaken to the core of my being. Amidst these circumstances, I wondered how I would maintain personal vitality and find joy in my professional vocation again.

It was during this time of wondering about my future that God began to give me an even greater capacity for compassion for others. He kindled a deep desire within me to want to understand and share with people how to develop a strategic plan to gain and sustain personal vitality in their ministry and people-helping practices. After all, this was the deep need of my current life experience at this moment in my own life.

What I learned was that developing a sustainable vitality plan would require periodic adaptation and adjustments as God walks us through different chapters and experiences in our lives. I also learned that maintenance of vitality, the ability to thrive and flourish, would require an intentional and focused effort. Self-care is essential and involves proactive attention to sustain serving effectiveness over time. If your vocation involves you living with the express purpose of honoring God by helping others under your sphere of influence, then it must be a top priority for you to maintain and replenish your vitality reservoir.

What follows in this chapter are the lessons that God revealed to me during my journey of recovery so I could continue to fulfill the calling God placed on my life.

How to Gain and Maintain Personal Vitality in a Stress–filled Vocation

It begins with being proactive and preemptive. You must be able to discern the difference between a healthy self-care and selfish-care. You first must clearly recognize the signs that your vitality is not what it needs to be in order for your life to be a blessing to those around you. The best asset you have in making a significant contribution in the world is yourself. If you fail to invest in yourself adequately—whether spiritually, educationally, emotionally, or physically, you damage and diminish the very tool you need to make your highest and best contribution.

The whole world, including human beings, moves based on energy. We are designed with a reservoir of vitality or energy. Just like lakes and oceans, our reservoirs are constantly emptying (evaporation and outflowing rivers and streams) and filling (fresh rainwater and inflowing mountain streams). Scripture reveals to us that the spiritual dimension of our being also contains springs and rivers of "living water."

Like most water bodies, dirt and debris will sink to the bottom usually forming an inert sediment layer. If we allow our reservoirs to become drained and depleted, pretty soon we start stirring up the sediment and muck and fouling the clean water supply we need to maintain a healthy and energized life. In contrast, if we allow our reservoirs to become dammed up with no overflow (we stop sharing our lives with others), the water supply stagnates and fouls. God designed us to expend our lives in a balanced way by releasing our vitality and gifts in service to others and replenishing the supply to keep our reservoir full and in a healthy, uncontaminated balance.

In this analogy, buried in the sediment of your reservoir are your old-nature tendencies including your poor attitudes, bad behaviors, and self-centered emotions that benefit neither you nor those God has called you to serve. If you make the mistake of thinking that you can expend more of your vitality without allowing your reservoir to refill and be renewed, your service becomes contaminated with unhealthy behaviors that actually undermine your missional goals and service.

As we've established from our research, it's in the low-vitality moments or seasons of life when we're uniquely vulnerable to attacks from the enemy. You actually hurt or damage yourself and others when your vitality reservoir is not providing you with healthy and clean (living) water. Nowhere in Scripture can you find an illustration that *working harder* (not to be confused with hard work) is a solution advocated by God.

Many of us know that vitality maintenance is essential to thrive and flourish, yet many of us tend to ignore the indicators that we're running low and starting to take in murky, unhealthy waters to keep us fueled. Your early warning signs (EWS) are like the depth indicator found in many reservoir bodies of water. When you see the water (vitality) level begin to drop, that should tell you it's time to pause your energy expenditure and allow the reservoir to replenish to keep things in a healthy balance.

To switch analogies for just a moment, ignoring your low vitality is like watching the fuel and oil supply gauges on your vehicle dashboard run down to low or empty and taking no precautionary steps to sustain your drive to your desired destination. An empty fuel tank won't damage a vehicle (it will only disrupt the trip), but an empty oil supply could burn up a car's engine and make the vehicle completely unusable without costly and time-consuming repairs. There is no more tragic or consequential situation than a people helper with a seized-up engine because their oil (an important biblical metaphor) system was not properly maintained. If you're not careful, you could end up in the junkyard, providing parts of your life to sustain other roadworthy servants.

It's essential that you identify and constantly monitor your early warning indicators. These can vary from person to person, so take the time to discover your warning indicators. Be sensitive to feedback from trusted others. For example, my wife Debbie seems to be more aware of my declining vitality than I am. Like a seismograph, she seems to be able to sound a warning when the slightest tremors signal an approaching earthquake in my life, enabling me to prepare and escape the damage.

You can find the expanded version of the Early Warning Signs Exercises for individuals and groups in the online workbook, chapter 14, at FullStrength.org/AtFullStrength.

The Wellbeing Domains of Life

While the models may vary, helpful wellness or wellbeing models exist that guide us to think about the various domains that make up our life experience. The models typically include at least the following six elements: spiritual, emotional, relational, physical, intellectual, and financial. These domains of life do not operate in isolation. They are all interconnected. If you struggle in one area, those struggles can negatively influence your overall thriving and flourishing.

In keeping with the vitality reservoir analogy, you could view these six wellbeing areas as mountain streams, each in their own way filling your vitality reservoir. While all these vitality streams are important, you only need to find the streams that are particularly renewing or energizing for you.

Here are some diagnostic questions that may help you discover the activities that tend to renew and replenish or drain and deplete your reservoir:

- Can you describe a time and context in which you experienced a feeling being energized and fully alive? This is your context of vitality.
  - Where were you?
  - What were you doing?
  - Who were you with?
  - Why was it especially renewing for you?
  - Was this activity something you can replicate on a routine basis?
  - What is the essential aspect of the activity you found so enjoyable?
- Can you describe a time or season in your life when you felt significantly lacking in vitality and resiliency? We refer to this as your context of vulnerability.
  - Where were you?
  - What were you doing?
  - Who were you with?
  - Why was this time or situation especially depleting of your vitality?
  - How can you avoid or manage situations like this in the future?
  - What was the essential aspect of the activity that was so draining?

The Vitality Streams of Life

In the following sections, we provide a series of diagnostic questions to help you think about and evaluate the current state of your vitality in each of six key areas of wellbeing. Further, based on the questions, it's our desire to help you discover and articulate the ways that you uniquely replenish your vitality in each domain. As you better understand where you are and the activities and relationships that renew and replenish you, it's our prayer that you'll be able to develop a more proactive and intentional approach to maintaining vitality in each of these vital areas of your life. I like to utilize the vitality wheel to illustrate the six domains.

The Spiritual Stream

Your spiritual wellbeing has everything to do with your *substance* in life. The key question that serves as a foundation for the spiritual stream or domain of life is: On what basis do you seek to please and relate to God?

The Spiritual Streams

If you seek to please God by attempting to manage the level of sin in your life, you could be living "under the law." The apostle Paul tells us plainly to get out from under the law (see Gal. 3:3) and learn to live in the realm of grace (see Rom. 6:14).

Contrary to Scripture, sin management or personal performance makes you responsible for your sanctification as represented by the following formula:

More right behavior + less wrong behavior = godliness

Instead, *grace living* makes God responsible for your sanctification: "For God is working in you, giving you the desire and the power to do what pleases him." (Phil. 2:13 NLT).

Hebrews 11:6 reveals the key to pleasing God: "And without faith [trust] it is impossible to please God."

We please God as we come to trust him and align our lives with the truths he has revealed about how to live a spiritual life. Not only are we *saved* by grace, but we are also *sanctified* by grace. Believing what God says about the spiritual life inspires obedience. If you walk in faith (trusting and believing him), as he teaches and instructs you to walk, the Holy Spirit will progressively sanctify your life making you more like Jesus day by day. You will naturally want and begin to sin less and less as your faith walk progresses and becomes more consistent.

If you through self-effort attempt to control your old nature and *manage* the sin out of your life, you will not experience a vital spiritual relationship with God. You will always feel as if you're falling short, which in fact you are. Only Jesus lived a perfectly sinless life. Obedience is the evidence of your sanctification, not the means.

Here are diagnostic questions that may be helpful in guiding you to renew your spiritual stream of life:

- What activities cause you to feel close to and connected to God?
- What steps do you need to take to incorporate more of these activities on a weekly basis into your life routines?
- What relationships cause you to feel close to and connected to God?
- What steps can you take to enjoy periodic fellowship with those people who help you experience the presence of God in your life?
- Based on whether you are a morning or evening person, are you able to begin or end each day with a meaningful time of fellowship with God in his Word, in prayer, in praise, in reflection, and in listening for his voice?
- What sacrifices would you have to make to give faithfully a portion of the best part of each day to strengthening your spiritual connection to God?
- Where have you seen God's faithfulness in recent days?
- When was the last time you spent more than three hours in solitude in order to listen to God?

◉ Are you involved in relationships that reflect a healthy accountability?

◉ During times of your life when you felt especially connected to God, what rhythms or routines were you following that supported that connected feeling? What happens when you allow other things to crowd out these routines?

◉ If God is pleased when, in faith, you trust him, in what areas or relationships are you not yet fully trusting him? How might your behavior change if you began trusting God in new and not-yet-surrendered-to-trust areas of your life?

◉ Is your focus more on doing or being?

◉ Do you have a Mount of Olives— a place of quiet reflection in your life?

◉ Are you free of bitterness or resentment?

◉ Where in your life might you lack a teachable spirit?

The Intellectual Stream of Wellbeing (learning and recreation)

◉ In what ways are you recognizing God's work through the adversities of your life? Do you recognize God's grace and blessings in daily living?

◉ Does a spirit of thanksgiving and gratitude characterize your life? If not, what steps can you take to become more appreciative of the blessings in your life?

◉ In what ways would you benefit from having a trusted accountability partner in your life?

For a helpful accountability tool, consider downloading the Full Strength Network's free MinistryPulse app on your smart phone. It can be found at MinistryPulse.org. The app allows you to export journal notes to the email account you register when you download the app. You can then easily forward and share your journal notes with an accountability partner. The app is designed to help you be more mindful about your own need for self-care and soul care.

The Intellectual Stream

Your mind or brain is an amazing, powerful, and complex organ by which you process your life experiences and interact with your environment. Your brain governs all your memories, imagination, creativity, curiosity, learning and building processes, and bodily functions. Protecting and exercising this part of your being is just as important as the other domains of your wellbeing.

A person who has lost his zeal for learning and growing is a person who is lacking in mental vitality. God created us with a spirit of curiosity and the responsibility to understand and "master" the creation, while at the same time stewarding the resources of the earth he designed to sustain us.

He also created us with a responsibility to steward (lead) ourselves and others through wholesome forms of positive, uplifting, and nurturing direction, persuasion, or influence based on the wisdom he has allowed us to accumulate in our life journeys (experiences) or through studying and comprehending wisdom he provides through other sources (education). Holy Scripture is the quintessential form of wisdom provided to us by God. Therein we find the "owner's manual" on how all things human are intended to work in an optimized way.

This coupled with our natural talents and spiritual gifting often places us (appointed by God or others) in a position of leadership responsibility involving others. Learning to lead yourself and others effectively is an acquired skill that deeply affects your intellectual reservoir of vitality. When executed poorly, it can deeply affect the vitality of those (children, coworkers, or work community) who are depending on you to lead wisely and well.

Blessed is the person who in humility has been endowed with a life-long hunger and quest for learning. How what we learn in this life will transfer to the next remains a deep mystery considering that our brain also returns to dust upon death. However, it is not illogical to presume that God will reward in some manner our quest for knowledge and wisdom in this temporal state of our existence into the eternal state of our existence as we fully enter and experience the kingdom of heaven.

Here are diagnostic questions that may be helpful in guiding you to renew your intellectual stream of life:

- Are you disciplined in some form of continuous learning to stretch and grow your mind?
- Do you read on average one book every couple of months?
- Do you have a unique hobby that gainfully occupies your mind apart from your professional duties?
- Do you enjoy engaging in stimulating conversations around interesting educational or vocational topics?
- Do you pursue reading in the art and science of effective leadership and management?
- When you watch television, are you drawn toward educational channels and networks?
- Do you enjoy learning about other people's careers?
- Who are the people who bring renewal to you and fill your reservoir of vitality? What kinds of activities do you like to do with them?
- When last did you spend time with a friend just for fun in a meaningful activity or a heart-to-heart conversation?

A significant part of learning is rooted in recreations stream. One of my favorite questions to ask a client is: "What do you do to de-stress?" Quite often the response is: "Well, I use to [blank], but I haven't done that for a long time."

Some people even feel guilty when they get involved in hobbies or recreational activities. They are often robbed of the joy of the activity by emotionally taking themselves out to the whipping post for wasting time. However, a balanced involvement in recreation actually contributes to our being a more effective worker, spouse or parent. So I ask:

- What brings renewal to you recreationally?
- When last did you do something simply for the fun of it?
- How are you able to de-stress?
- What brings renewal to you emotionally?
- What activities when you finish them make you say, "That was good—a true gift from God!"

The Financial Stream

Biblical financial wisdom and financial stewardship are critical well-being areas, especially for pastors and church staff who may not always receive compensation commensurate with their levels of education, when compared to secular professions.

We're grateful that ministries like the Ron Blue Institute for Financial Planning, Crown Financial, Financial Peace University, and other faith-based organizations are available to help educate pastors and congregations on the issues surrounding the use and management of personal finances. Full Strength Network also exists to help pastors and church staff find financial advisors, counselors, and advisors who can assist ministry leaders in gaining a deeper perspective into what Scripture teaches about biblical financial wisdom and stewardship.

Based on our experience, several critical areas must be understood and managed wisely and well by people influencers. Spiritual leaders must embrace, model, and instruct on the topic of biblical financial wisdom and stewardship. To avoid instruction and education on this critical area of discipleship is tantamount to spiritual malpractice given all that Scripture has to teach on this subject. Scripture promises blessing on those who manage their finances in accord with biblical principles.

God owns everything. Any possession that comes into our hands comes with a stewardship responsibility to be used in a manner that glorifies God. Our possessions are one of our most important stewardship-management areas.

Living within your means in accord with biblical financial wisdom helps you maintain your vitality reservoir. Living outside your means rapidly depletes your vitality and adds an overarching chronic stress to every aspect of your ministry leadership.

Here are diagnostic questions that may be helpful in guiding you to renew your financial stream of life:

- Do you have and follow a budget that restrains or guides you into not spending more than your weekly or monthly household income?
- If your church is not paying you a wage that is sufficient to cover your household expenses from month to month, have you considered scaling back your household expenses, having your spouse work, or taking on a second job so as not to use debt to live from month to month?
- Are there at least two or three trusted lay leaders (advocates and accountability partners) with whom you can be fully transparent regarding your financial position as a paid member of the church staff?
- Are you carrying large sums of education debt? Have you disclosed and discussed this debt with the lay leaders of your church to see whether they are willing to help you accelerate the payoff of this debt?
- Are you disciplined in the use of credit cards so that you avoid the heavy interest penalties that result from carrying balances on credit cards?

◉ While the benefit is still available and under guidance from legal and tax advisors, is your church providing you a housing allowance, if you qualify, to legally minimize your tax ability to the lowest possible level?

◉ If married, are you and your spouse in one accord regarding living sacrificially, perhaps at or near poverty levels, in order to fulfill your shepherding call from God? If not, are you willing to engage a counselor or coach who can help you both evaluate the authenticity of your call?

The Physical Stream

Without question, we are fearfully and wonderfully made. To believe that we evolved from inert matter eons ago in some ancient sludge pool into the complex human beings that we are today, in our thinking, takes more "faith" to believe than that we were created by an intelligent, all-powerful, relationship-minded Designer.

Healthy physical activity has much to contribute to the quality and quantity of your vitality reservoir. Proper sleep, exercise, sunlight, and healthy eating are major contributors to your mental focus, mood balance, and longevity. People who exercise regularly and who have nutrition-centric eating habits generally have a more positive outlook on life. Recreational activity, when it involves physical energy, is the more pleasant aspect of your physical wellbeing simply because it is fun and enjoyable. But the other aspects of maintaining your physical wellbeing require a stewardship mindset that to some may seem laborious.

Chronic exhaustion is another of the established factors involved in vocational people helpers burning out or disrupting their meaningful work and calling by means of some disqualifying moral failure. Your emotional and rational processes are compromised when exhaustion begins to characterize how you live your life. Many sleep studies recommend seven to eight hours of sleep per day. Sleep disorder studies indicate that a lack of restorative sleep strongly correlates with vehicle and work-related accidents, costly job performance errors, mood disorders, depression, and eventually, a number of major illnesses.

Sufficient physical exercise each week is the fastest-acting, lowest-cost, mildest antidepressant available. Exercise produces endorphins in the bloodstream that positively affects the serotonin levels in the brain. Serotonin, a brain-balancing hormone, helps maintain brain health, positively affecting such things like your emotions and ability to concentrate.

Natural light on the retina of the eye affects the melatonin levels in your body, which eventually affects the serotonin levels in the brain. This helps explain Seasonal Affective Disorder (SAD) for people who live in areas with less sunlight during winter months. People who do not get sufficient exposure to sunlight each day are prone to have deficient levels of Vitamin D, with the deficiency contributing to depression and mood destabilization. Counselors in northern states with shorter periods of sunlight are accustomed to seeing their client loads increase in winter months. Lack of exercise and sunlight are potential contributing factors in low vitality and for those vulnerable to depression.

Being hugged by someone from whom you want to receive affection actually releases endorphins into the bloodstream that positively affects your mood. Guilt-free sexual intimacy (i.e., sex as designed and intended by God) releases large doses of mood-supporting endorphins into the blood-stream. Married couples, especially as they age, typically have different levels of desire for sexual intimacy, so frank and honest discussion is required to ensure that emotional or relational dysfunction does not occur as a result of one or the other partner's need for physical gratification in sexual activity. Scripture does indicate that spouses need to be sensitive and responsive (within bounds) to the sexual needs of their partners. This sensitivity should be viewed as a safeguard to protect the relationship.

Here are diagnostic questions that may be helpful in guiding you to renew your physical stream of life:

◉ Have you established, and do you maintain as a habit, a regular, daily time to wake and go to bed resulting in a sacred rhythm of getting adequate and uninterrupted sleep each night?

◉ Have you established, and do you maintain as a habit, a regular pattern of physical exercise involving both aerobic (cardio) and anaerobic (strength) training several days out of each week?

◉ Are you educated on the importance of how to fuel and sustain your body's health through proper nutrition?

◉ Are you consuming empty and vitality-depleting calories and foods on a regular basis?

◉ Are you addicted to sugar?

◉ Are you consuming proper amounts of clean, healthy water on a daily basis to meet your body's daily water intake effectively?

◉ Following prescribed sun protection protocols, do you expose yourself to sufficient sun or natural light on a daily basis?

◉ If married, have you and your spouse had honest discussions regarding the importance of expressing physical intimacy in mutually satisfying ways?

The Emotional Stream

As discussed previously in this chapter, your emotions are an essential aspect of your being. In his book, *The Soul of Shame*, Curt Thompson, MD, shares that:

Emotion holds a place of primacy in the realm of human behavior. . . .

The derivation of the word emotion includes its Latin root, *a-motion*, which means "to precede movement." This suggests that whatever emotion is, it gives rise to human movement. . . . Hence, emotion is of primal significance when it comes to us doing anything.

Another important aspect of emotional salience involves its role in our anticipation of the future.

The challenge is that emotion can so dominate my mind's landscape that it becomes difficult to extract myself from what I anticipate I will feel in the future and shift my attention to the present moment.[2]

It's almost amusing that we emotionally react (we're moved to words or actions) based on how we anticipate we're going to feel in the future if certain events turn out a certain way, which may or may not occur in that way. In truth, we can't predict the future or know in advance how others are indeed going to act, yet we respond in advance of factual events actually occurring. Given that our emotions work in this manner (they trigger us to movement in words or actions before we actually analyze the facts with our minds)—this makes learning how to manage and control our emotions an essential life skill.

Here are a series of diagnostic questions designed to help you discover the degree to which you control your emotions, or they control you:

- As I think about my day-to-day emotional response pattern, what feelings are my emotional defense apparatuses trying to protect me from?
- Is it rational that I should try to protect myself from feeling those feelings, or am I only limiting or hurting myself by allowing my emotions to control me unduly?
- Am I willing to dig, alone or with the help of others, to discover why I fear and avoid discovering the causes of my feeling responses?

- What facts might I believe about myself that I'm afraid to confront or deal with? Are these true or false facts that I'm allowing to control me in certain areas of my life?
- To what extent am I able to manage my emotions, or to what extent do they actually control me?
- Are there any areas of my life where experiencing certain emotions (e.g., shame) force me into unhealthy mask-wearing, hiding, or avoidance behaviors that I believe help me to protect myself?
- What areas of shame in my life are causing me to hide from God or from others?
- Do I frequently get upset with myself that I react with words or emotions, then later have regret wishing I would have stayed in better control of myself?

Here are diagnostic questions that may be helpful in guiding you to renew your emotional stream of life:

- What brings renewal to you emotionally?
- What activities, when you finish them, make you say, "That was good . . . a true gift from God!"
- Fear of something that might occur in the future plays a large part in influencing emotions. What steps can you take to start identifying, confessing, and giving those fears over to God (remember Heb. 11:6, our trust or faith in him pleases him)?
- What aspects of God's love are you not understanding or experiencing such that fear (of punishment or rejection) is still controlling your emotions and keeping you from coming to maturity in God's love for you? (Meditate on 1 John 4:18.)
- Have you come to understand that confessing your sin struggles to other trusted believers positions you to receive (experience) their love and assistance to help address and overcome your area of weakness or struggle?

When my shame drives me to hide, I'm literally closing myself off from the power of love that is the very thing I need for healing and freedom.

It can be especially difficult for some of us to identify the activities that are truly emotionally renewing. It may be helpful to ask others about their activities that emotionally renew them.

It is also important to discern the difference between emotional relief and emotional renewal. For example, addictive behaviors can relieve anxiety or depression but continue to deplete your reservoir of precious energy resources. Unhealthy activities such as chronic complaining, excessive eating or drinking alcohol, spending money needlessly, and sexually acting out can give a temporary relief that results in more depletion. These are counterfeits of what God intended for us that flow from the sewer pipe (sin nature and living in a sin-filled world) at the bottom of our reservoirs.

The Relational Stream

The relational stream has everything to do with your sense of connectedness in life. God created us as relational beings. He created us to be in healthy relationship with himself, with others, and with ourselves. Our relationships with others include special consideration for those who are married and for married couples with children. The Hebrew word *shalom* carries with it the idea that we be "at peace" in our relationships with God, self, others, and our environment.

It's very possible to be involved in large numbers of relationships in our lives, without enjoying real friendships and companionship. On a practical level, the writer of Ecclesiastes captures the importance of having at least a few deep relationships as essential to our life journey:

> Two people are better off than one, for they can help each other succeed. If one person falls, the other can reach out and help. But someone who falls alone is in real trouble . . . A person standing alone can be attacked and defeated, but two can stand back-to-back and conquer. Three are even better, for a triple-braided cord is not easily broken. (Eccl. 4:9–10, 12 NLT)

In the sixth chapter of Ephesians, the apostle Paul talked about putting on the whole armor of God. This passage is about spiritual warfare, but it also contains insights about the importance of close relationships. Roman armor covered the vital organs like the head and protected mainly the front side of the body. Roman solders often did battle in a formation called the "tortoise" position. If one soldier was struck down in battle, the remaining solders would step over the fallen soldier as protector and continue battle in a back-to-back position protecting each other and their fallen comrade from further injury.

Scripture describes the intimacy of relationship that exists among the members of the Trinity. In his role as rabbi, Jesus enjoyed an "inner circle" relationship with Peter, James, and John, as well as other close relationships with other disciples. One of the great errors of many pastors is the belief that it's wrong or inappropriate to enjoy close intimate relationships with a few people, including members from among your own congregation. You need such relationships and they are to be cultivated to maintain relational health. Isolation and loneliness have been identified as among the causal criteria leading to a ministry-damaging or ministry-destroying moral failure.

For me as a counselor, one of the saddest comments I hear comes from leaders in the church setting. They are surrounded by relationships yet many ministry leaders feel isolated. They often feel that there is no true friend or person with whom they can relax and just be a human, with all their frailties. The loneliness and isolation often drain a ministry leader's vitality reservoir without setting off any early warning alerts. Extra effort on the part of pastors and church staff may be required to plug this relational leak in the vitality reservoir.

In the biography, *Winston's War*, author Michael Dobbs states, "Great men are almost always failures as fathers!"[3] In God's household, a pastor's spouse and children must be given priority as those members of the congregation most in need of the pastor's shepherding care. To fail as a spouse and parent is to fail as a spiritual leader.

Here are diagnostic questions that may be helpful in guiding you to renew your relational stream of life:

In Friendships

- ◉ Who are the people who bring renewal to you and fill your reservoir of vitality? What kinds of activities do you like to do with them?
- ◉ When last did you spend time with a friend just for fun in a meaningful activity or a heart-to-heart conversation?
- ◉ What activities bring true connectedness in your personal friendships? In your professional relationships?
- ◉ Who are people that if you lost them you would wish you had taken more initiative in the relationship?
- ◉ Who are the people you might someday wish you had gotten together with more?
- ◉ What are situations that are difficult for you to enter into, but when you do, you are usually glad you did?

- How about the crucial conversations that you know need to take place that may make all the difference in the world?
- Who are those willing to be "in your face" when they think you need to be set straight?
- What are the characteristics of people you most enjoy being around and when you're with them, you are energized by the social engagement? (Use these insights as clues to identify candidates for your relational "inner circle.")
- What are the activities that you enjoy doing with other people, such that the activity and the fellowship enjoyed during the activity are relaxing and refreshing?
- Who are the people in your life that, when you are with them, make you want to be a better person simply by virtue of their examples and their perspectives on life and living?
- Do you have close friends who are willing to challenge you when they observe you behaving in a manner that does not align with your expressed beliefs, attitudes, and behaviors?
- Do you have a trusted accountability partner?

In Marriage

- Recall three or four special moments in your marriage. What was the activity that was present? How did you treat each other?
- What activities bring a sense of renewal and connectedness in your marriage?
- When did you last go out and do an activity with another couple just for fun?
- Who are the people who encourage you in your relationship with your spouse?
- Do you know at any given time what has been important to your spouse in the last seventy-two hours?

- What are the principles that you live by, bring a vitality to your marriage?
- What expressions or activities leave you and your spouse feeling valued? Appreciated? Loved? Renewed?
- Is the expression of gratitude a frequent occurrence in your marriage?
- What steps do you and your spouse take to celebrate your lives together and make new and rich memories together?

In Family

- What activities bring a sense of renewal and connectedness in your family? It may vary with each family member.
- What expressions and activities leave your children feeling valued and connected to you? What activities with your children leave them feeling renewed and blessed?
- What principles do you want to engrave in the hearts of your children?

In all your relationships, here are three very helpful questions that provide a shortcut to improving relational health. Asking these questions periodically and carefully, listening for the verbal and nonverbal responses that will pay huge relational health dividends:

- What one or two key things should you start doing to improve your relationship?
- What one or two keys things should you stop doing to improve your relationship?
- What one or two keys things should you continue to do to sustain your relationship?

Putting It All Together

At first reading, considering all that must be managed to maintain vitality across six domains of wellbeing may seem overwhelming. You may be thinking that your life is already busy without piling on more activities and responsibilities. The goal of this chapter is not to channel you into working harder, but to channel you into working differently so that you can consistently maintain your vitality. Incremental success is always better than grand failure. Adopting effective vitality rituals and strategies is not about doing more or working harder. It is about discovering the activities that God has given you that than can be renewing.

What we are encouraging you to do is find those activities that uniquely maintain and renew your energy and vitality levels and work enough of those activities into your weekly routine so that these activities help you remain in a positive state of thriving and flourishing. You may not necessarily need to excel in managing all six domains of wellbeing to maintain your vitality reserves; however, you will likely need to focus on several areas at once to stay encouraged and remain in a positive energized capacity to care for others.

So let's develop a strategic plan by applying simple questions to each of the six domains. Flowing from the stream of each domain, what are the activities, practices, rituals, and relationships that bring you vitality?

1. **Pick a domain from the vitality wheel.**
   Name of the Domain: (Example: Physical)

2. **Write down a few of the activities, rituals or relationships that renew you.**

   (Example #1: Biking and Walking)

   (Example #2: Going to the health club)

3. **Go through each of the other domains and do the same.**

   Identify the activities, rituals, and relationships God has given you for your enjoyment and renewal.

For a helpful accountability tool, consider downloading the Full Strength Networks free MinistryPulse app on your smartphone. The app allows you to export journal notes to the email account you register when you download the app. You can then easily forward and share your journal notes with an accountability partner. The app is designed to help you be more mindful about your own need for self-care and soul-care.

You can also find what we call "Strength Journeys" that are helpful for your mindfulness and insight on our website.

To build a summary of your Vitality Strategies, you can find a helpful chart in the online workbook in chapter 14. Go to: FullStrength.org/ AtFullStrength.

Balancing Principles of a Strategic Vitality Plan

Imagine that you are driving in a powerful thunderstorm with very poor visibility. The storm has caught you at a disadvantage, as you notice again that your windshield wiper blades are worn out. Of course, you fully intended to get them changed. Unfortunately, it is too late. It is easy to forget during weeks of sunshine, but now you have to wait it out at the side of the road.

Many of us take the windshield-wiper approach to life. We have the best intentions to make those important changes when life is turbulent. But when the clouds disperse, so goes the willpower. A mature response to authentic change requires that we go into training, not just trying. Trying is making the effort, but training is arranging our life around the people, principles, and practices that allow us to someday become that which we cannot presently be.

More vitality is possible for you in the future when you train yourself in the disciplines and practices that bring vitality. Even though you cannot prepare for every hardship that comes your way, you can establish a pattern of attitudes and behaviors that allow you to regain your balance and increase your vitality. Also, being creative can help you regain your balance and find renewed vitality.

These balancing principles of a beneficial vitality plan can help you innovate the way you gain and maintain the vitality necessary to be a blessing to others. Let's take a look at these balancing principles.

The Six Balancing Principles

The first balancing principle is that *some of the activities should be able to cross the seasons or change with the seasons.* For example, one of my favorite activities recreationally that renews vitality is bicycling. The problem is that because I live in the Midwestern part of the United States, cold and icy winters can get in the way of bicycling. Therefore, I need activities that are more conducive for winter weather or activities that cross the seasons.

Whatever the activity you enjoy that brings vitality, keep in mind that, if it does not cross the seasons, it would be good to consider a different activity for the other seasons or identify activities that are for all seasons.

The second balancing principle is that *some activities should be short in duration and others long in duration.* If your favorite activity is playing golf or shopping, you need several hours. However, you don't always have three to four hours available without neglecting your responsibilities or family.

Because you have already made a list of activities in the eight areas of living a balanced life, you may want to go back to your list and identify the practices and activities that are both short and long in duration. The most useful activities are those that can be done in both shorter and longer periods of time.

Do you like to read or play a musical instrument? These kinds of activities fit both categories. If your calendar is too full with work and family responsibilities, it might be difficult to get together with a friend. However, with some effort you might find that some of your friends may enjoy meeting you for a brief breakfast appointment or for a cup of coffee. I've met with a friend for breakfast for about an hour each week for over eight years. We do other things together but seldom find the time to do those activities. However, the breakfast time keeps our friendship alive and strong.

The third balancing principle of a beneficial vitality strategy is that *some activities should be able to cross a number of the categories.* Actually, the more categories an activity crosses, the more beneficial it can be to help gain and maintain vitality. In my life, an activity that crosses almost all the categories is going out for a cup of specialty coffee at a place that is quiet. Sometimes I read the newspaper, a book, the Bible, or write in my journal, or work on personal goals—which fit the categories of recreational, mental, spiritual, and emotional vitality.

Riding a bike to the coffee place can add exercise (physical vitality). Meeting my wife can make it marital or one of my kids a family vitality exercise. Meeting a friend will add the social-relational component. This one activity includes the categories of social, family, and/or marital. I can do it in the winter or the summer so it crosses the seasons. It also fits the next category of being able to be done in solitude or with another person.

The fourth balancing principle of a beneficial vitality strategy is that *some activities should be solitary in nature and others involve being in community.* Striking a balance between solitary activity and being involved with others is evidenced in healthy people. Those who cannot be alone and those who withdraw from others live in unhealthy extremes. I am not suggesting that those with a high preference for introversion are unhealthy. Introversion basically means that the person is energized or revitalized by his private world. Neither do I suggest that those who are highly extroverted are unhealthy. Extroversion basically means that a person primarily gains energy and becomes revitalized by activity with others.

However, the person who does not have both solitude and involvement with others is lacking balance in life. Different people have different levels of need for solitude and being in community with others—but both should be present.

What kinds of activities do you like to do in solitude that bring vitality? Some people like gardening, playing music, and reading.

Others like more energetic activities like jogging, biking, hiking, and other outdoor activities.

What kinds of activities do you like to do with others or even large groups of people that bring vitality? The important point is that you should find a balance based on whether you are an extrovert or introvert by preference. Balance usually comes through an activity that is the opposite of your bent. If you are extroverted, learn to practice solitude. If you are introverted, step out and get more involved with others. These activities may seem unnatural at first but you may find that they bring a fresh perspective and vitality to your life.

The fifth balancing principle is that *some activities should be process focused and others product focused.* An example of this principle in the physical area is exercise. Let's say that you want to exercise three times each week. That is a process-focused activity. The objective is to continue with the activity with no end in sight. You can exercise for different reasons. It can be an effort to keep your body in good condition, which is process focused. You may also exercise to lose weight, which is product or outcome focused.

The sixth balancing principle of a beneficial vitality strategy is that *some activities should be focused on giving, whereas others are focused on receiving.* If all the activities are based on receiving, we risk becoming self-indulgent. We must remember that self-indulgence will never fill our reservoir with vitality. It is a counterfeit that, at best, can give a false sense of being filled. That is why people who have a lifestyle of being *takers* never seem to be satisfied or content.

You have heard that it is better to give than it is to receive. Those who are deeply involved in a life of service know this well. Nothing can fill us with vitality more than doing something truly sacrificial for others. On the other hand, many people who are caretakers by nature can from time to time find their reservoirs nearly empty. Many caring people freely give but have broken receivers. They have a difficult time asking for help and receiving help from others. This too can be unhealthy.

When we, as vocational caregivers, will not receive the help of others, we are robbing them of the joy of giving. In order for someone to receive the blessing of giving that brings vitality, there must be a gracious receiver. How is your balance when it comes to being a sacrificial giver and a gracious receiver?

Now that you have identified activities that bring vitality in the six domains of life, you might want to take the time to go back and identify how each of these principles apply to the activities. It may require you to make some adjustments.

Our Need for Solitude and Reflection

I would be remiss if I failed to mention one of the most important of all the categories. It is not on the Vitality Wheel simply because of its importance, and yet it is consequentially neglected in our culture. It is a practice that has fallen through the cracks—the practice of solitude.

Wisdom can be found in odd places. For example, I noticed this message on the package of a box of Sleepytime® Tea:

Usually, when the distractions of daily life deplete our energy, the first thing we eliminate is the thing that we need the most: quiet, reflective time. Time to dream, time to contemplate what's working and what's not, so that we can make changes for the better . . . learn how to pause.

We allow the urgent matters of life to crowd out and cause us to neglect the important matters of life. We live life under the tyranny of the urgent.

One of the never-urgent but critically important elements of a healthy life is a planned time for solitude, planning and evaluating, considering the nonproductive activities that we should eliminate from our lives, and spending time with important people. Solitude and reflection have been pushed out of our lives by the fast-paced busyness of our contemporary culture.

The practice of modern life could easily be called an *urgency addiction*. Instead of setting priorities and putting "first things first" (Covey's second habit), we have condemned ourselves to a life on the treadmill of busyness, living with a false belief that if we just run a little faster we can get everything into a peaceful, enjoyable alignment, where all will be well. This belief is not based on truth; it's a lie.

One of the biggest challenges we will face in life is to resist wanting or believing that we need to *do more*. Only in dedicated moments of solitude and reflection can we take the time to evaluate priorities and trim away urgent things to make room for things that are important. Being busy creates the illusion of accomplishment and importance, when in fact busyness is undermining both of these virtues.

God did not speak to Elijah in the mighty windstorm. He did not speak to Elijah in the earthquake. He did not speak to Elijah in the fire. He spoke to Elijah with a gentle whisper (see 1 Kings 19:11–12). If we don't schedule times of solitude and reflection into our lives, we will miss the voice of God.

In Psalm 46:10 we read, "Be still, and know that I am God." Have you effectively invited God in to help you evaluate your life's priorities, your life's direction, and the choices you make in how you will invest your time and resources?

Eugene Peterson offers these biting thoughts on busyness:

The word *busy* is the symptom not of commitment but of betrayal. It is not devotion but defection. . . .

I am busy because I am vain. I want to appear important. Significant. What a better way than to be busy? The incredible hours, the crowded schedule, and the heavy demands on my time are proof to myself—and to all who will notice—that I am important.

I am busy because I am lazy. I indolently let others decide what I will do instead of resolutely deciding myself. I let people who do not understand . . . write the agenda for my day's work because I am too slipshod to write it myself. . . .

It was a favorite theme of C. S. Lewis that only lazy people work hard. By lazily abdicating the essential work of deciding and directing, establishing values and setting goals, other people do it for us; then we find ourselves frantically, at the last minute, trying to satisfy a half dozen different demands on our time, none of which is essential to our vocation, to stave off the disaster of disappointing someone.[1]

The Saturation Effect

Dr. Richard Swenson explains why we are often unaware that overload and burnout are creeping up on us. Initially, we are energized by new activities added to an already heavy load, but then we find ourselves uncomfortable in an overextended state. Swensen calls this phenomenon *saturation*. He offers this analogy:

Picture yourself in a chemistry lab with a flask of hot water. Your task is to progressively add salt to the flask. Initially, the salt totally dissolves in the hot water. As you keep adding salt, it soon reaches a point where it will no longer dissolve, it just now settles on the bottom—the solution has reached its saturation point.

If we add additional hot water, the salt once again begins to dissolve. As we remove the heat and the water begins to cool, that salt will crystalize because cold water lacks the same capacity to absorb salt as does hot water.

In life, we tend to keep adding more and more activities, commitments, and debt to our lives. At first, these activities will dissolve in the heat of our enthusiasm, but soon a saturation point will occur. For many, the answer is to turn up the heat by working harder and going faster. But when exhaustion and cool down occurs, life is a supersaturated, crystalized mess.[2]

Solitude and reflection are the safety gauges that keep us from reaching states of saturation and supersaturation. Without the safety gauges, you deplete your vitality reservoirs and place yourself at risk of burnout, or worse, of becoming vulnerable to a mortal blow by the enemy that can take you out of vocational ministry altogether.

One of the biggest challenges in our culture is to resist doing more. You have to take time and be still long enough to evaluate the purposefulness of your activities. Too much of the activity that gives you your sense of routine and security often drives you to distraction and sometimes exhaustion. Too much activity blocks out the voice of correction and change. You cannot hear God speak as clearly in the flurry of activity. When you commit to saying yes to one commitment, you are always saying no to something else.

We need to recognize that all our treadmill of doing so much is not always productive. Sometimes it is mindless and driven, shrouded in self-protection. Many of us are fearful of solitude, having to listen to our own inner voices or the still small voice of God's Spirit. We keep on moving when in fact we should be still—still enough to evaluate and to hear.

When Psalm 46:10 says, "Be still and know that I am God," does it mean that if we are never still we don't really know God all that well? The greater challenge is not to *do*, but rather to *be* in the place where you can hear; not to hear the old and familiar, but to hear again what God thinks about your life's priorities, direction, and choice of activities.

Why is it that we don't plan more solitude into our lives? Again, let me suggest that many are anxious about the results of listening to their own inner voices and God's still small voice that can only be heard in silence. We by nature are self-protective. Sometimes we will even go to great lengths to protect ourselves from the truths about ourselves. Another reason we do not plan more solitude into our lives is that we have become convinced that time in solitude is wasted time—being lazy.

Dr. Charles Ringma, in his book, *Dare to Journey*, asserts that it is because we are fearful of solitude: "We try to do more while our energies ebb away and we become like uprooted trees with our roots wildly groping for the sky."[3]

Dr. Ringma believes that solitude is . . .

....

[F]uel for the journey, and more importantly, it is the discipline that will shape the very fabric of our being.[4]

For it is not to others that we should first of all turn; instead, we should create the necessary space to meet with God Himself.[5]

We need to resist making unhelpful distinctions where we play off one thing against another. Prayer, for example, is not opposed to work; and the search for solitude is not opposed to active involvement in our world. These seeming opposites belong together. Prayer leads to work, and work needs to be done prayerfully. Similarly, solitude is not simply a withdrawal from the world in order to be renewed and refreshed. It is also finding a new center of inner quietness and certitude from which we act in the midst of a busy and demanding world.[6]

It is not the place where we recharge our spiritual batteries and then continue to live as we have lived before. It is not the place where we catch our breath in order to madly reenter the race. It is not the place where we simply find some quietness before we plunge into the world with its babble of voices.[7]

Another leader in promoting the importance of planning solitude into our lives is Henri Nouwen. Nouwen's many thought-provoking books are woven with reminders of the importance of solitude. Nouwen speaks of solitude as experiencing an important and transforming "loneliness that cannot be removed by any other sinful human being."[8]

Nouwen continues to assert that

- Solitude is the furnace in which transformation takes place.[9]
- Time given to inner renewal is never wasted.[10]
- The place of solitude is not a private therapeutic place . . . it is the place of conversion.[11]

The Practice of Solitude

Time is among our most precious commodities this side of heaven. Yet we use it as if there is an endless supply. We can take it for granted. We rush around in our hurry-sick society as if we can gain more time. Being still and knowing God is quickly becoming a lost art in our technologically connected world. Harvey Mackay captures the importance of time in his poem "Time is Free":

Time is free, but it's priceless.
You can't own it, but you can use it.
You can't keep it, but you can spend it.
Once you've lost it you can never get it back.[12]

Hurry sickness causes us to devalue time. The thought of spending it on solitude is unnerving for many people.

As a clinician, my work is primarily with vocational people helpers such as social workers, ministers, physicians, nurses, missionaries, and so on. I'm puzzled to realize how uncomfortable many can be with solitude. It has become my belief that an appreciation of solitude does not come naturally to most people. It is a learned appreciation and one that produces a deeper character.

Howard Thurman, the man who brought inspiration to the civil rights leader, Martin Luther King Jr., writes these words concerning our need to practice solitude:

We must find sources of strength and renewal for our own spirits, lest we perish. There is a wide spread recognition of the need for refreshment of the mind and the heart. It is very much in order to make certain concrete suggestions in this regard. First, we must learn to be quiet, to settle down in one spot for a spell. . . . We must, each one of us, find his own time and develop his own peculiar art of being quiet. . . . The first step in the discovery of sources of strength and renewal is to develop the art of being still, physical and mental cessation from churning. This is not all, but it is the point at which we begin.[13]

The following sections offer some simple suggestions to begin the practice of solitude.

Place

Find a perfect place that will work for you. It must be a quiet place that will be disruption free and one that you will enjoy returning to time after time.

Time

Find the ideal time of day that works best for you. If you're a morning person, first thing in the morning may be ideal. If you're a midday or evening person, schedule in solitude during these best parts of your day. Solitude and reflection are so important that it's good to allocate the best time of day for you to practice it.

Duration

Find an ideal length of time that works well for you. Your times of solitude may be short in the beginning, but as your practice skills improve, you will likely find yourself setting aside longer periods of time for solitude and reflection. Eventually, this practice may lead to setting aside an entire day or a periodic solitude sabbatical often called a silent retreat. You may find yourself being drawn to include times of Scripture reading, prayer, praise, and worship into your times of solitude.

Purpose

You may find it helpful to designate your times of solitude for a specific purpose. For example, you may want to journal your thoughts when dealing with a specific decision that you struggle to make. You may want to designate specific solitude times to reflect and evaluate how you're doing on one of the six domains of wellbeing. Answering this series of questions is always helpful: "What should I start doing? What should I continue doing? What should I stop doing?"

Our Ultimate Role Model

If Jesus, as God in flesh, consistently practiced times of solitude, then we should follow his example. Christian leaders and those in people-helping professions must set the example on this important practice or life discipline. We serve no one well when we live frantic, overloaded, and exhausted lives. Jesus understood the importance of self- and soul-care.

In the four Gospel accounts, there are ten occasions and nine reasons that Jesus removed himself from the crowds to be alone for renewal and focus. *(You can find a comprehensive chart by going to chapter 15 of the online workbook at* FullStrength.org/AtFullStrength.*)*

It is important for each of us to find our Mount of Olives. When and where is the place in your life that you can find the solitude that is renewing both spiritually and emotionally?

If You Are Never Still

An old university professor friend after recovering from a life-threatening heart attack once told me that a passage in the Bible that became real to him was "Be still and know that I am God" (Ps. 46:10).

He said to me, "If we are never still, how much do we really know God?"

It is not easy to "be still" in our culture where life changes at an exponential tempo. We will not find our Mount of Olives, our quiet center, unless we are very intentional in doing so. It will not come by accident. However, if we do not discover the obedience of being still in order to know God, it may come through his *making* us be still. It is in this stillness that we can truly know God who will be our only true security and significance this side of heaven.

May you hear the voice of God as you learn to practice solitude and reflect on what makes life worth living. Our prayer is that you will live life *At Full Strength* and that you will succeed in navigating the risks of deeply investing in the wellbeing of others in response to God's call on your life.

Appendix

I Am Your Security and Significance, I Am in Control

I am he, I am he who will sustain you. I have made you and I will carry you. . . . With whom will you compare me or count me equal?
—Isaiah 46:4–5

Remember this, keep it in mind, take it to heart. . . . Remember the former things, those of long ago; I am God, and there is no other; I am God, and there is none like me. I make known the end from the beginning, from ancient times, what is still to come. I say, "My purpose will stand, and I will do all that I please." (Isa. 46:8–10)

Do not call conspiracy everything this people calls a conspiracy; do not fear what they fear, and do not dread it. The Lord Almighty is the one you are to regard as holy, he is the one you are to fear, he is the one you are to dread. He will be a holy place. (Isa. 8:12–14)

Forget the former things; do not dwell on the past. See, I am doing a new thing! Now it springs up; do you not perceive it? I am making a way in the wilderness and streams in the wasteland. (Isa. 43:18–19)

Do you not know? Have you not heard? The LORD is the Everlasting God, the Creator of the ends of the earth. He will not grow tired or weary, and his understanding no one can fathom. He gives strength to the weary and increases the power of the weak. . . . those who hope in the LORD will renew their strength. They will soar on wings like eagles; they will run and not grow weary, they will walk and not be faint. (Isa. 40:28–31)

Can a mother forget the baby at her breast and have no compassion on the child she has borne? Though she may forget, I will not forget you! See, I have engraved you on the palms of my hands; your walls are ever before me. (Isa. 49:15–16)

"I know the plans I have for you," declares the LORD, "plans to prosper you and not to harm you, plans to give you hope and a future. Then you will call on me and come and pray to me, and I will listen to you. You will seek me and find me when you seek me with all your heart." (Jer. 29:11–13)

Names and Roles of God

Creator of the universe, Maker of heaven and earth
Almighty God and the All Powerful Omnipotent One
All-knowing omniscient God, Lord Adonai—"Sovereign One"
Yaweh and Elohim—"Everlasting God"
Abba and Emmanuel, El Shaddai—"All Sufficient," Holy One,
    Righteous Judge
Great King of Glory, a Tower of refuge and strength, Your Stronghold
Jehovah—The Great "I Am"
Jehovah Jirah—"I Am Provider"
Jehovah Rapha—"I am Healer"
Jehovah Shalom—"I am Peace"
Jehovah Rahe—"I am Shepherd"
Jehovah Shammah—"I am Present"
Jehovah Palet—"I am Deliverer"
Jehovah Gael—"I am Redeemer"
Jehovah Magen—"I am Shield"
Jehovah M'Kaddesh—"I am Sanctifier"
Forgiving, gracious, merciful God of unfailing love
Yeshua and Messiah, faithful and true
Bread of Life, Consuming Fire
Your Comfort and Confidence, the God of all compassion
Deliverer, your Dwelling Place
Door and the Good Shepherd
Shade and Shield, Source of Strength
Your Stronghold, your Song, your Stream of Living Water.
Light of the World, Way, Truth, and Life
Wonderful Counselor, Mighty God, Everlasting Father
Prince of Peace, King of Kings, Lord of Lords
The Alpha and the Omega,
The Beginning and the End.

—taken from The Holy Bible

Notes

Introduction

1. Ed Viesturs and David Roberts, *No Shortcuts to the Top* (New York, NY: Broadway Books, 2006), back cover.

2. Cited on www.elephantjournal.com/2008/07/there-are-old-climbers-and-bold-climbers-but-no-old-and-bold-climbers/, accessed October 2018.

3. Viktor Frankl, *Man's Search for Meaning* (Boston, MA: Beacon Press, 2006), 65–66.

4. *SBL Greek New Testament,* 1 Timothy 6:19b, www.biblestudytools.com/sblg/, accessed October 2018.

Chapter 1

1. Dennis Howard, director of Vitality Care Institute, LMHC, LCSW, "The Crosshairs Research Project" research findings were compiled (Fort Wayne, IN: 2014). This study was based on data collected on 633 cases records involving ministry, nonprofit, and humanitarian workers in counseling and coaching records over a twelve-year period from 2001–2013.

2. Howard, "The Crosshairs Research Project."

3. Howard, "The Crosshairs Research Project."

4. Howard, "The Crosshairs Research Project."

Chapter 2

1. Dennis Howard, director of Vitality Care Institute, LMHC, LCSW, "The Crosshairs Research Project" research findings were compiled (Fort Wayne, IN: 2014). This study was based on data collected on 633 cases records involving ministry, nonprofit, and humanitarian workers in counseling and coaching records over a twelve-year period from 2001–2013.

2. Howard, "The Crosshairs Research Project."

3. Howard, "The Crosshairs Research Project."

4. Howard, "The Crosshairs Research Project."

5. Howard, "The Crosshairs Research Project."

6. John Gottman and Robert Levenson, "What Predicts Change in Marital Interaction Over Time? A Study of Alternative Models," *Family Process* 38, no. 2 (June 1999):143–158, https://doi.org/10.1111/j.1545-5300.1999.00143.x.

7. John Mordechai Gottman, *What Predicts Divorce?: The Relationship Between Marital Processes and Marital Outcomes* (Hillsdale, NJ: Lawrence Erlbaum Associates, Inc., 1994), 783–784.

8. Gottman, *What Predicts Divorce?*, 783–784.

9. *SBL Greek New Testament,* 1 Timothy 6:19, www.biblestudytools.com/sblg/, accessed October 2018.

Chapter 3

1. The American Institute of Stress, *What is Stress*, www.stress.org/what-is-stress, accessed October 2018.

2. John Wooden with Steve Jamison, *Wooden: A Lifetime of Observations and Reflections On and Off the Court* (Chicago, IL: McGraw-Hill, 1997), 58.

3. C. S. Lewis, *The Four Loves* (New York, NY: Harvest Book, Harcourt Brace Jovanovich, Inc., 1960), 169.

4. Tim LaHaye, *How to Win Over Depression* (Grand Rapids, MI: Zondervan Corp., 1974), 155.

5. Marshall Goldsmith, PhD, *What Got You Here Won't Get You There* (New York, NY: Hyperion, 2007), 35.

6. Peter Drucker, https://www.azquotes.com/quote/864759.

Chapter 4

1. Michael Card, *Why?,* www.songlyrics.com/michael-card/why-lyrics/, accessed October 2018.

2. Corrie ten Boom, www.goodreads.com.

3. Paul David Tripp, *Dangerous Calling: Confronting the Unique Challenges of Pastoral Ministry* (Wheaton, IL: Crossway, 2012), 92–93.

4. The Toxic Triangle mentioned in this book was developed by the author in 1996. It is not the same as Hogan's Destructive Leadership Triangle, but readers might find this resource helpful: A. Padilla, R. Hogan, R. B. Kaiser, *The toxic triangle: Destructive leaders, susceptible followers, and conducive environments* (Leadership Quarterly, vol. 18, 2007), 176–194.

Chapter 5

1. Henry Cloud, *Necessary Endings* (New York, NY: Harper Collins, 2010), 122.

2. Cloud, *Necessary Endings,* 139.

3. Cloud, *Necessary Endings,* 141.

Chapter 6

1. Merriam-Webster Online Dictionary, www.merriam-webster.com/dictionary/anthropology, accessed October 2018.

2. John Gottman, PhD, *10 Lessons to Transform Your Marriage* (New York, NY: Crown Publishing Group, Random House Publ., 2006), a general theme throughout the book.

3. Jimmy Dodd, conversation with Jimmy at SonScape Retreat Center, Colorado: Woodland Park, Full Strength Ministries Think Tank, March 30, 2015.

4. John C. Maxwell, *The 360° Leader: Developing Your Influence from Anywhere in the Organization* (Nashville, TN: Thomas Nelson, Inc., 2005), 142–143.

5. Randy Alcorn, *The Grace and Truth Paradox: Responding with Christlike Balance* (Colorado Springs, CO: Multnomah Books, 2003), 88.

Chapter 7

1. Charles Ringma, *Dare to Journey—with Henri Nouwen* (Carol Stream, IL: NavPress Publishing Group, 2014), 72.

Chapter 8

1. Robert Robinson (1735–1758), *Come Thou Fount of Every Blessing*, http://hymnary.org/text/come_thou_fount_of_every_blessing, accessed October 2018.

2. Edwin Arlington Robinson, *Richard Cory,* en.wikipedia.org/wiki/Richard_Cory, 1897.

3. Theory on the meaning of *sincere* is discussed at https://english.stackexchange.com/questions/343644/does-the-theory-that-sincerely-originated-from-without-wax-hold-any-merit, accessed November 2018.

4. Dennis Howard, director of Vitality Care Institute, LMHC, LCSW, "The Crosshairs Research Project" research findings were compiled (Fort Wayne, IN: 2014). This study was based on data collected on 631 cases records involving

ministry, nonprofit, and humanitarian workers in counseling and coaching records over a twelve-year period from 2001–2013.

5. Karl Barth, *Church Dogmatics, The Doctrine of the Word of God,* vol. 1, part I (Edinburgh, United Kingdom: T & T Clark Internationl, 2004), 231–234.

6. Paul David Tripp, *Dangerous Calling: Confronting the Unique Challenges of Pastoral Ministry* (Wheaton, IL: Crossway, 2012), 102.

7. Humility Paradigms based on multiple conversation while working with the staff of the Master Peace Retreats (a ministry of the Masterworks Foundation under Ambassador Enterprises located in Fort Wayne, IN, 2007–2011).

8. Robert Hastings, "The Station", www.inspirationalarchive.com/2810/the-station/.

9. Edward Mote (1834), *My Hope is Built on Nothing Less,* https://hymnary.org/text/my_hope_is_built_on_nothing_less, accessed October 2018.

Chapter 9

1. Michael Jordan, "*I've missed more than 9,000 shots . . .*" thinkexist.com/quotation/I-ve_missed_more_than-shots_in_my_career-i-ve/216033.html, accessed October 2018.

2. Charles Swindoll, *Quotable Quotes,* www.goodreads.com/quotes/267482-the-longer-i-live-the-more-i-realize-the-impact, accessed October 2018.

Chapter 10

1. Howard Thurman, *The Creative Encounter: An Interpretation of Religion and the Social Witness* (New York, NY: Harper & Brothers, 1954), 52–53.

2. Jessica Shaver, "I Told God I Was Angry" www.dailystrength.org/group/post-traumatic-stress-disorder-ptsd/discussion/poem-i-told-god-i-was-ang_1, published October 5, 2006.

3. Stephen R. Covey, *First Things First* (New York, NY: Simon & Schuster, 1994), 150–151.

Chapter 11

1. Charles Spurgeon, *Lectures to My Students,* (Philadelphia, PA: Icthus Publication, 2014), a compilation of his addresses delivered to the students of The Pastors' College, Metropolitan Tabernacle, 856. Lecture 11, 131-140, www.gotothebible.com/HTML/downcast.html.

2. Daniel G. Amen, MD, *Change Your Brain, Change Your Life* (New York, NY: Crown Publ. Group, 1998), 203–207.

3. Les Carter, PhD, *Imperative People* (Nashville, TN: Thomas Nelson Publ., 1991), 51.

4. Larry Crabb, PhD, *Finding God* (Grand Rapids, MI: Zondervan Publishing House, 1993), 62.

5. John Gardner, *Self-Renewal: The Individual and the Innovative Society* (New York, NY: W. W. Norton & Company, 1981), 97.

6. Amen, *Change Your Brain, Change Your Life*, 56.

7. Amen, *Change Your Brain, Change Your Life*, 64.

Chapter 12

1. Steve Ewing and John B. Lundstrom, *Fateful Rendezvous: The Life of Butch O'Hare* (Annapolis, MD: Naval Institute Press, 1997), 78–79, 155.

2. Origin and meaning by Online Etymology Dictionary, etymonline.com/word/vocation.

3. Jacques Ellul and Geoffrey W. Bromiley, *The Judgment of Jonah,* (Eugene, OR: William B. Eerdmans Publishing, 1971), 25.

4. Origin and meaning by Online Etymology Dictionary, etymonline.com/word/career.

5. Origin and meaning by Online Etymology Dictionary, etymonline.com/word/mission.

6. Origin and meaning by Online Etymology Dictionary, etymonline.com/word/vision.

7. Gary Keller with Jay Papasan, *The One Thing: The Surprisingly Simple Truth Behind Extraordinary Results* (Austin, TX: Bard Press, 2012), chapter 14: "Live by Priority, Goal Setting to the Now", 219.

Chapter 13

1. Quote by Mother Teresa of Calcutta, www.goodreads.com/quotes/139677-the-greatest-disease-in-the-west-today-is-not-tb, accessed October 2018.

2. Larry Crabb, PhD, *Finding God* (Grand Rapids, MI: Zondervan Publishing House, 1993), 62.

3. Cited at https://www.education.ne.gov/wp-content/uploads/2017/07/JohnWooden.pdf, accessed October 2018.

4. Donald W. McCullough, *Waking from the American Dream* (Downer's Grove, IL: InterVarsity Press, 1988), 76–77.

Chapter 14

1. Denny Howard, *2002 Personal Journal* (Fort Wayne, IN: unpublished, October 2002).

2. Curt Thompson, MD, *The Soul of Shame* (Downers Grove, IL: InterVarsity Press, 2015), 49–51.

3. Michael Dobbs, *Winston's War: A Novel of Conspiracy* (Naperville, IL: Sourcebooks Landmark, 2009).

Chapter 15

1. Eugene Peterson, *The Contemplative Pastor: Returning to the Art of Spiritual Direction* (Christianity Today, Inc., 1989), 17–19.

2. Richard A. Swensen, MD, *Margins: Restoring Emotional, Physical, Financial, and Time Reserves to Overloaded Lives* (Colorado Springs, CO: NavPress, 1992), 78.

3. Charles Ringma, *Dare to Journey—with Henri Nouwen* (Carol Stream, IL: NavPress Publishing Group, 2014), 1.

4. Ringma, *Dare to Journey*, 1.

5. Ringma, *Dare to Journey*, 2.

6. Ringma, *Dare to Journey*, 7.

7. Ringma, *Dare to Journey*, 14.

8. Henri Nouwen, *Heart Speaks to Heart* (South Bend, IN: Notre Dame, Ave Maria Press, 1989), 21.

9. Henri Nouwen, *The Way of the Heart: Desert Spirituality and Contemporary Ministry* (New York, NY: Random House Publ., 1981), 20.

10. Henri Nouwen, *The Road to Daybreak: A Spiritual Journey* (New York, NY: Doubleday Press, 1988), 20.

11. Nouwen, *The Way of the Heart*, 27.

12. Harvey MacKay, *Time is Free,* www.goodreads.com/quotes/79511-time-is-free-but-it-s-priceless-you-can-t-own-it, accessed October 2018.

13. Howard Thurman, *Deep Is the Hunger* (New York, NY: Harper & Row Publishers, 1951), 175–176.

Authors' Recommended "Know and Grow" Strength Resources

- ◉ **Livstyle.com:** comprehensive assessments for individual and team growth for both profit and nonprofit enterprises
- ◉ **MinstryPulse.org:** an online growth journal to keep you mindful of your wellbeing